Behind Enemy Lines

Behind Enemy Lines

Civil War Spies, Raiders, and Guerrillas

WILMER L. JONES, PHD

Taylor Trade Publishing
Lanham • Boulder • New York • London

Published by Taylor Trade Publishing
An imprint of The Rowman & Littlefield Publishing Group, Inc.
4501 Forbes Boulevard, Suite 200, Lanham, Maryland 20706
www.rowman.com

Unit A, Whitacre Mews, 26-34 Stannary Street, London SE11 4AB, United Kingdom

Distributed by NATIONAL BOOK NETWORK

British Library Cataloguing in Publication Information Available

The hardback edition of this book was previously cataloged by the Library of Congress as follows:
Jones, Wilmer L.
  Behind enemy lines : Civil War spies, raiders, and guerrillas / Wilmer L. Jones.
    p. cm.
  Includes bibliographical references and index.
    1. United States—History—Civil War, 1861–1865—Secret service. 2. United States—History—
Civil War, 1861–1865—Underground movements. 3. United States—History—Civil War,
1861–1865—Commando operations. 4. Spies—United States—Biography. 5. Guerrillas—United
States—Biography. I. Title.
  E608. J66 2001
  973.7 85—dc21

00-048821

ISBN 978-0-87833-191-8 (cloth)
ISBN 978-1-63076-086-1 (pbk. : alk. paper)
ISBN 978-1-63076-087-8 (electronic)

∞™ The paper used in this publication meets the minimum requirements of
American National Standard for Information Sciences—Permanence of Paper for
Printed Library Materials, ANSI/NISO Z39.48-1992.

Printed in the United States of America

To My Family:
my loving wife, Carol,
my son, Scott, and
my daughter, Christa

Contents

Contents

If I am entitled to the name "spy" because I was in the secret service, I accept it willingly; but it will hereafter have to my mind a high and honorable significance. For my loyalty to my country, ... I am called "traitor," farther North a "spy" ... instead of the honored "Faithful."

ELIZABETH VAN LEW, UNION SPY

In no other way does the enemy give us so much trouble, at so little expense to himself, as by the raids of rapidly moving small bodies of troops harassing, and discouraging loyal residents, supplying themselves with provisions, clothing, horses, and the like, surprising and capturing small detachments of our forces, and breaking our communications.

ABRAHAM LINCOLN

I have only a short time to live. Only one death to die. And I will die fighting for this cause. There will be no more peace in this land until slavery is done for.

JOHN BROWN

Vengeance is in my heart, death in my hand; blood and revenge are hammering in my head.

"BLOODY BILL" ANDERSON

Introduction

SINCE 1865, books and magazines depicting the glories of battles like Gettysburg and Antietam and the leadership qualities of men such as Robert E. Lee and Ulysses S. Grant have proliferated the field. For many the Civil War was fought only on the battlefield. Other elements of the conflict, just as interesting, have not received the same level of coverage. *Behind Enemy Lines* examines these other aspects of the war.

One of the less explored areas was intelligence gathering and espionage, which would play a key role in the Civil War. President Abraham Lincoln was quick to realize this, stating that it was important to prevent vital military information from falling into the hands of the enemy. At the outset of the war, the war departments in both Washington and Richmond did not have an organized intelligence unit. Although not a full service for the Union, Allan Pinkerton's Detective Agency was the first in American history to fill that role. The Confederate government had no such organized agency, but at first they were more successful in gathering information than the Federals. Before the war ended, the situations had reversed.

Mounted military raids were another aspect of the Civil War that involved action behind enemy lines. Many of these raids adopted the classic hit-and-run tactic of attacking the enemy where he least expected it, and then quickly disappearing. Raids led by such notables as J.E.B. Stuart, John Singleton Mosby, and Hugh Judson Kilpatrick were conducted with uniform troops under the authorization of their governments. As raiders, they were expected to treat noncombatants with the same care and respect that was required of regular army troops. If captured, they were to be treated as prisoners of war. Any captured materials and supplies were to be turned over to their governments.

For the first two years of the Civil War, Confederate cavalry proved superior to their Union counterpart. The South utilized this advantage by conducting numerous raids behind enemy lines. These raids were more effective than those conducted by the Union. As a result, Confederate raiding operations are given more coverage in *Behind Enemy Lines*.

Standard Confederate guerrilla operations, led by bushwhackers such as William Quantrill and "Bloody Bill" Anderson, were often gory and terrorized civilians and military troops alike. Robbing and looting all in their path, the guerrillas made their own rules, gave no quarter, and often slaughtered innocent civilians as well as enemy soldiers. If captured, they could expect to be treated as criminals and hanged. They were admired, fed, and protected by local civilians but were considered dangerous to the Confederate high command and unproductive to their cause.

Behind Enemy Lines is divided into three basic parts: spies, raiders, and guerrillas. Each section describes some of the events and people who contributed to this phase of the war. I have selected from the breadth of information available that which was the most interesting to me. It is my hope that the reader will be motivated to further explore the subject.

This book was written because of my many years of interest in the Civil War. Having read extensively about the battles and battlefield heroes, I was curious to know more about that part of the war about which less has been written. *Behind Enemy Lines* is the result of that search. I hope you will enjoy reading it as much as I did writing it.

WILMER L. JONES, PhD
Towson, Maryland

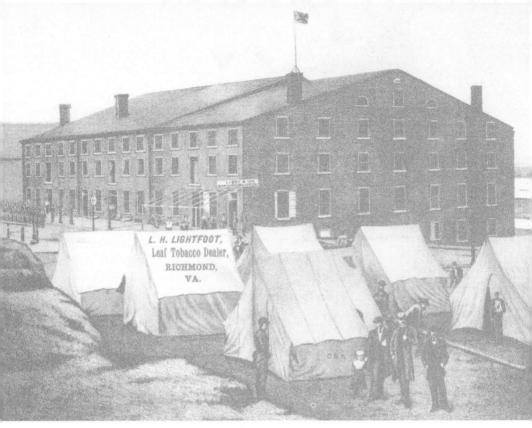

Part 1　　　A Web of Deception

BLUE AND GRAY SPIES

ON the early evening of February 22, 1861, not twelve hours after his Philadelphia speech, President-elect Abraham Lincoln had dinner at the Jones House in Harrisburg, Pennsylvania. Before he completed his meal, he was summoned from the table. Lincoln changed his clothes, put on an overcoat, and gathered a hat and a shawl which he later used as a disguise. Then he hurried from the hotel.[1]

Lincoln, a master politician, was using his long trip from Springfield, Illinois, to Washington, D.C., to let the people see their new president and to win their support. He made numerous stops along the way; at each he was met with friendly crowds and made brief speeches. Before the state assembly at Trenton, New Jersey, Lincoln promised to do everything within his power "to promote a peaceful settlement of all our difficulties." As always, he called upon his gift for words, saying he needed their help to "pilot the ship of state" through the perilous waters ahead because "if it should suffer wreck now, there will be no pilot ever needed for another voyage."[2]

Eleven days earlier when Lincoln had boarded a special train in Springfield to begin his trip, several hundred of his supporters were there to wish him luck and bid him farewell. "My friends," Lincoln told them, "no one, not in my situation, can appreciate my feelings of sadness at this parting." In concluding he said: "Trusting in Him who can go with me, and remain with you and be everywhere for good, let us confidently hope that all will yet be well. To His care commending you, as I hope in your prayers you will commend me, I bid you an affectionate farewell." The crowd responded by calling out, "We will pray for you."[3]

On February 21, Lincoln arrived in Philadelphia. Now, after what he considered a very successful trip, he faced the final leg. The most difficult and dangerous part of the trip lay ahead in Baltimore. For some time Lincoln had been warned that his life was in danger. Like Washington itself, Baltimore contained a strong secessionist element, and its chief of police, George P. Kane, could not be counted on to provide adequate protection for him. This would provide a perfect opportunity for an attack on Lincoln. But Lincoln was determined to reach Washington by the regular route, and he had turned down an offer by an Ohio chemist to provide him with a gold-plated suit that could be worn over his undershirt.[4]

By the time Lincoln reached Philadelphia, word of an assassination conspiracy had arrived from several sources. The first was from detective Allan Pinkerton, founder and operator of a private detective agency in Chicago, now on special assignment. He told Lincoln of Baltimore ruffians, "plug-uglies," who were planning to murder him. Pinkerton urged Lincoln to cancel the next day's Philadelphia speech and visit to Harrisburg and instead go to Washington that night. General Winfield Scott, who warned Lincoln that bands of rowdies in Baltimore were threatening violence when he passed through the city, also urged him to make a secret night trip. Senator William Seward informed him that 15,000 men were organized to prevent his passage through Baltimore and were planning to blow up the railroad tracks and set fire to the train. Lincoln finally agreed to use the Pinkerton agency to protect him but insisted on keeping his appointments in Philadelphia and Harrisburg. Lincoln declared he would rather be "assassinated on the spot" than to give in to the threats of traitors.[5]

Lincoln was taken by carriage to a siding of the Pennsylvania Railroad, where a locomotive and a single, empty passenger car were waiting. Lincoln quietly boarded the train and occupied the berth reserved for an "invalid" passenger. There he was met by a large, muscular man named Ward Hill Lamon, an Illinois lawyer who had ridden the circuit with him and was Lincoln's personal bodyguard. Lamon carried with him an arsenal of four pistols, two large knives, a blackjack, and a pair of brass knuckles.[6]

Later, Lamon recalled Lincoln's feelings: "It was with great difficulty that he could be persuaded to make that 'clandestine escape' from Harrisburg to Washington. He protested that it was cowardly and most humiliating to him, but as General Scott and Mr. Seward had so earnestly advised it, he yielded to it under protest."[7]

For the first part of the trip the railroad tracks to Philadelphia had been cleared of traffic, and the telegraph lines from Harrisburg had been cut as a precaution in the event that persons unfriendly to Lincoln might try to send word that he was on the move. When Lincoln arrived in Philadelphia, he was met by Allan Pinkerton. Pinkerton had more than 200 security guards hired by

Allan Pinkerton (left) and President Lincoln meet with General John McClernand to discuss spy operations in 1862. (Library of Congress)

the railroad and had stationed them at every bridge and road crossing between Harrisburg and Baltimore. The President-elect and Lamon were whisked into a carriage and driven from the Pennsylvania Railroad Station to the Philadelphia, Wilmington, and Baltimore Railroad Station. There Lincoln was taken quietly to the regular night train for Baltimore; from Baltimore he would make a connection for Washington.[8]

The rear portion of the sleeper car had been reserved for one of Pinkerton's operatives, a Mrs. Kate Warne, and her "invalid brother" (Lincoln), who retired almost immediately upon arriving. She was joined by Lamon, Pinkerton, and two other well-armed bodyguards. At around midnight the train carrying Lincoln moved toward the nation's capital. As the train sped past each bridge and crossroad, the watchman in his turn raised a lantern to signal that all was well.[9]

Lincoln's train arrived at Baltimore's Calvert Street depot at about 3:30 A.M. Baltimore was the point of greatest danger for him because of the strong anti-Lincoln sentiments there. This danger was compounded greatly by the crude railroad facilities that connected the Calvert Station with the Camden Station. Lincoln's car, like all other cars going to Washington, had to be drawn individually by horses for a short distance through the city streets to the Camden Station, where another locomotive would take it to its destination. During this brief trip, Lincoln's car was most vulnerable to attack. Yet the transfer was made without a problem; the city was sound asleep. At the Camden Station, however, Pinkerton was disturbed to find that the engine scheduled to pull Lincoln's car to Washington had not yet arrived. They were forced to wait for more than an hour. On the platform outside, a drunk sang "Dixie" over and over again.[10]

It was 6:00 A.M. on February 23 when Lincoln arrived in Washington. There Lincoln was met by his old friend and ally, Congressman Elihu B. Washburne. Stretching his long legs, Lincoln said: "Well boys, thank God this prayer meeting is over." Then Pinkerton, Lamon, Washburne, and Lincoln sped off to Willard's Hotel, where Lincoln would reside until his inauguration.[11]

Pinkerton sent a code telegram to Mrs. Lincoln, still at Philadelphia with her sons: "PLUMS DELIVERED NUTS SAFELY." She was relieved by the news of her husband's safe arrival.[12] Ten days later Lincoln would solemnly swear to preserve, protect, and defend the Constitution of the United States as he became the sixteenth president.[13]

After Lincoln's clandestine trip to Washington, he quickly became aware of

the importance of gaining information about the enemy's movements and operations before they occurred. It would signal the beginning of a deadly contest
of spies and counterspies, of men and women who associated with the enemy
in their towns and camps to gather intelligence. In President Lincoln's view,
intelligence — the business of acquiring information about the enemy's plans
and movements — should play an important part in his military commanders'
strategy. In 1862 he wrote to his western generals that knowledge of the enemy's
movements was "the most constantly present, and most difficult" of the problems they had to solve. This knowledge, Lincoln believed, was necessary if the
Union armies were to take advantage of their superior numbers to offset the
Confederates' shorter march to any point of concentration. If Union generals
knew in advance where Confederate generals planned to concentrate their
armies, they had a chance to beat them to the location and occupy the better
ground.[14]

When the Civil War began, both armies had a core of professionally trained
officers, but neither had an established intelligence service; it was not until the
middle of the war that they did. Spying was left to the amateurs because, in
the minds of the U.S. military, espionage was considered less than honorable.
Few people were attracted to serve in this capacity, and military planners preferred to ignore it. George Washington, however, had seen the importance of
gathering intelligence and had organized and financed an operation during the
Revolutionary War.[15]

Washington advanced more than $17,000 of his own money to finance espi-
onage and counterespionage activities. He organized an intelligence network
around New York City, where the British headquarters were located. This lead
to the capture of British Major John Andre and the exposure of Benedict Arnold
as an American traitor. The most famous of Washington's agents was the one
who was caught, Nathan Hale. While Hale proved to be a courageous hero, as
a spy he was incompetent. Revolutionary spies, because of their success in maintaining secrecy, were almost entirely unknown for more than a century. After
the war there was little need for an intelligence department within the army.[16]

The United States remained without an intelligence service until the Mexican War. In the Mexican War, General Winfield Scott employed a Mexican
national and bandit, Manuel Dominguez, and some cohorts to spy for the Americans. They achieved some success in revealing the Mexican army's movements,
but their use ended with the war.

The inflammatory nature of the Civil War sparked patriotic fervor on both sides, leading those who were unable to bear arms to consider spying. The task was fairly easy since both sides spoke the same language, shared the same moral code, and were familiar with each other's geography. The skills most necessary to be a successful spy were daring and resourcefulness. The spy's role was to infiltrate an enemy's camp, inspect his fortification, determine his strength and, if possible, plans for attack, watch his movements, and secretly report the findings. The fact that romanticism was associated with spying helped to offset the risk of death if caught.[17]

Before the war, secret societies opposed to the government conducted occasional undercover operations. In the North there were groups who favored peace and supported the Democratic Party. One such organization was the Order of American Knights. They had all the characteristics of a secret society: oaths, rituals, strict security regulations, and an "inner ring," the Sons of Liberty. Members identified each other using a copper coin with a head on one side; thus, they became known as "Copperheads."[18] In the Midwest, however, Copperheads wanted their states to leave the Union and plotted for ways to get them to secede. Although these organizations were supposed to be secret societies, all were easily infiltrated by federal agents. In Baltimore, Allan Pinkerton's operatives uncovered a plan by the Knights of Liberty, a secret society, to assassinate Lincoln. Later they broke up a plan to invade Washington. The leaders of these plots were jailed, putting an end to the society's work in Washington.[19]

When the Civil War began, the South had an espionage system already in place. It was highly efficient, with spies already placed in the offices of the federal government, especially the War Department. Often the Confederates knew the Yankees' plans soon after they had been reached and well before the Union troops in the field. The federal government had been operational for over seventy years, allowing Confederate sympathizers to be placed through normal hiring procedures. This network could be counted on to relay important information to Southern operatives in Washington. The Union, however, could not target a government that did not exist prior to the war. This made it difficult to infiltrate the Confederate government once it was formed. Furthermore, Washington was a Southern community populated predominantly by Southerners. This made it easy for residents to spy on the camps that circled the city and report the size and movements of troops.[20]

As the war continued, the Union intelligence service improved to the point that it challenged its Confederate rivals, but it was never able to completely stop the flow of information to the South. Southern spies were able to penetrate the highest Union headquarters and government offices until the end of the war. One Confederate spy went undetected and throughout the war continued to work in the office of General Lafayette Baker, chief of the Union's secret service. Confederate agents were in Washington on such a regular basis that one of the hotels kept a room permanently reserved for their use.[21]

The Confederate spy rings of Rose O'Neal Greenhow and Benjamin F. Stringfellow were the first in Washington. Both were in place before the war began. The Union had no comparable rings in place in the South before the war. The most effective Union spy organization, directed by Elizabeth Van Lew in Richmond, was in operation because of her own initiative.[22]

At the outset of the war, other factors favored the South's spy efforts. They were able to gain valuable information from those officers who resigned from the U.S. Army to serve the Confederacy, but there was no similar movement of Southerners to the North. There were few safe houses for Union operatives in the South, while the Confederates had an extensive network established in the North.[23]

Early Confederate foresight enabled Colonel Thomas Jordan, an officer on Union General Winfield Scott's staff, to establish spy operations in Washington. At the outset of the war, when most of the officers with Confederate sympathies resigned their commissions, Jordan stayed in Washington to study Scott's war plans and organize a spy ring. One of Jordan's acquaintances was the widow Rose O'Neal Greenhow. Before he left Washington to join General P.G.T. Beauregard's staff, Jordan gave her a cipher for encoding dispatches and arranged for a system of couriers to deliver her messages southward. With Greenhow's help, Jordan was able to establish a thriving spy network. Greenhow was able to supply information to the Confederacy before the First Battle of Manassas, which helped lead to a Confederate victory.[24]

Colonel Jordan was replaced by Major William Norris, whose organization in Richmond grew to at least sixty operatives, all of whom were involved in maintaining the communication lines with the North and supplying information to the Richmond government. Nevertheless, when information of the enemy's field operations was available, it sometimes was ignored. On April 12, 1863, Major Norris provided General Robert E. Lee with information about the size of Major General Joseph Hooker's Army of the Potomac before they crossed the Rappahannock. Although Norris's information proved fairly accurate, General Lee ignored the report, believing it had no validity.[25]

Confederate General Thomas "Stonewall" Jackson was probably the general who made the greatest use of intelligence. For him, there were only four pieces of information needed before facing the enemy: the position of the enemy, the number of troops and their movements, the generals in command, and the location of the headquarters of the commanding general.[26]

In the North the first step in establishing a military intelligence service came when Major General George McClellan assumed command of the Army of the Potomac. He brought with him the well-known railroad detective, Allan Pinkerton. Prior to his return to the U.S. Army, McClellan had been associated with the railroads in Chicago and had employed Pinkerton as a detective. McClellan knew that he needed such a man with him.[27]

Pinkerton and his operatives had been successful in catching criminals; using the same techniques for catching spies, they met with success, too. When they tried to gather intelligence, however, they were less successful, having little idea what information an army needed, where to find it, or how to evaluate it. They were still floundering when McClellan was relieved of command in November 1862.[28]

Pinkerton's secret service consisted of a core of detectives, the most capable of whom was Timothy Webster, who was hanged in Richmond in 1861. During the Civil War the term "secret service" was a generic term used to describe any organization that gathered information by covert means. One of Pinkerton's successful methods of collecting information was the interrogation of runaway slaves as they came into Union lines. When Pinkerton found a slave who could read and write, he would attempt to send him back behind enemy lines to spy.[29]

General Winfield Scott, the senior Union officer on active duty, hired Lafayette Baker as an intelligence officer, giving him the same title as Pinkerton, Head of the Secret Service. While Pinkerton was in the field with McClellan, Lafayette Baker was responsible for counterintelligence activities in Washington. In the West, Major General Ulysses Grant was forming his own military intelligence organization; it would serve him through the war. Grant's choice to head the intelligence operation was Brigadier General Grenville Dodge. In addition to his role as spymaster, Dodge also held the dual role of regimental commander. Although untrained in the area of espionage, Dodge became a proficient spymaster and was of great value to Grant and General William T. Sherman. One of Dodge's favorite methods of collecting information was to send his chief of staff, Captain George Spencer, behind enemy lines under a flag of truce with a message to be delivered in person to the Confederate commander. Spencer was usually successful in passing through to the commander and, in doing so, collected valuable information about troop size and deployment.[30]

One of Dodge's most able operatives was Philip Henson, who had many characteristics that made him an ideal spy. He was born and lived in the South and had no need to fake his accent. As a person who traveled a lot, he knew the territory as few others did. Henson was naturally friendly, always willing to share his whiskey wherever he went, and had a way of ingratiating himself with people of every social status. Although a Southerner, he was opposed to secession and had a strong love for the Union. At the outset of the war, Henson did not wish to fight for the Confederacy, so he persuaded the owner of a Mississippi cotton plantation to hire him as an overseer, a position that exempted him from military service. In late 1862, when Grant invaded Mississippi, Henson took the oath of loyalty to the Union. Many of his neighbors were coerced into taking the oath; Henson did it because he believed in it.[31]

But Henson did more than swear allegiance to the Union — he agreed to spy for General Dodge. In a short time Henson and an unwitting accomplice, Jesse Johnsey, were on their way to Vicksburg, where Johnsey's sons were serving in the Confederate army. With the help of Henson's whiskey and an explanation that they were going to see "our boys in Vicksburg," they were able to gain entrance to the city. Assisted by a Confederate captain who introduced them to General John Pemberton, the two were free to move about the city. Henson was able to take mental notes of the city's defenses and troop deployment. Dodge was so pleased with the information that he gave Henson a horse named Black Hawk.[32]

Dodge frequently provided his spies with seemingly important information that they could use to gain the confidence of enemy officers. Dodge allowed Henson to take schedules for Union projects to Lieutenant General Leonidas Polk, who was so impressed by the information, he put Henson on his own espionage payroll.[33] At other times during his service as a spy, Henson worked as a double agent for at least three Confederate generals. Armed with passes from various Confederate commanders, and one from Dodge, Henson was able to make his way from camp to camp, gathering vital military information.

In May 1864, Henson's luck seemed to run out. Sent to spy on the activities of the Confederate's famous cavalryman, Nathan Bedford Forrest, he was arrested in Tupelo, Mississippi. Unlike other Confederate officials, Forrest was not fooled by Henson's persuasive personality. For months Henson was held in a tiny, windowless room known as the "sweat box." What happened next is unclear. In 1865, however, Confederate authorities, in their desperation to find men for the army, agreed to allow Henson to serve in the 26th Mississippi under General Lee in Virginia.[34]

All captured spies were not as lucky as Henson. On November 19, 1863, two of Dodge's agents captured a Confederate spy, twenty-one-year-old Sam Davis of Smyrna, Tennessee. Incriminating material intended for delivery to General Braxton Bragg was found sewn into his saddle and cavalry boots. Most embarrassing to Dodge was a penciled draft of his own monthly report. The document had been taken from his desk, probably by a slave who worked in his office.[35]

Dodge himself undertook the interrogation and repeatedly offered young Davis not only a chance to live, but also his freedom in return for information about his leader. Davis refused, even though he knew that his co-conspirator and leader, Captain Henry Shaw, was being held in the same jail on an unrelated matter. Dodge pleaded with Davis to give up the name of his leader, but it was no use. Davis continued to refuse to identify Shaw or reveal any other secrets. "I would die a thousand deaths before I would betray a friend or my country," he said. Dodge had no choice but to turn him over to a court-martial board.[36]

Found guilty of spying, Davis was sentenced to be hanged on November 27. Dodge repeatedly offered to commute the sentence if he would give him the names of the others involved, but Davis refused to cooperate. The night before his execution, he wrote a final letter to his mother. "I have got to die tomorrow morning," he began. "Mother I do not hate to die."[37]

The next morning Davis once again was offered the opportunity of saving his life. A witness later wrote that Davis told Dodge that to answer his question would be a betrayal. Davis refused to save his own life at the expense of his friend's. One of Davis's last statements on the scaffold was that he forgave the executioner for what he was about to do. Davis then turned and said, "I am ready." Henry Shaw watched the execution from his jail cell and would survive the war, but with the reputation as the man who lived because Davis had died.[38]

When Grant went east to take command of the armies there, Dodge remained in the West. Directing the operations of an efficient network of spies in the east was Colonel George H. Sharpe, on the staff of General George Meade. By mid-1863 the Sharpe organization, having replaced Pinkerton's agency, was the most professional spy operation since the days of George Washington. The federal army had finally surpassed the Confederacy in its ability to gather intelligence. By the conclusion of the war, Sharpe had placed approximately 200 agents throughout the entire Confederacy. Colonel Sharpe followed Pinkerton's practice of using special ethnic groups, local Indians, and African Americans. Sharpe realized the importance of transmitting data rapidly and was constantly experimenting with new and novel ideas for increasing the speed. One such idea was the use of hot-air balloons. Unfortunately the balloons proved very susceptible to rifle fire.[39]

During the Battle of Gettysburg, Sharpe supplied General Meade with important information about Lee's army, its size, location, and possibility of reinforcements. After the final day of the battle, July 3, 1863, Sharpe gave General Meade a complete report on Lee's situation, indicating that Lee was now too weak to attack. He recommended that Meade attack immediately before Lee had a chance to retreat. Meade did not act on his recommendation, and this inaction remained a sore point with Sharpe the rest of his life.[40]

The information collected by spies for the Confederacy was often ignored, too. From the beginning the Confederate secret service operated as a part of the War Department, but the agency connections with individual commanders varied and in some cases were tenuous. Robert E. Lee, for example, was a general of the old school. He believed that war should be fought by men in uniforms and on the battlefield. He considered spying as a dirty affair of which he wanted no part. "I have no confidence in any scout (spy)," he once said. As a result of Lee's attitude toward espionage, the Confederacy's main secret service operated at a distance from him and the Army of Northern Virginia. Major Norris's organization had difficulty coordinating information with the commanding generals. Much valuable information was either late in arriving or ignored. In addition, Lee's generals, including James Longstreet and J.E.B. Stuart, preferred to rely on their own spies. In the confusion that resulted, it was not uncommon to find a single agent who worked for a field commander at some times and for Norris's secret service at other times.[41]

Throughout the war the press provided detailed information about troop movements, strategies, and orders of battle. Had Confederate commanders placed spies on the staffs of their adversaries, they probably would not have had any better information than that supplied by the Northern press. Braxton Bragg, commanding general in the West in 1862, subscribed to several Northern newspapers using the name of a Confederate sympathizer. Robert E. Lee was also known to have frequently read papers from New York and Philadelphia. Major William Norris, chief of the confederate secret signal bureau, had Northern papers regularly delivered to Jefferson Davis every morning. Union generals also read Southern newspapers but did not find them as informative.[42]

The Civil War saw the arrival of new technology that was useful not only for the military but also for espionage. The telegraph was used effectively for military and governmental messages, and although operatives could not use it in enemy territory, it provided a method of moving information in a rapid manner once it got to a telegraph outpost. With the invention of the telegraph, the military had a rapid means of communicating with their forces without having to worry about their courier being captured by the enemy. When it became apparent that telegraph lines could be tapped and valuable information gained by the enemy, messages had to be sent in cipher with the hope that, if they were intercepted, the enemy would not be able to decipher them. Even enciphered messages were not always safe, thanks to the art known as code-cracking or cryptanalysis. Both sides used ciphers, and both tried to break their opponent's messages with varying degrees of success.[43]

Most cryptologists distinguish between codes and ciphers. Ciphers are messages in which individual letters in the original text are replaced with other letters or symbols. This replacement can result from substitution or by transposition, where the letters are rearranged. A cipher can express any idea the original language can. The sender or receiver only has to know the system for translating the text.[44]

The cipher system had to be not only secret, but easy to use. During the Civil War, a disk with a set of brass wheels was used. To encipher each letter of a message, first the key letters on the inner wheel of the disk were lined up with the letter A on the outer wheel. Then the operator found the appropri-

This brass wheel allowed spies to encode and decipher messages. Each letter in the outer wheel corresponds to a letter with the inner wheel, so, for example, the word "assassinate" would read "bttbttjobuf." (Museum of the Confederacy, Richmond, Virginia)

ate message letter on the outer wheel and the cipher letter on the inner wheel. An alternate to the disk was the cipher square. Of course, it was possible to read an enciphered message without the key by deducing the system used to create it.

Codes provided a more secure method of sending messages. When a code was used, complete words or phrases were replaced with other words, numbers, or symbols. The use of a code required both sender and receiver to have a code book listing words and their code replacements. Although messages written in code were almost impossible to break and read, the sender was limited to the words and thoughts included in the code book.[45]

Although Civil War messages were written in both code and cipher, cipher messages were used more frequently. The Confederates used a rather sophisticated cipher, but Union cryptologists occasionally were able to decipher their messages. The South, however, seemed to be completely unable to crack the Union cipher. The success or failure of each side's cryptologists was due to the types of secret writing they chose and their approaches to breaking the code or cipher.[46]

The cipher used by the Union was developed in 1861 by Anson Stager, general manager of the Western Union Telegraph Company. When George McClellan became the commander of the Union army, he recruited Stager as his communication chief and adopted his system. Although this system was simple to use, it was so successful that in the entire course of the war not one communique was ever deciphered. Confederate forces became so desperate that intercepted Union messages were printed in Southern newspapers seeking assistance in deciphering them, but to no avail.[47]

The most useful characteristic of Stager's cipher system was its simplicity. The words in the message were transposed by the sender according to a predetermined formula. Although the text was scrambled beyond recognition, the recipient would know how to reconstruct the words in the correct order.[48]

It is difficult to understand why, after such an auspicious beginning, the Confederates would have so little success in breaking the Union cipher. Perhaps the Confederates did not devote much energy to cryptanalysis because they enjoyed more successes with other methods of gathering intelligence, such as using spies and cavalry patrols.

Abraham Lincoln kept in close contact with the cipher operations. During the war he spent more time in the War Department telegraph office than in any other place except the White House. Lincoln kept a close watch on the daily operations of the war by reading the dispatches of his generals as well as any deciphered Confederate communiques.[49]

Federal cipher-breaking successes were due primarily to three of the most experienced operators of the Union army: Charles A. Tucker, Albert A. Chandler, and David H. Bates, who were labeled the "Sacred Three." In December 1863, the Sacred Three's most notable accomplishment occurred. A postal censor in New York discovered a suspicious message addressed to Alexander Keith in Halifax, Nova Scotia, who was known to have connections with Confederate agents. The letter was sent to the Sacred Three in Washington to be deciphered. The solution showed evidence of an important Confederate spy ring in New York City and indicated that they were planning to ship engraved plates to New York in order to print Confederate money. The South, which lacked much of the technology necessary to print money, had employed engravers in New York to build presses for them. On December 31, 1863, U.S. marshals raided the engraving shop, confiscating the machinery, plates, and several millions in Confederate money.[50]

The Union War Department was very sensitive to the necessity of keeping their ciphers secret. As a result, guidelines were established for who could use the ciphers and how they could be used. The operators who controlled the ciphers were kept independent of the commanders they served. They reported to the War Department through Stager, providing daily logs of messages sent, and the names of the sender and recipient.[51]

The Union and the Confederacy found another covert use for the telegraph, in addition to sending enciphered messages and tapping the lines to gain information. It was possible to break into an enemy's line and send bogus messages and information. Both Union and Confederate forces employed this process, usually at the local army level where ciphers were not used.[52]

Another invention that came into its own about this time was the camera, with both sides employing photographers as spies. They photographed troop encampments with particular emphasis on the weapons and troop size. The famous Civil War photographer Alexander Gardner was employed by Allan Pinkerton to assist him with spying. Gardner photographed areas of geographic interest to McClellan for use in making maps. General Sherman used the same technique to produce maps during his Atlanta campaign and his march to the sea.[53]

In addition to the individual spies, several unique spy groups were active during the war. From the earliest days of the Civil War, the Confederacy had a secret operation in Canada. It was originally intended to support the growth of a peace movement in the North, with an emphasis on the defeat of Lincoln in the election of 1864. Later the operation expanded to include a variety of efforts to disrupt the Northern war effort. These actions included raids, attempts to free Confederate prisoners held in the Northern camps, and the creation of false information.[54]

The Canadian operation also functioned as a relay point for communication between England and the Confederacy. Throughout the war the South continued to hope that England would join them in their efforts. In addition to her covert operations, Rose O'Neal Greenhow served as the Washington and Toronto go-between. The Toronto group also worked closely with the Copperheads in an attempt to foment riots, hoping to cause the Union to divert troops from the front line.[55]

On October 19, 1864, the Toronto operatives, in need of money, staged a bank robbery in St. Albans, Vermont, a small town conveniently located just 20 miles from the Canadian border. The robbery was successful and the agents returned with $200,000 in gold and U.S. currency. Most of the conspirators, including their leader, Lieutenant Bennett Young, were captured by Canadian authorities. When pressed by the federal government for the return of the bank robbers, Canadian officials refused, since they believed the Confederates were on a military mission. None of the raiders was sentenced for their actions.[56]

The Canadian operatives were also involved in acts of sabotage and the destruction of federal property. In November 1864, they came to New York intent on "torching" the city. They selected nineteen hotels as targets and hoped to create a riot similar to the earlier draft riots in New York. Their efforts were only partially successful; a few hotels did suffer fire damage, but the total effect was not what was desired.[57]

In December 1864, Confederate operatives in Canada, under the leadership of Thomas Hines, planned to kidnap Vice President–elect Andrew Johnson on his way to Washington for the inaugural. Two attempts were made, but both failed. They were never able to get the Copperheads to rise up, despite spending over a million dollars to fund the operation. This failure was due primarily to the excellent counterespionage efforts of the Union. By this late stage of the war, the Union had developed a very sophisticated counterespionage organization and had surpassed the Confederacy in all phases of spying.[58]

The greatest sources of military intelligence for the federal government during the Civil War were runaway slaves, who escaped by the thousands to the North. It is estimated that during the war approximately 700,000 slaves escaped to the Union. Allan Pinkerton was one of the first to recognize their value as providers of information; as early as the fall of 1861, his agents interrogated slaves as they entered Union lines.[59]

Some African American spies were successful in infiltrating the homes of high Confederate officials. One was a man named William A. Jackson, who was Jefferson Davis's coachman. Jackson was able to listen to conversations in Davis's home and in the presidential coach before passing the information to Washington. Another African American, Mary Touvestre, worked in the home of a Confederate engineer and overheard him discussing the remodeling of the C.S.S. *Merrimac.* She was able to steal a set of plans for the remodeling and took them to Washington.[60]

Furney Bryant, an escaped slave, headed a black spy ring in the Carolinas and played an important part in helping the Federals capture a large collection of Confederate silver coins. In 1863, Bryant enlisted in the Union army and served out the war there.[61]

The Dabneys, an African American couple, kept Union General Joseph Hooker supplied with information using an ingenious method. Mrs. Dabney sent messages to her husband by hanging her laundry out to dry in a predetermined pattern. Colors were used to designate various Confederate generals. A gray shirt stood for James Longstreet. When Mrs. Dabney took it off the line, it meant he had gone to Richmond. When a white shirt was moved to the west end of the line, it indicated that Ambrose P. Hill's corps had moved upstream. A red shirt was used to depict Stonewall Jackson's movements. As long as the two armies remained in the area, the Dabneys, with their clothesline telegraph system, continued to provide useful information to General Hooker's scouts.[62]

The most famous African American to participate in spying activities was Harriet Tubman, known in the South by her code name "Moses." She made numerous trips into the South to assist slaves in their flight to freedom in the North. In the process she would gather information useful to the federal government and military.[63]

As the war progressed, General Dodge continued to expand Pinkerton's initiative of using slaves as Union spies. By their own unwillingness to accept the innate abilities of African Americans, the Confederacy provided the Union with a unique spy system that continued to operate throughout the war.

Civil War spies caught by either the Confederacy or Union were initially imprisoned for varying lengths of time. In most cases the spies were exchanged after a period of time so that any information gained would be of little use to the enemy. Spies were usually exchanged in an even swap unless one was of particular importance. Operatives caught in civilian clothes were always classified as "spies." When a military man was captured, it was important to him to be classified as a "scout" rather than as a "spy." While both normally operated behind the lines gathering information, scouts were usually treated as prison-

Belle Boyd, a Confederate spy who refused to sign the Oath of Allegiance to the United States. (Dictionary of American Portraits, Courtesy Confederate Museum)

ers of war, while spies faced the possibility of being executed. In many cases it was difficult to ascertain whether the person caught with information was a spy or just a courier. The importance of the information carried was often used to make the determination.[64]

In the Washington area, captured Confederate spies were placed in the Old Capitol Prison. Civilians imprisoned could be released only if they signed an oath of allegiance to the United States. Belle Boyd and Rose O'Neal Greenhow, two famous Confederate spies held there, refused to sign such an oath. When Belle Boyd was finally released, she was required to sign a statement pledging not to return north of the Potomac River as long as hostilities still existed.[65]

Union sentiments regarding the execution of Confederate spies changed in 1862 when Pinkerton's agent Timothy Webster was hanged in Richmond. On January 25, 1863, James Williams was the first Confederate spy to be hanged. Military records, however, indicate that the number of spies executed by either side was small. To preserve anonymity, spies carried no documents to identify them. Therefore, when a spy was executed, the record often only included the event but did not name the person.[66]

During the Civil War, spying was uncoordinated. The intelligence collected was often slow in being forwarded to the field and proved of little importance after the fact. The Confederate secret service bureau was never centralized in the modern sense. As a result, it was limited in authority, scope, and effectiveness. There is little evidence, for example, that General Lee considered the reports he received from the secret service any different from the numerous other pieces of information that reached him. The Confederates were the first, however, to implement all-out war. As the war progressed, they became more aware of what would be required to win it. The practice of espionage was in opposition to the sense of chivalry, fair play, and honor that were part of the old South. That the South was forced to involve themselves in these practices shows how grim the struggle to survive had become.[67]

At the beginning of the war there were no rules for covert operations, so spies had to learn on the job. While doing so, they made mistakes that sometimes cost them their lives. Spying during the Civil War was in its infancy and did not play a major role in the outcome of the war. Through their bravery and dedication, however, Civil War operatives helped to establish a foundation upon which U.S. intelligence could build. Twenty years after the Civil War, the War Department formally authorized the military to organize their own intelligence services.[68]

1

Union Private Eye

ALLAN PINKERTON

THE Union's debacle at Manassas in July 1861 shocked the North out of its expectation of a quick victory. Lincoln began to make plans for a longer war, plans that should have preceded the Union advance on Manassas. Major General George McClellan had achieved victory in western Virginia in mid-July, and Lincoln called him to Washington to command the Army of the Potomac. McClellan arrived in the capital five days after the battle at Manassas and began organizing the forces around Washington. Only thirty-four, but ambitious, he had begun a very promising career as a civilian. After resigning from the army in 1857, McClellan had become vice president of the Illinois Central Railroad and then superintendent of the Ohio and Mississippi Railroad. In 1861 he returned to the army as a major general of the Ohio volunteers.[1]

McClellan brought Allan Pinkerton and his nationally known detective agency with him to command his personal intelligence service. Before the war, Pinkerton had enjoyed a close friendship with McClellan, and the Illinois Central Railroad was under contract with the Pinkerton Agency for police protection.[2] Pinkerton, a forty-two-year-old Scotsman, was born August 25, 1819, in the slums of Glasgow. His father was a police sergeant. When Pinkerton was ten years old, his father was crippled by injuries received in a workers' riot. In 1830, when his father died, young Pinkerton was forced to drop out of school to support his widowed mother and her other children.[3]

Young Pinkerton's first job was as an errand-boy for a friend of his father. He later recalled working from dawn to dusk for pennies. Later he worked as an apprentice to a pattern maker, but soon he became a cooper (barrelmaker). His powerful physique and attractive personality helped him gain leadership in his trade union. He also became active in the Charterist movement, an organization whose goals included forcing the government to provide social benefits for the citizens of Scotland. When the Charterists turned to violence and terrorism, Pinkerton was forced into hiding from the police. While "underground," in 1843 Pinkerton married; he and his bride made their way to Nova Scotia, then to Chicago, and finally to a settlement of Scots at Dundee, Illinois.[4]

At Dundee, Pinkerton started a flourishing cooperage business. While cutting wood on one of the islands in the Fox River, he accidentally uncovered a hide-out for a gang of counterfeiters. He led a raid on the camp, capturing the whole gang. Local merchants, who were suffering heavy losses from bogus currency and were not satisfied with the local law enforcement agencies, offered to hire Pinkerton on a part-time basis to watch out for counterfeiters. After being responsible for several more arrests, Pinkerton decided he enjoyed detective work more than making barrels.[5] These experiences gave Pinkerton a taste

---

Previous page:
Allan Pinkerton, the original "private eye." His security agency continues to flourish in the 21st century. (Library of Congress)

of law enforcement. In 1846 he was named deputy sheriff in his home county; soon after he took a job with the sheriff of Cook County. This position led to his employment as the first detective on the Chicago police force.

Pinkerton's success as a detective attracted the attention of several railroad owners whose lines had been hit by a series of robberies. In 1850, at their urging, Pinkerton resigned from the police force and set up a private detective agency, one of the first in the nation. From the beginning, his agency specialized in railroad security. By 1860, it was flourishing and broadening its scope of operation.[6]

The company's logo — a wide-awake human eye, with the slogan "We Never Sleep" — became well known. In time it led to the expression "private eye" as a nickname for private investigators.[7] The agency was very strict about the business it would conduct, and all prospective clients were thoroughly checked before a case was accepted. Pinkerton developed a code of conduct under the title of *General Principles*, which all agents were expected to follow. The rules that Pinkerton set for his agency's operations were an indication of the moral character of the man.[8]

Pinkerton's methods were often unconventional. Using all sorts of bizarre disguises, he and his operatives pursued criminals with dogged persistence, bringing them to court with sufficient evidence to ensure conviction. His services were varied. He dealt with embezzlers, bank and train robbers, counterfeiters, and murderers. Despite Pinkerton's active involvement with all types of criminals, his face was not widely known, mainly because he usually worked in disguise.[9]

When the Civil War began in April 1861, Pinkerton offered his services to Lincoln, writing "I have in my force from sixteen to eighteen persons on whose courage, skill, and devotion to their country I can rely. If they with myself as head, can be of service in the way of obtaining information of the movements of the Traitors or safely conveying your letters or dispatches or that class of Secret Service which is the most dangerous, I am at your command."[10] Pinkerton had already earned Lincoln's gratitude by warning him before he took office of an assassination plot by secessionist sympathizers in Baltimore and ensuring his safe entry into Washington. In a meeting with the president and his cabinet, Pinkerton outlined his ideas. Lincoln's advisors urged him to accept the offer, saying Pinkerton had already proved his value by uncovering the Baltimore plot. Lincoln, however, delayed in making a decision.[11]

Before Lincoln could act, Pinkerton received a letter from General McClellan asking him to come to Cincinnati quickly and secretly. Using his pseudonym "Major E. J. Allen," which he used throughout the war, Pinkerton went to meet with McClellan. McClellan wanted Pinkerton to serve on his staff. Pinkerton explained that Lincoln had shown similar interest, but there had not been a firm commitment. McClellan appealed to Lieutenant General Winfield Scott to settle Pinkerton's dilemma. After consulting Lincoln, Scott endorsed the project and Pinkerton lost no time in joining McClellan.[12]

The friendship between Pinkerton and McClellan is perhaps one of the strangest relationships of the time. Pinkerton was a self-made man from the slums of Glasgow who, in America, had risked his life helping slaves escape to freedom by way of the Underground Railroad. McClellan was a well-born West Pointer whose friends and associates were railroad executives and other men of means who had little concern for the cause of freedom. But Pinkerton and McClellan did share some things in common. Both placed great importance in details and were excellent organizers; both were cautious, patient, and believed firmly in the art of maneuvering in battle. McClellan had stated, "No prospect of a brilliant victory shall induce me to depart from my intention of gaining success by maneuvering rather than fighting." Pinkerton's skill in producing detailed reports and his work ethic were welcomed by McClellan; as a result the two enjoyed mutual trust and respect for each other.[13]

In his memoirs, Pinkerton called himself chief of the "United States Secret Service," a name his organization never really possessed. During the Civil War, "secret service" was a term used to describe any organization that gathered information by covert means. Although the Pinkertons did gather information, they were not unique in that respect. Pinkerton's agency was not national in scope, working primarily in the eastern theater of the war. It was organized to operate in two different ways. When McClellan was in the field, Pinkerton would go along as a member of his staff in charge of gathering information about the enemy. When in Washington, his agency would receive their orders from the War Department. Their task then was to investigate all persons suspected of being Confederate sympathizers.[14]

Pinkerton's organization was not a government bureau; he remained a civilian whose agency was under contract to the army. He refused to disclose the names of his agents, even to the War Department, which paid their salaries. On his monthly pay vouchers he only gave the initials of his employees, listing them as "Operative A," "Operative B," etc. Secretary of War Edwin M. Stanton tried to force him to reveal their names, but he insisted that it was necessary to keep the information a secret in order to ensure their future success as operatives. Pinkerton continued with this policy and was able to draw the full amount of their pay right up to the end of his service. This was one of the few defeats Stanton would suffer as secretary of war, being forced to pay the salaries and expenses of agents whose backgrounds and loyalty he had no way of checking.[15]

About the same time that Pinkerton went to work for McClellan, General Winfield Scott realized he needed an intelligence officer, too. He hired Lafayette Baker, who assumed the same title as Pinkerton — Head of the Secret Service. This led to confusion within the government as well as within the two services. It was not uncommon for agents of one agency to arrest agents from the other, believing them to be Confederate spies. The two agencies continued to operate independently throughout the war with no effort to coordinate their efforts or to eliminate competition between the two.[16]

When Pinkerton went into the field with McClellan, Baker was in charge in Washington. Baker confined his work to Washington, mostly in the area of counterintelligence and investigating government fraud. Baker was unyielding in his efforts. Later, during the war, he accused a woman in Washington of selling presidential pardons. Believing he had an excellent case, Baker reported it to President Lincoln, who actually was signing the pardons for her clients. Lincoln ordered Baker to drop the investigation, but Baker refused, causing a permanent rift between the two.[17]

Lincoln's most immediate concern was keeping the border state of Kentucky in the Union. "I think to lose Kentucky is nearly the same as to lose the whole game," Lincoln wrote. The divisions over secession were running very deep within the state. On May 2, 1861, Governor Beriah Magoffin declared Kentucky officially neutral, but few expected that fragile position to last.[18]

McClellan asked Pinkerton to gather more information about the situation in Kentucky and other Southern states. On occasion Pinkerton would take to the field himself; for this assignment he volunteered to attend to it personally. McClellan enthusiastically assented. The trip would take Pinkerton through three states: Kentucky, Tennessee, and Mississippi. While in Confederate territory, he would be Mr. E. J. Allen from Augusta.[19]

Wearing civilian clothes, E. J. Allen departed by train for Louisville, Kentucky, the first stop on his trip. After casually talking to a variety of people and determining the sentiments of the most influential, he sent his report to McClellan. In it he reported that Kentucky was in a peculiar position. The governor's sentiments were not favorable to the Union. "Although the popular feelings of the people were deeply pro-slavery," he wrote, "and the state's commercial bonds with the Deep South strong, the patriotic example and teaching of Henry Clay had impressed upon [the people] a reverence and love for the Union higher and purer than any mere pressing of selfish advantage." He predicted that Kentucky would not join the Confederacy and that within a short time their citizens would be joining the Union cause. He was correct in both predictions.[20] In Bowling Green, Kentucky, Pinkerton found a great deal of sympathy for the Union, but there was widespread fear that many slaves, if freed, would turn on their former owners and murder them.[21]

After purchasing a horse, E. J. Allen traveled to Nashville, Tennessee, where he talked leisurely with Confederate soldiers. They found him to be a "Yankee-hating Georgian" and were willing to tell him what they knew of Confederate defense plans. In one conversation he spoke to a surgeon who revealed his plan for destroying an invading Northern army. It consisted of poisoning barrels of whiskey, which would be loaded on a commissary wagon; then the wagon would be disabled and abandoned on the route of the oncoming Union troops. When asked for his opinion of the plan, Pinkerton's response was, "Are you sure that some of your friends won't find the whiskey first?"[22] Pinkerton was pleased to find that, although the secessionist element was more united and outspoken in Nashville, there was some evidence of pro-Union feelings. This is the last time he would encounter such feelings as he got further and further into the Deep South.

Pinkerton's next stop was Memphis, Tennessee, which was considered a strategic position and a prize the Union hoped to take early in the war in order to control the Mississippi River and split the Confederacy. Memphis connected the rich plantations to the south by rail with Charleston, South Carolina. Pinkerton later wrote of the dangerous atmosphere for Union sympathizers in Memphis in mid-1861: "Here to be known or suspected as a Union man was to merit certain death. . . . Here rebeldom was rampant and defiant."[23]

Pinkerton made his way to the Gayoso House, one of Memphis's most elegant hotels, where the headquarters of Confederate Brigadier General Gideon J. Pillow was located. Pillow was in charge of the fortifications at Memphis.

Pinkerton registered at the hotel and took up residence there. He wore no disguise, except a slight alteration of his beard. The ease at which he operated was his greatest disguise. Pinkerton quickly made friends, and after just a few days there, he was drinking and smoking cigars with General Pillow. In his memoirs he wrote of his experience: "He [Pillow] little dreamed when on one occasion he quietly sipped his brandy and water with me, that he was giving valuable information to a sworn foe."[24]

E. J. Allen spent several days in Memphis touring the earthworks and fortifications under construction and talking to the workmen during the labor. Pinkerton committed what he saw and heard to memory until he returned to his hotel room, where he made notes about it. Later this information would be very important to the Union commanders. All seemed to be going smoothly until one evening the hotel's African American porter informed him that he was in great danger. He told Pinkerton if he didn't leave in a hurry, he would be a "dead man before morning." A Confederate spy had recognized him in the lobby and was certain he was not E. J. Allen from Augusta, Georgia. The rebel spy had seen him in Cincinnati with McClellan less than three weeks earlier. With the assistance of the porter, Pinkerton slipped down the back stairs and was able to make his escape. Reasoning that those in pursuit of him would expect him to head north, he went south, using little-known roads. While his pursuers headed north, Pinkerton galloped into Mississippi.[25]

Pinkerton continued to gather information as he traveled through Mississippi. He planned to spend several days in Jackson, the capital, before going on to Vicksburg and across the river into Louisiana. After checking into a hotel, he was soon walking about the city, observing military preparations. Through careful questioning, he was able to acquire important military information about Vicksburg and Louisiana.

One morning while being shaved by the hotel barber, he was recognized. Years before, Pinkerton had been a customer at the barber shop in the Sherman House in Chicago, where the barber had worked. Now the barber recognized Pinkerton and referred to him by name. When he continued to insist that he knew him, Pinkerton pulled the greatest bluff of his life. He leaped toward the barber and threatened to "whip him on the spot" if he continued to imply that he was a Yankee. Pinkerton turned to the crowd that had gathered and told them that the barber had insulted him, that he had never been in Chicago, and that "he did not know Mr. Pinkerton or any of his gang." Then he invited the entire crowd to join him in the nearby hotel bar for a drink. All accepted, and there, they toasted the Confederacy and drank to Confederate President Davis.[26]

Pinkerton's drinking companions were satisfied for the time, but not wanting to push his luck, he slipped away to the hotel stable, mounted his horse, and rode north as fast as he could. When he arrived in Cincinnati and reported his findings, McClellan was pleased with the thoroughness of his report.

By the end of 1861, Pinkerton's force had grown to twenty-four; of them, only five served behind enemy lines. Pinkerton's main source of information was not from spying on the enemy, but from interrogation of prisoners, deserters, and refugees. His method of interrogating was very systematic. In addition to routine questions about Confederate numerical strength, fortifications, and armament, questions were asked about their health, food and forage, clothing and shoes, condition of horses and harness, re-enlistment prospects, military and civilian morale, the condition of roads and railroads, and the nature of the Southern economy.[27]

All informants, refugees, deserters, and captured prisoners of war were subject to the same interrogation routine. Unfortunately all the information received was written up by clerks who were unable to screen that which was useful from that which was not. The reports were often wordy, and little effort was made to compare new information with earlier reports. The report writers were under instruction to give just the facts and not to editorialize. For several months McClellan received volumes of information, more than he had time to read or interpret properly.[28]

The most reliable information came from deserters, especially European immigrants or Northerners who had been impressed into Confederate service. Some claimed to have planned to desert from the time they entered the army. As a result they often made mental notes about the Confederate army in order to improve their chances of being welcomed by the Federals. The greatest number and the most cooperative class of informants were the black refugees. Their information was limited, however, because they had lived mostly on farms and plantations and had little access to military installations or operations.[29]

As McClellan's intelligence gatherer, one of Pinkerton's important tasks was to determine the strength of Confederate forces facing the Army of the Potomac. Pinkerton and McClellan trusted each other to the degree that each would accept the claims of the other. When Pinkerton reported his findings,

McClellan never questioned them. Unfortunately Pinkerton's estimates were often inflated.[30]

Lincoln questioned the number of troops in the Army of the Potomac. By the War Department's count, 108,000 men had been sent to the Peninsula, yet General McClellan reported only 85,000. The difference was due to the way the counts were made. The War Department counted all men in McClellan's army at a given time, including officers and fighting men, noncombatants, those on special duty and on sick call, and even those in the guardhouse. McClellan's count was much lower because he only included enlisted men who were actually present for duty. There was nothing wrong with McClellan's method of counting, but he was obligated to explain his method when reporting his army's size. His obstinate refusal to explain what he was doing reduced his credibility with Lincoln. Moreover, McClellan did not count the Confederate army the same way he counted his own. On the Peninsula, Pinkerton provided McClellan with estimates of Confederate strength based on the number of rations issued to the enemy troops. Consequently his totals were often overestimated.[31]

Pinkerton's miscalculations of enemy strength had a devastating effect on McClellan's 1862 Peninsula campaign. His information confirmed McClellan's fears that Confederate forces outnumbered his own. When Pinkerton estimated that the Union army faced 150,000 Confederates, McClellan called for reinforcements for his army of 120,000, believing success would require an attacking force of twice that. In reality, McClellan already outnumbered General Joseph Johnston's army of 50,000 by more than two to one.

After the bloody battles of Seven Pines and Fair Oaks, General McClellan believed he was in a position to end the war, stating, "the final and decisive battle is at hand." He was certain that the capture of Richmond would end the war and enshrine his name in history; it might even make him president of the United States. Although impatient with McClellan's slowness and his constant complaint about not having enough troops, Lincoln accepted his strategy and agreed to his request for reinforcements, sending Major General Irvin McDowell's army south to strengthen him for his next move. McClellan had insisted that these reinforcements were vital because of the information provided by Pinkerton. Pinkerton continued to believe that General Johnston's forces outnumbered McClellan's and that his army was still on the rise. This gave McClellan an excuse to wait, plan, reorganize, and demand more men and supplies —

anything except attack.[32] As a result, the Peninsula campaign dragged on into a series of battles that ultimately forced McClellan to withdraw and helped to extend the war.

Although Pinkerton was in error in estimating troop size, he was able to select competent operatives. One of his most talented was Timothy Webster,. who operated repeatedly behind enemy lines, gathering information and sending it north to Pinkerton. Under suspicion of being a spy on several occasions, Webster was able to talk his way out of trouble. For more than a year, Webster was able to carry out many daring operations.

Pinkerton was one of the first men to recognize and take advantage of the talents of slaves and freedmen for gathering information. Southerners often underestimated the ability of African Americans to spy, believing they were not intelligent enough or capable of independent thought. The Confederates' unrealistic assessment of African Americans increased their value as spies. In addition, Southerners believed that their slaves knew little about what was going on. Actually, those servants who worked about the house probably knew as much as their owners.[33]

One of Pinkerton's most successful black spies was John Scobell. In his memoirs, Pinkerton described Scobell as "a remarkably gifted man.... The manner in which he performed his duty was always a source of satisfaction to me." Scobell and his wife were freed before the war. Scobell's wife remained in Richmond as a cook while he went north, where he was recruited as a spy by Pinkerton. Pinkerton recalled that "he had only to assume the role of a light-hearted darky and no one would suspect his real role." Scobell returned to the South, operating on his own. Hiring himself out as a day laborer and cook among various Confederate camps, he was able to collect information about troop strength and movements. When other Union spies were discovered and captured, Scobell was left to continue his work without being questioned.[34]

Pinkerton's sometimes unsuccessful effort in gathering accurate information was not due to lack of energy or organization. "My shrewd and daring operatives," he later wrote, "men and women, trained for the work, moved in and out among the Rebel troops at all times and places." The information provided by Pinkerton's agents and reported to McClellan was voluminous. They not only identified the enemy units, but contained information and minutiae about morale, supplies, and equipment, down to the description of buttons on Confederate uniforms. Such information, although useful, failed in the most important category of all — the accurate estimation of the enemy's strength.[35]

Although Pinkerton's ability to gather reliable intelligence all the time may be questionable, he excelled as a spy catcher. His greatest success was the apprehension of Rose O'Neal Greenhow, a widow and Washington socialite with strong Southern sympathies. Rose moved in the highest political and social circles because of her good looks and charm. Taking advantage of this, she was able to get important military information from men who found her irresistible. Allan Pinkerton did not succumb to her charms, however, and it was he who was responsible for her arrest.[36]

In the summer of 1862, Lee's invasion of Maryland caught Pinkerton without his spies in place. As a result, he contributed little to the ensuing campaign. After the Battle of Antietam, McClellan was removed from command of the Army of the Potomac, and Pinkerton followed his chief back into civilian life. When he returned to his detective business, it became the duty of Lafayette Baker's secret service to carry on the counterespionage work in Washington and to protect the president. Baker was not as conscientious as Pinkerton had been in protecting Lincoln. On April 14, 1865, John Wilkes Booth was able to assassinate the president. Although a man from Baker's service had been on assignment that evening to guard Lincoln at Ford's Theater, Baker was never able to explain his absence.[37]

Following the war, Pinkerton expanded his agency's operations, with his major clients still being railroads and express companies. The agency's first contact with armed train robbery came in 1866 with the holdup of an Adams Express Company car on the Ohio and Mississippi Railroad by the Reno gang. Pinkerton moved in and, with secret operatives, managed to put the gang out of business within two years.[44] As the number of train robberies increased in the Midwest and South, the demand for Pinkerton's National Detective Agency grew.Pinkerton's two sons, William and Robert, joined the firm and proved to be as talented as their father in chasing criminals. The agency's methods were effective. It let it be known that once a file was opened on a fugitive, it was never closed until he was captured or dead. While their agents were often able to infiltrate outlaw gangs, leading to their arrest, the major part of the agency's success was due to its persistence. The agency claimed it would spend $20,000

Lafayette Baker was Pinkerton's greatest rival. Both men named themselves "Chief of the United States Secret Service," but President Lincoln was killed on Baker's watch.
(National Archives and Records Administration)

to catch a robber who stole $200. After the war the Pinkertons, under the able leadership of their founder Allan Pinkerton, had well earned its motto, "The Eye That Never Sleeps."[38]

By 1882 Pinkerton was still going to the office from time to time. By now the agency was being run by his two sons and had branched out in all directions. During the winter of 1883–84, Pinkerton was bedridden after suffering a paralytic stroke. He seemed to rally a bit during the summer of 1884 and was able to get up and about. One day in early June he went for a walk, tripped on the sidewalk, fell, and bit his tongue. Gangrene set in, and after three weeks of intense pain, he died on the afternoon of July 1. Pinkerton's devotion to his agents was evident even in death. One of the requests in his will was that the graves of Timothy Webster and other Pinkerton agents buried near him in Graceland Cemetery "never be sold, graveled or aliened in any matter whatsoever."[39]

Allan Pinkerton created a vast organization that fought crime from petty pilfering to grand larceny and from street mugging to murder. His name became a household word around the world. Until the development of the Federal Bureau of Investigation in 1908, the Pinkertons acted as a national police force. Many of the principles of crime detection which Pinkerton developed are still used today.[40]

The evaluation of Allan Pinkerton's performance as a spymaster during the Civil War, however, is not as clear cut. As the organizer and chief of the first official United States secret service, some see Pinkerton and his operatives as courageous people who proved to be of incalculable value. They cite Pinkerton's safe delivery of Lincoln to Washington, the important arrests of Confederate spies in Washington and Baltimore, his collection of information for General McClellan, and the agency's service behind enemy lines during several Union campaigns.[41]

Others see Pinkerton in another light. They give him credit for his counterespionage work, an activity similar to the undercover work he had done before the war with burglary rings and which had been a specialty of his detective agency. In dealing with military intelligence, however, he was not always able to separate fact from rumor. He and his interrogators, they say, exercised the power of judge and jury over those brought to them for questioning. On their recommendation a deserter or prisoner-of-war could be paroled or imprisoned based on information given during the interrogation. As a result, the information given was often what the prisoner thought the interrogators wanted to hear.[42]

Although a few of Pinkerton's operatives, including himself, ventured deep into enemy territory, most operated in Richmond. On rare occasions when they did go behind enemy lines, they seldom went beyond the front line, not attempting to ascertain enemy strength in the rear.[43] The most important criticism of Pinkerton's espionage efforts is in the area of estimating Confederate troop strength. In 1864, Pinkerton's troop estimates were made public and compared to the actual numbers. They aroused both anger and amusement. It was a sorry conclusion for Pinkerton, a man who had served his country well.[44]

2

Union Double Agent

TIMOTHY WEBSTER

URING the Civil War, Timothy Webster was considered one of the most conscientious and effective Union spies. When he was arrested in Richmond in April 1862, the Union's espionage efforts suffered a severe loss. Webster's arrest and conviction as a spy came as a complete surprise to Jefferson Davis and the Confederate government. He had been trusted with valuable documents to deliver to Rebel agents in the North. As retribution for the embarrassment he caused them, Webster was sentenced to death by hanging, the first such penalty during the Civil War.[1]

Timothy Webster was born in Newhaven, Sussex, England in 1821. By the time he was twelve years old, his family had immigrated to the United States. He grew up in Princeton, New Jersey, and became a New York City policeman. His effectiveness as an officer of the law was soon recognized by a friend of Allan Pinkerton, who recommended him for detective work. Pinkerton offered him a position with his agency. Webster, realizing this was a good opportunity, accepted. As a Pinkerton agent, Webster's work was excellent, and he quickly became one of their top operatives.[2]

For the eight years before the war, Webster was a premier detective in the Pinkerton agency. By his undercover work, he discovered the plot to assassinate Lincoln in Baltimore. In his memoirs, Pinkerton praised Webster for his efforts: "He amongst all the force who went with me, deserves the credit for saving Mr. Lincoln, even more than I do."[3]

When the Civil War began and Pinkerton went to work for General George McClellan, he took many of his agents, including Webster, with him, requiring them to make the transition from detective to spy. Many of Pinkerton's agents never completely understood the requirements of being an effective spy. Webster, however, successfully made the change and quickly became Pinkerton's top operative. "Any man meeting Webster," according to Pinkerton, "would be immediately impressed with his conviction." During his career, Webster lived up to this assessment.[4]

Timothy Webster's first assignment was to spy on Confederate army units forming in Kentucky and Tennessee. He arrived in Louisville early in May 1861 and rapidly made friends with Southern sympathizers there. He used his own name and claimed to be a resident of Baltimore. Continuing his trip, he went to Memphis, stopping at Bowling Green, Kentucky, and then Clarkesville, Tennessee. Along the way he continued to make friends and gather information, which he sent back to Pinkerton in Washington. Webster's reports were always filled with useful details: "An army officer from Fort Dover, on the Cumberland River, said 500 men well armed, with 32-pounders (iron) were there to guard the river."[5]

Previous page:
Timothy Webster was the first spy in the Civil War to be hanged. His loss was a severe blow to the Union Secret Service.

(Reprinted with permission of Pinkerton, Inc.)

On his last trip to Memphis, Webster found himself being followed. By a few discreet inquiries, he learned that the man shadowing him was a member of the local "Safety Committee." Undeterred, Webster continued to act as normally as possible, not altering any of his routines. While registered at the Worsham House, he ingratiated himself with a group of Confederate officers in the hotel bar and quickly convinced them that he was a rabid secessionist. "He practically mesmerized you into thinking he was whatever he decided to be," a colleague noted. His deception was so convincing that, after several drinks, the officers insisted on buying him a "secession hat" (a Confederate officer's hat).[6]

The next morning his "shadow" was still with him when he left the hotel and walked to the train station, where he boarded a train for Chattanooga. At Grand Junction, when he changed to a northbound train, Webster noticed he was still being followed. At Jackson, Tennessee, he inquired about trains to Humboldt. Giving the impression that he would be there for several days, he asked about hotel accommodations. He made no attempt to keep his destination a secret, making sure that his pursuer heard it. At Humboldt he got off the train and quickly stepped behind a pile of baggage. His shadow, assuming he had gone to the hotel, hurried off in that direction. In a few minutes Webster boarded a train that took him north toward Ohio and safety.[7]

Webster's next operation took him to Baltimore, now under military rule. His assignment was to infiltrate the Knights of Liberty, a gang of armed Confederate sympathizers who were believed to be responsible for the violence in Baltimore. As a result of riots in April, some key Baltimore citizens, including the chief of police and members of the board of police commissioners, had been arrested and were being held in custody at Fort McHenry. To establish himself as a man of means with Southern leanings, Webster secured quarters at the prestigious Miller's Hotel. Within a short time Webster had made contact with members of Knights of Liberty and had no difficulty in gaining their confidence. Again he posed as a "diehard secessionist."[8]

While in Baltimore Webster worked in conjunction with another Pinkerton operative, John Scully, who acted as his courier when it was not safe for him to deliver information to Pinkerton. In order to make certain that they could get past Southern sentries, Webster devised a simple trick. He and Scully went to a photographic gallery, where they posed holding a Confederate flag between them. Both men kept a copy of the photograph in their wallets in the event they were stopped when going through Confederate lines.[9]

Webster often made trips to Washington to deliver information to Pinkerton personally. Occasionally he would be forced to take some of his new friends from Baltimore with him. Although it prevented him from delivering his report, it did provide him with the opportunity to meet other secessionists who had not been suspected before, persons that Pinkerton would be happy to learn about.[10]

One evening while Webster was enjoying himself in a Baltimore bar with some of his newly acquired friends, a dangerous situation developed. A man by the name of Bill Zigler accused him of being a Union spy, claiming he had seen him in Washington the day before. Webster willingly acknowledged that he had been to Washington, but Zigler insisted that he had seen him talking to Pinkerton. Webster quickly took action; calling him a scoundrel and a liar, he knocked Zigler to the floor. Zigler jumped up with a knife, only to face Webster's pistol. "Coward!" shouted Webster. "It would serve you right if I shot you down like a dog." Webster told him to leave the room or he would shoot him. Zigler backed down, putting his knife away, and left. His friends at the bar apologized for Zigler's behavior and assured Webster of their friendship and support. The incident not only solidified his position with the rebel enthusiasts but brought him a chance to infiltrate the Knights of Liberty.[11]

The Knights of Liberty were a secret organization. To gain membership required an initiation. As part of his initiation, Webster was blindfolded and taken to their secret meeting place. While still blindfolded, he was presented to the "Most Noble Chief." After swearing undying obedience and allegiance to the secessionist cause, his blindfold was removed; Webster was now a member of the Knights of Liberty.[12]

As ridiculous as Webster's initiation into the Knights of Liberty had been, the organization's goals were not. Webster learned that they were a part of a larger plot to invade Washington. The plan was to have the Baltimore rebels attack the capital from the north, while Confederate forces crossed the Potomac and approached from the south. When Pinkerton learned of this, the decision was made to put an end to the Knights of Liberty.

As a member of the Knights of Liberty, Webster was called upon to speak at one of their meetings. At the same time he made arrangements with Pinkerton for a large-scale raid. The raid was to take place at the climax of his speech so as not to bring suspicion upon him. At the appointed time, Union troops battered down the door. As the Knights of Liberty scurried about in panic, Webster escaped through a window. Many ringleaders of the society were arrested, including two leading Baltimore newspaper editors. After a hearing, some were imprisoned at Fort McHenry; the others were released after taking the federal oath of allegiance. The freed conspirators congratulated Webster of his miraculous escape, never suspecting him of complicity in the raid.[13]

By October 1861 things in Baltimore had settled down, so Webster was sent to Richmond. He was smuggled across the Chesapeake Bay with a group of Southern sympathizers, landing at Gloucester Point where Confederate troops under Colonel Charles H. Crump were stationed. Webster went boldly to Crump's headquarters, convincing him to provide passes for them. At Richmond he registered at the Spotswood Hotel and began a reconnaissance of the city's defenses.[14]

After a time he returned to Baltimore, where he again made contact with paroled members of the Knights of Liberty and was able to get information concerning a scheme to smuggle supplies to the South. Webster notified Pinkerton, and the cargo was seized at the docks.[15]

While in Baltimore, another threat to Webster's security occurred — he was arrested as a Confederate spy. Imprisoned for hours, Webster finally got word of his situation to Pinkerton. He feared that an order by Pinkerton for his release would be suspicious. Because word of his arrest had spread throughout Baltimore, he could not just walk out of a federal prison as if nothing happened without jeopardizing his cover. A plan had to be developed.[16]

While a crowd of onlookers gathered, Webster was taken under guard from the prison and placed in a police van. The officer in charge ordered the driver to head for Fort McHenry. On a lonely place on the road, Webster was allowed to jump from the wagon and disappear into the night. Again Webster's credibility among the city's Confederate sympathizers was enhanced when stories detailing his dramatic escape appeared in several Baltimore papers.[17]

Armed with credentials from the Knights of Liberty and letters of introduction from Baltimore secessionists, Webster set out for Richmond again. This time he went to see the editor of the *Richmond Examiner*, explaining that his business required him to make frequent trips to Washington and Baltimore and that he would act as a messenger for the paper. His pleasing personality and affable approach convinced the editor of his sincerity, and an agreement was reached.[18]

Now with a letter of introduction, Webster went to see William Campbell, son of a Baltimore secessionist friend. With the help of Campbell, he soon circulated freely in Confederate society and was able to make friends with some of the leading political and military persons, including Brigadier General John Winder. Through this contact, Webster was able to arrange an interview with the Confederate secretary of war, Judah Benjamin, whom he convinced of his sincerity and interest in the Southern cause. Webster offered his services to deliver dispatches to Southerners in the North; he was now playing the dangerous game of double agent.[19] Webster carried mail and important dispatches to Confederate agents in the North, but they were delivered only after having first been read by Union officials.

At the War Office in Richmond, Webster obtained a pass to visit Manassas, which allowed him to visit other military installations. At Fredericksburg he was given complete run of the camp, making good use of the opportunity to collect information. After a complete inspection, Webster returned to Washington and Pinkerton's office.[20] Pinkerton forwarded the information, which proved very valuable to McClellan. To show his appreciation, McClellan secretly had a letter of thanks smuggled to Webster for his effort.

Webster continued to move freely between Baltimore, Washington, and Richmond, delivering Benjamin's messages. He had an excellent memory and his reports were classic. Although he was in constant danger, he was still able to report explicit details of every item of military importance. One of his reports, a thirty-seven-page document, included the smallest details of Richmond's fortifications. In addition to the height and locations of breastworks, the types, numbers, and locations of guns and the number of troops, his report also included such information as the percent of soldiers without shoes and the price of various food items.[21]

In his lengthy report, however, there was one important inaccuracy, one that had calamitous consequences for McClellan. Webster's estimate of Confederate strength around Richmond was overstated by 40,000 men. Pinkerton did not question the figures and merely passed them on to McClellan. Assuming the estimate of Confederate strength was accurate, McClellan delayed his offensive campaign and requested more troops. This inaction angered both Lin-

Allan Pinkerton tried everything he could think of to save Webster, but President Davis was determined to make an example of him.

(Dictionary of American Portraits)

coln and Stanton and helped to establish McClellan's reputation as the general with the "slows."[22]

For civilians, too, Webster reported suspicious instances of illegal trading with the enemy. He carried messages, dispatches, and other items both ways. He once took a special horse-bit to General Joseph Johnston. Dispatches sent North were carefully examined in Washington before they were delivered. Those going South contained enough factual information to convince the Confederates, but not enough to cause harm to the Union efforts.[23]

On one occasion a Union surgeon, who was defecting to join the Confederate army, was sent to Webster for help in getting past the Union pickets. When Webster learned he was also carrying an important message to Secretary Benjamin, he offered to help, planning to meet him in the morning. In the meantime he arranged to have the doctor followed by an ex-slave. When they met the next day, the doctor was distressed; he had been robbed the preceding night by a black man who took his papers. Webster consoled the doctor, telling him he had only lost the papers and could still report verbally. The doctor was even more troubled, explaining that the papers were sealed and he had no idea what they contained. Webster was sympathetic but thought, "I know, and soon McClellan will know too."[24]

One of Webster's last trips to Richmond was unusually difficult and was to have serious repercussions for his health. Escorting the wives of two Confederate officers and their children across the Potomac, they encountered a storm which caused the small boat to run upon a sandbar off the Virginia shore. Webster quickly came to aid of the women and children on board, making several trips to assist them to reach the shore. Then the shivering party walked through the icy rain to a nearby farmhouse, where they dried out as best they could before a fire. Webster gave the only blanket to the women and children and tried to sleep in his wet clothes. As he lay down to sleep, he noticed an unwrapped packet that had fallen from the coat of one of the women. It was addressed to Judah Benjamin and contained maps of the country surrounding Washington with the numbers and locations of federal troops. After taking note of the information, Webster placed the package back into the woman's coat. This was information to which only someone in the federal government would have access. Acting on Webster's information, Pinkerton was able to arrest a Confederate spy in the U.S. provost marshal's office.[25]

Webster returned to Richmond the next morning, but he quickly came down with a severe case of inflammatory rheumatism — the result of his exposure in the icy waters of the Potomac. He was forced to go back to Washington and was confined to bed for several weeks. Webster never did fully recover his strength and would suffer continued pain from the rheumatism.[26]

By January 1862, believing he had completely recovered from his illness, Webster made another trip to Richmond. It was his last. He was accompanied by Hattie Lawton, one of the agency's best female operatives. When they reached Richmond, the weather turned cold and damp, aggravating his rheumatism again. The pain increased to the point that Webster was not able to travel and was confined to his hotel room. Lawton and Scobell, who was acting as her African American servant, stayed to care for him. Prostrated by his illness, Webster was neither able to return to Washington nor send a message to report his condition.

When Webster's regular reports stopped coming, Pinkerton became concerned. In a few days he learned of his most trusted agent's condition. Pinkerton dispatched agents John Scully and Pryce Lewis to Richmond to find out what had happened. Lewis believed the assignment was too risky for two, reminding Pinkerton that "one man can remember a story and stick to it." Still Pinkerton insisted on sending them both.[27]

The two men reached Richmond without incident, but upon their arrival they were soon spotted as suspicious characters and followed. Once they learned of the whereabouts of Webster, Scully and Lewis paid him a visit along with their Confederate "tails." After their visit, both Scully and Lewis were arrested and held for questioning. Although not arrested, Webster was now considered a suspicious character, too.[28]

The next morning, confident that their arrest was merely routine, Scully and Lewis were taken to General John Winder's office for questioning. Interrogated by Winder and Captain Sam McCubbin, the two agents insisted they were old friends of Webster and were just passing through Richmond. They had almost convinced their captors of their innocence when Lieutenant Chase Morton entered the room. Earlier in the war, Morton's father, Senator Jackson Morton, had been arrested by Scully and Lewis. Morton immediately recognized them. Handcuffed and charged with espionage, they were both taken to the Henrico County jail. While in prison, the two somehow got hold of a well-tempered knife and were able to saw through the steel bars. The process was slow, but finally they completed the sawing and, along with a few other prisoners, were able to escape. Unfortunately Scully and Lewis were discovered by a Confederate patrol just a short distance from the safety of the Union lines at Fredericksburg. Taken back to Richmond, where the news of their escape had become well known, the two Union spies were greeted by a crowd who came out to see them.[29]

Lewis and Scully were now imprisoned in Castle Goodwin, a filthy fortress that had once been a market for slave trading. The two men were separated, and Lewis was placed with a group of Confederate deserters. He had been there but a short time when he was involved in a second escape attempt. The deserters were in the process of tunneling their way to the street outside when they were discovered, and the attempt was foiled. As a consequence, Lewis was transferred to another cell and manacled in solitary confinement.[30]

Scully and Lewis were both tried, convicted of espionage, and sentenced to be hanged on April 4, 1862. But there was still a glimmer of hope for them. Scully was Irish and Lewis, English; neither had become American citizens, so they were still legally British subjects. Lewis wrote a note to the British Consul in Richmond, demanding the protection of the British government. When John Cridland, the acting British Consul, received the note, he visited Lewis in prison. Cridland was not too encouraging, saying he thought there was little chance he could save them, but he promised to examine the evidence against them. At this time, however, Cridland's intervention on behalf of England would mean a great deal, as Lewis knew. The Confederacy was desperately courting England to intervene in the war on the South's side; Lewis reasoned that the execution of two British-born Union spies would not be well received by the English.[34]

After Cridland examined the trial's transcript, he concluded that Scully and Lewis were tried before they could prepare a proper defense. This, he believed, caused the trial to be tainted with a "reversible error." Cridland presented this information to Secretary of War Benjamin, who prided himself on upholding justice and adhering to the law. As a result, he overruled the court-martial of both men and postponed their execution for two weeks.[32]

Just before their scheduled hanging, the two condemned men received word of their stay of execution but were advised that things still looked dark for them and that they should tell the authorities all they knew. Lewis stood firm, denying that Webster had any connection with Pinkerton or any of his agents, but Scully broke down and told the whole story. Because Webster had been so well connected with Confederate officials, Winder had refused to believe that he was a Federal operative. It was only after Scully's confession that Winder was convinced. As a result of Scully's willingness to tell all, both men's lives were spared.[33]

On September 29, 1863, Lewis and Scully were released from prison as part of a party of 150 Union prisoners-of-war being repatriated. Erroneous information was spread that Lewis, as well as Scully, had betrayed Webster. The error was compounded later when Hattie Lawton reported the same thing. Lewis had to fight hard to clear his name. The stigma of his betrayal hounded him most of his life. It was not until 1903 that his name was finally cleared. The years leading up to this proved hard for him, and in 1910 he ended his life by jumping off the top of the Times Building in New York. Neither man ever worked for Pinkerton again.[34]

Webster's luck finally ran out, and he and Lawton were arrested and charged with espionage. When Pinkerton learned of the capture of his agents, he immediately asked McClellan to send a delegate under a flag of truce to bargain for their lives, but the general refused. McClellan believed that to do so would be an admission that they were spies and that might result in their instant execution. After McClellan refused, Pinkerton went to see Secretary of War

Stanton.[35] As a result, Lincoln called an emergency session of the Cabinet to discuss the matter. Stanton promised to do all he could to save Webster's life, but he would do nothing for Scully and Lewis, who he believed had betrayed their companion to save their own lives.[36]

Stanton sent Pinkerton and Colonel Thomas M. Key of McClellan's staff under a flag of truce to deliver a message to Jefferson Davis. Stanton's message reminded Davis that Washington had not mistreated Confederate spies they had captured and that none had been hanged. He asked that Webster's life be spared. But typical of Stanton's rigid personality, the note also cautioned that if Webster were hanged, the Union had no choice but to hang a Confederate spy in retaliation. Prior to this time it had been the Union's policy to incarcerate spies for a period of time and then exchange them for Union prisoners.[37]

President Davis was unmoved by Stanton's request. There was just enough of a threat for the proud Davis to refuse clemency to Webster. He agreed to commute the death sentences of Scully and Lewis, but Webster must hang; an example would have to be made. When McCubbin delivered Davis's decision to Webster, he requested to be shot by a firing squad rather than to be hanged. Webster felt he deserved an honorable end. Hattie Lawton was at Webster's bedside when Winder informed him that his request had been refused. She told Winder that Webster would show them how a Union man could die and warned him that Washington would neither forget nor forgive Webster's treatment. Three years later her threat came to fruition when the South appealed for clemency on behalf of John Beall and Robert Kennedy, two Confederate agents captured in New York. They were hanged after their request to be shot was denied.[38]

On April 29, 1862, Webster, with Lawton at his side, was helped to a carriage and driven to the fairgrounds at Camp Lee, where he was greeted by a large crowd of spectators and a high scaffold. Webster was shocked to learn that his execution was to be public, an indication of Davis's feelings about Stanton's undiplomatic threat.[39] Southern newspaper accounts said that Webster collapsed, begging for mercy, and had to be carried to the gallows. This was not true. Webster was so crippled by rheumatism that he could not walk on his own. Although he had to be assisted up the steps, Webster still made it on his own feet.[40]

In the absence of an official hangman, one of the prison guards was used as a substitute. As a result the execution was horribly botched. When the trap was sprung, the knot slipped and Webster fell to the ground with a sickening thud. In great pain, Webster lay on the ground until two guards could carry him back up the stairs, again to face the hangman's noose. This time the noose was adjusted so tightly that Webster's face turned red. As he gasped for air, he uttered: "Strangled! I suffer a double death!" Again the trapdoor opened and Webster's body fell through; this time the rope held. Timothy Webster was the first American spy to be executed in America since Nathan Hale in 1776.[41]

Hattie Lawton was allowed to accompany Webster's body to a Richmond funeral parlor. That night Webster was buried in the paupers' section of Richmond cemetery in an unmarked grave. When Pinkerton learned of this, he vowed to find his grave and return his body to Northern soil. After the war he was able to do this, thanks to the efforts of another federal spy who took careful note of the burial spot. In his postwar memoirs, Pinkerton reflected on Webster's courage and contributions to the Union cause, writing that he had "suffered in a glorious cause and died a martyr's death."

3

"Crazy Bet"

ELIZABETH VAN LEW

LIZABETH Van Lew had the right combination of age, marital status, and eccentricity to be an effective spy. Southerners often dismissed as harmless women known as "spinster ladies." Such was the diminutive Richmond figure who was referred to as "Crazy Bet."[1]

Union Major General Benjamin Butler dubbed her "my correspondent in Richmond," and Lieutenant General Ulysses Grant considered her valuable enough to provide personal protection for her when the Union army entered Richmond. Yet the only surviving tribute to her is a boulder marking her grave in Shacke Cemetery in Richmond with the inscription: "Elizabeth L. Van Lew, 1818–1900: She risked everything that is dear to man — friends, fortune, comfort, health, life itself — all for the desire of her heart — that slavery might be abolished and the Union preserved."[2]

One of the most successful spies for the Union, Van Lew was the most incongruous. She was a member of the Virginia aristocracy and lived on one of the highest hills in Richmond. Although very much a lady, she became the most hated woman in the Confederacy. The three-story Van Lew mansion on Church Hill contained huge rooms, a library where she kept her horse, and on the third floor, beneath the attic, a secret room where she hid escaping Union soldiers.[3]

Van Lew was born on October 15, 1818, to a wealthy family. Her parents, John and Eliza, were Northerners who met in Richmond after her father moved there for his health. John Van Lew was able to establish a successful chain of hardware stores in Richmond. He was a loving father who adored his three children. "I remember my father coming in at night and waking and taking us up in our long white gowns to sit awhile on his knee to be pressed to his heart," Van Lew recalled. Her parents were intellectuals who enjoyed reading; a sizable sum was budgeted each year for the purchase of books. The Van Lew house became a center of social gatherings where many famous and prominent people were entertained. Among their friends were Chief Justice John Marshall and the Lee families of Richmond. Edgar Allan Poe once read his poetry in their parlor. In 1843 Van Lew's father died after a prolonged illness. John Van Lew left the house and other real estate to his wife. To each of his children he left a $10,000 endowment.[4]

Van Lew was sent north for an education. It was here that her attitude toward slavery was shaped. She was greatly influenced by her governess in Philadelphia and the abolition movement in the North. One incident stood out in her mind, the sale of two slaves that separated a mother from her child. The separation was so traumatic for the mother that she died. The situation had a long-lasting effect on Van Lew. After her father's death, she convinced her

---

Previous page:

Elizabeth Van Lew's espionage during the Civil War made her the most hated woman in the Confederacy.

(Valentine Museum, Richmond, Virginia)

mother to free their nine slaves. With part of her inheritance, she purchased the freedom of the relatives of the Van Lew slaves.[5] Her former slaves were very loyal to the family and, after being freed, stayed on as servants. Several became important links in the communication network she established with the Union army during the war.[6]

Well before the Civil War began, Van Lew was a staunch abolitionist. "Slave power," she wrote in her diary, "is arrogant, is jealous and intrusive, is cruel, is despotic." The Van Lew estate soon became a haven for runaway slaves and a station for the Underground Railroad. Because of her outspoken views on slavery and its practice, Van Lew was considered an eccentric by members of Richmond's society. Social leaders believed she had acquired her abolition beliefs while attending school in Philadelphia; they did not consider her a true Southerner because both of her parents had come from the North. Van Lew, however, loved the South and was proud of being a Southerner; it was slavery that she hated.[8]

When the Van Lews' abolitionist views became known throughout Richmond, they were subtly excluded from some of the social events to which they formerly had been invited. Although Van Lew was considered attractive as a young lady, she did not marry. By the time she was forty years old, she had lost that beauty, having a sharp nose and piercing blue eyes, giving her the classic "old maid" look. With a reputation for being eccentric, soon she was referred to as "Crazy Bet."[8]

In 1863 General Robert E. Lee ordered all horses in the Confederacy confiscated for his cavalry. When three of Van Lew's beautiful white coach horses were taken, she was determined not to lose her last animal. Van Lew had her servants spread straw on the floor of the library, where she kept the horse for the duration of the war. This served to confirm her neighbors' opinion that she was crazy.[9]

After the fall of Fort Sumter, with the Confederate flag flying over Richmond, Van Lew committed herself to saving the Union. "Never," she later wrote, "did a feeling of more calm determination and high resolve for endurance come over me."[10] She was determined to do all that she could to see that the slaves were freed and the nation reunited. Van Lew was not alone in this determination. Richmond's population contained a number of Union supporters who were opposed to secession; she tried to elicit their help in her plans to supply information to the North. Those Richmond citizens who were believed to be loyal to the Union were ridiculed, and their lives were often in danger. "Mobs went to private houses to hang the true of heart," she wrote. "Loyalty now was called treason, and cursed. If you spoke in your parlor or chamber to your next of heart, you whispered."[11]

Although espionage was never proved against them, public opinion condemned the Van Lew family for their Northern sympathies. Early in the war a Richmond paper wrote of them: "While every true woman in this community has been making articles for our troops, or administering to our sick, these two women have been spending their opulent means in aiding and giving comfort to the miscreants who have invaded our sacred soil." Throughout the war, Van Lew continued to be harassed. "I have had brave men shake their fingers in my face and say terrible things," she wrote. She went to see Jefferson Davis himself to ask for protection. When he didn't respond, Van Lew invited Lieutenant Gibbs, commandant of Libby Prison, to board his family in their house.[12]

Despite continued threats from local Confederates, Van Lew went on with her plans. The family owned a small farm near Richmond, adjacent to the James River and Osborne Turnpike. Because of its excellent location, it became the first of five points along the James River used by the Van Lews to pass information to federal forces at Fortress Monroe in Hampton, Virginia.[13]

Van Lew took advantage of her Crazy Bet image. Even before the war, she had been considered strange. Now she emphasized her strangeness — talking to herself, allowing her hair to fall in disarray, and wearing old and shabby clothing. Behind Van Lew's cover was a clever woman capable of improvising as the need arose.[14]

Despite Van Lew's eccentricities and her outspoken opinions on slavery, her mother and brother remained moderate in their views. As a result, their plush home continued to serve as a gathering place for some of Richmond's prominent citizens. They entertained various Confederate officers and government officials, who unwittingly revealed pieces of information which Van Lew forwarded to her Union contacts in the North.[15]

Information was delivered by her servants carrying baskets of eggs. One of the eggs had been drained and its contents replaced with a message written on very thin paper. Sometimes messages were smuggled out in a basket with a false bottom. Notes were also carried in the soles of servants' shoes. For security measures, Van Lew tore the messages into several pieces, each sent by a different courier using different routes. Messages were often written in cipher or with a clear ink that became visible when dipped in milk.[16] Van Lew's courier system worked so well that not a single of her servants was ever caught by the enemy.

Van Lew's first opportunity to get information for the Union came in July 1861 when Union prisoners were brought to Richmond after the First Battle of Manassas. After she learned of the poor conditions in the Libby Prison where Union officers were being held, Van Lew requested permission to minister to them. When her request was refused, she contacted Confederate Secretary of the Treasury Christopher Memminger, an acquaintance of her family. She reminded him of a sermon he had given on Christian charity. Memminger gave his permission, giving her a note which would allow her to enter the prison.[17]

Van Lew made frequent visits to the prison, bringing food and medicine purchased with her own money. At first she simply sent military information to Union headquarters. Then she persuaded Confederate doctors to transfer the seriously wounded Union officers to hospitals in Richmond. In addition to bringing the men supplies and clothing, Van Lew brought books with split spines in which to hide notes, and food on a platter that had a false bottom where information could be hidden. In order to draw suspicion away from herself, she played out her Crazy Bet role. She wore odd combinations of clothing and walked through the city mumbling to herself. As a result, the guards at the prison considered her harmless. Through her visits she was able to collect valuable information about Confederate troop movements observed by prisoners after they were captured.[18]

Once the information was collected, various methods were used to get through enemy lines. Van Lew's couriers had a ready alibi, for they were traveling to the family's farm on the outskirts of Richmond. Her servants traveled through Confederate lines so frequently that after a while sentries did not bother to stop them. Van Lew joked that her delivery service was better than the Confederate postal service.[19]

The federal prisoners were not Van Lew's only source of information. She listened carefully to the conversations of the Confederate guards at Libby, who often were careless in their talk. She developed a friendship with the prison's commandant, Lieutenant David Todd, by bringing him buttermilk and gingerbread. With the friendship came information. Later, when Todd was replaced by Lieutenant Gibbs, she convinced him to move his family into the Van Lew mansion as boarders. Gradually Van Lew's circle of operatives widened. When

Libby Prison, from which Van Lew helped Union soldiers escape.
(Library of Congress)

her mother joined the espionage ring, she was able to get clerks in the Confederate war and navy departments in their confidence. Van Lew's greatest achievement, however, was placing one of her former slaves, Mary Bowser, in the Confederate White House. As a servant in the dining room, Bowser had access to many of President Davis's personal conversations.[20]

Bowser had been educated in a Quaker school for African Americans in Philadelphia after being given her freedom by the Van Lews. Van Lew persuaded a friend to use her as an assistant whenever she helped at a function at the Confederate White House. Bowser pretended to be illiterate so as not to raise suspicions. Eventually she was able to work her way into a permanent position in the executive mansion. From 1863 until the end of the war, Bowser worked for the Davis family. On several occasions she was present when Davis met with Robert E. Lee and members of the Confederate cabinet. Bowser also had access to the president's office and had the opportunity to read dispatches and orders to be given to Confederate commanders. She was said to have a photographic memory; everything she saw on Davis's desk, she could repeat word for word.[21]

In addition to espionage work, Van Lew established a network of safe houses to help escaping prisoners return to Union lines. Close to Libby Prison, the Van Lew mansion was a safe house as well. On February 9, 1864, when federal officers escaped from Libby Prison, their success was due to a large degree to Van Lew's careful planning. A few of the prisoners dug below the street to a nearby vacant lot. They were able to keep the operation a secret until the night of the escape. When the secret was leaked, hundreds of prisoners jumped at the chance. Before the guards were aware of what was happening, 109 men had escaped; some of them spent the night in the Van Lew mansion.[22]

After the 1864 escape, Van Lew wrote to General Butler at Fort Monroe, pleading for a raid on Richmond to free the thousands of Union prisoners being held there. At Belle Isle on the James River, prisoners were forced to sleep in the open with little or no covering and were dying at the rate of ten per day. During the winter of 1863–64, more than 400 Union prisoners died, many of whom froze to death.[23]

Butler passed the information along to Stanton, and a plan was developed to send 3,500 cavalrymen under Brigadier General Judson Kilpatrick and Colonel Ulric Dahlgren to free the prisoners. The raid ended in disaster when Kilpatrick was turned back by a strong Confederate force. Dahlgren was killed and ninety-two of his men taken prisoner. Papers were found on Dahlgren's body which showed that his orders were to burn Richmond and assassinate President Davis. When the news was made public, Southerners were outraged. Jefferson Davis was incensed by the plan and ordered that Dahlgren be buried in an unmarked grave. The burial was held at night in secret. A witness hiding in the cemetery, sent by Van Lew, noted the burial spot and reported its location to her. Later that night, Crazy Bet went to the cemetery and marked the spot. Later, Van Lew had several of her employees dig up the body and take it to Yellow Tavern, where it was reburied and the spot marked. When the war ended, Van Lew informed the family of the actual burial site and helped them to retrieve it.[24]

As the war progressed, the Union command recognized the value of Van Lew's contributions. During the early part of the conflict she had communicated with General Butler. Later her communications went directly to General Grant. Her couriers passed Confederate pickets daily with messages hidden in the soles of their shoes. They were seldom questioned. As a cover they carried flowers which Van Lew had picked from her garden every morning. Later, these flowers would be found on General Grant's table.[25]

After a while General Winder began to suspect that Van Lew was smuggling fugitives and information to the Union, but he couldn't prove it. He ordered his men to search her mansion. They failed to find anything, missing the hidden panel on the attic staircase and the room behind it where escaped Union prisoners were hidden. A few hours after the search, dressed in filthy clothing and carrying a moth-eaten parasol, Van Lew went to see General Winder. Playing her role as Crazy Bet, she chastised him for what she called conduct "unbecoming of an officer and a gentleman." General Winder apologized.[26] In February 1865, the secret service made another attempt to determine if Van Lew was a spy. They sent an English agent to Richmond, who uncovered several Union sympathizers and agents, but they were unable to implicate her.[27]

Despite Van Lew's deviousness, her diary revealed that she believed herself to be under constant surveillance and in danger. In 1915 a *New York Times* article stated that "there was not a moment during those four years [of the Civil War] when Lizzie Van Lew could hear a step behind her on the street without expecting to have somebody tap her on the shoulder and say 'you are my prisoner.'" Still, she persisted, sending whatever information she could obtain.[28]

In 1865 the way finally was clear for Grant's army to enter Richmond. Van Lew saw the tumult and chaos all about her as the evacuation began. She told a neighbor it would be good to see the war over, and now many young lives would be saved. When her neighbor reacted by saying that anything would be better than to fall under the U.S. government, Van Lew knew it would be useless to talk with her.

Later that day, Elizabeth Van Lew raised an American flag from a flagpole on her roof. It was the first Union flag to fly in Richmond in four years. A crowd gathered outside, threatening to tear down the flag and burn down her house. Van Lew refused to be intimidated. "I know you all," she said, calling them by name. "General Grant will be in the city within the hour; if this house is harmed," she said, "your house shall be burned by noon." The mob dispersed.[29]

When General Grant heard that Lee had evacuated Richmond, he sent Union cavalry into the city to protect Van Lew and her family. The Union soldiers found her inside the Confederate War Department office, saving papers left by the fleeing Southerners. She had gone to the offices to collect documents she felt General Grant might find valuable.[30]

One of the first things Grant did when he entered Richmond was to visit Van Lew at her mansion to thank her. Later Grant would put his thanks in a letter, writing: "You have sent me the most valuable information received from Richmond during the war."[31]

When the war ended, Van Lew continued to live in the mansion on Church Hill. She was broke, having spent everything she had on her efforts to help the Union. Both Van Lew and her brother needed to find employment in order to survive. General George Sharpe did what he could to obtain a government grant for the family for their service and sacrifice during the war. A small grant was provided, enough so that the house could remain in the family. Near the end of Van Lew's life, the family of Lieutenant Colonel Paul Revere of Boston, whom she had aided in Libby Prison, provided some financial assistance.[32]

Efforts were made by former Union prisoners to have her compensated for her service to them, but nothing came of it. When Ulysses Grant became president in 1869, he appointed her postmaster of Richmond with an annual salary of $1,200. She lost the position when Rutherford Hayes became president in 1877. Later she received a clerical appointment in the Post Office Department in Washington.[33]

Van Lew remained a social outcast for the rest of her life, being shunned

General Grant sent his cavalry to protect Elizabeth, who insisted on flying an American flag from the Van Lew mansion, pictured above.
(Library of Congress)

by the citizens of Richmond. "I live here in perfect isolation," she wrote. "No one will walk with us on the street, no one will go with us anywhere. And it grows worse and worse as the years roll on and those I love go to their long rest." When her mother died in 1875, not enough friends were available to serve as pallbearers.[34]

During the summer of 1899, Van Lew suffered from congestive heart failure; she lived her remaining months in the family mansion with her forty cats. She died on September 25, 1900, in her home on top of Church Hill and was buried in the family cemetery. Only a few relatives were in attendance. A simple marker was placed on the grave until two years later, when a large stone arrived from Massachusetts, a gift from the Revere family.

Van Lew once wrote in her journal: "If I am entitled to the name 'spy' because I was in the secret service, I accept it willingly; but it will hereafter have to my mind a high and honorable significance. For my loyalty to my country, I have two beautiful names — here I am called, 'traitor,' farther North a 'spy' — I am called a 'spy' instead of the honored 'Faithful.'"[35] It seemed to be a fitting epitaph.

Into the twenty-first century some of the classic old homes of Richmond, including Jefferson Davis's residence, have been preserved. Not so the Van Lew mansion on Church Hill. In 1911 the building was torn down so that a school could be erected in its place. Richmond had taken its final revenge on Elizabeth Van Lew.

4   *Siren of the Shenandoah*

BELLE BOYD

SEVENTEEN years old when the Civil War began, Belle Boyd soon shot and killed a Union soldier. At the age of nineteen, Boyd was a prisoner of the Union, having been captured as a spy. During the Union occupation of the Shenandoah Valley, she associated with the enemy soldiers and, using her wits and feminine charm, obtained useful information for the Confederacy. Southern newspapers called her the "Joan of Arc of the South" and "Siren of the Shenandoah." Northern reports referred to her as a camp follower and an overrated spy. Belle Boyd was the most famous of the female spies of the Civil War. Her notoriety was not due as much to her success as a spy as to her love of publicity and fame, behaviors that professional spies usually try their best to avoid.[1]

Born in Martinsburg, Virginia, on May 9, 1844, Boyd was the first of eight children of Mary Rebecca and Benjamin Reed Boyd. In 1844, Martinsburg was a thriving community and was known as the "Northern Gateway to the Shenandoah." During the Civil War, Martinsburg would join several Virginia counties to form the state of West Virginia. When Martinsburg came under Union occupation in 1861, Boyd's career as an operative for the South began.[2]

Boyd's father was a prosperous store owner, whose wealth enabled the family to live comfortably and to own several slaves. The Boyds were a closely knit family and protective of one another. "I passed my childhood as all happy children usually do, petted and caressed by a father and mother, loving and beloved by brothers and sisters," Boyd recalled. As a child, Boyd was vivacious, energetic, athletic, and an accomplished rider. An impulsive tomboy, she raced her horse through the woods and dominated her brothers and sisters as well as other children her age. One day her parents were entertaining some friends at dinner, but eleven-year-old Boyd was not allowed at the table because her parents believed she was too young for such social functions. Suddenly the eating and conversation were interrupted by a loud noise. The door swung open violently, and a horse and rider dashed into the dining room, stopping at the table. Boyd sat firmly in the saddle, in perfect command of the situation. When Belle's father asked for an explanation for her actions, she replied: "Well, my horse is old enough, isn't he?" In this case, and in others years later, her defiance of authority was tolerated, and punishment was not forthcoming.[3]

Boyd attended school in Martinsburg with her brothers and sisters, but when she was twelve, her parents sent her to the exclusive Mount Washington Female College in the Baltimore suburbs. At Mount Washington she studied the classics, music, and French. In 1859 the abolitionist John Brown and his band violently attacked the government arsenal at Harpers Ferry, only fifteen miles from Boyd's home. Despite the troubles brewing throughout the nation, life contin-

---

Previous page:
Belle Boyd exchanged her debutante ball gown for a gray Confederate uniform.
(William L. Clements Library, University of Michigan)

ued. Boyd graduated from Mount Washington and eagerly awaited her debut, a social custom of the time that introduced a young woman to society. As a debutante, Boyd dreamed of parties, pretty dresses, suitors, and dances, as did other fifteen-year-old young ladies of her social status.

In the winter of 1860–61, Boyd spent time in Washington. She soon learned that the residents had strong Southern sympathies, openly expressing them. With the election of Lincoln as president in 1860 and the firing on Fort Sumter, Boyd returned to Martinsburg. She believed, as most Southerners did, in the sovereignty of the states and their right of secession. It was this passion and devotion to the South and their cause that led her to serve the Confederacy, regardless of what the consequences might be.[4]

By the age of seventeen, Boyd had grown into a compelling young woman whom some considered beautiful and who knew how to use her charm to captivate men. She would put these traits to good use for the Southern cause. "My duties were painful in the extremes!" she later wrote, "but I allowed for one thought to keep possession of my mind — I was doing all a woman could do in her country's cause."[5]

When the war began, Boyd's father quickly joined the Confederate army, serving under Stonewall Jackson in the Shenandoah Valley. The Boyd family appeared to have a love for serving the Confederacy and for espionage, as not only Boyd, but at least three of her relatives served as spies. Belle Boyd, however, can claim the title of being the youngest of the Boyd spies; she was only eighteen.[6]

In 1861 Union troops occupied Martinsburg. On July 4, while celebrating the nation's birthday, several federal soldiers had a little too much to drink. They decided to visit the Boyd home to remove the Confederate flag that flew from the second-story window and replace it with the Stars and Stripes. Arriving at the house, they demanded entrance. Mrs. Boyd stood at the doorway, refusing to allow the soldiers to enter and declaring that her family would rather die than have the Yankee flag fly above their house. When one soldier shouted obscenities at Mrs. Boyd and pushed his way through, Boyd appeared in the hallway with a pistol. She fired into the group, mortally wounding one of the men. As she later recalled, "I could stand it no longer. My indignation was aroused beyond my control. My blood was literally boiling in my veins. I drew out my pistol and shot him." After the shooting, the Union soldiers withdrew, taking their bloody comrade with them and leaving the flag behind. The man died three days later.[7]

Arrested, Boyd was taken before a tribunal of Union officers. She explained that the soldiers were violating the sanctuary of her home and that she was only defending her family. After reviewing the evidence, the officers ruled that she had committed justified homicide. As a result she was only reprimanded and released. A guard was posted outside her home to prevent a reoccurrence of the act and reprisal by friends of the deceased soldier. Boyd's impulsive action would exemplify her behavior throughout the war and establish her reputation.[8]

When Boyd recalled the shooting incident in her memoirs, she was not remorseful: "Shall I be ashamed to confess that I recall without one shadow of remorse the act that I saved my mother from insult and perhaps death? That the blood I then shed has left no stain on my soul, imposed no burden upon my conscience?"[9]

The shooting of the Union soldier marked the beginning of Boyd's career as a Confederate operative. She was determined to provide the Southern army with whatever information she could find about the movements and size of enemy troops. In order to gather this information, she had to break with the rigid, conventional behavior of young ladies of the day. While she did not deviate from the moral code, she did go beyond common social restrictions. She shocked her friends by waving to both Confederate and Union soldiers in the street and by visiting enemy military camps to talk to officers in their tents. She danced and flirted with the occupying Yankee troops, captivating them to the point that they would talk freely when with her. Boyd claimed that it was necessary to be on good terms with the enemy if she wanted to gather information.

Although Belle Boyd was not considered beautiful by all, she was described as "very attractive … quite tall, with a superb figure … and dressed with much taste." The fact is, Boyd did not have to be pretty to get her way with men. She had a winning personality with Union troops and was most obliging in taking care of their needs. One Northern paper referred to her as an "accomplished prostitute." It was difficult for anyone not to give the Siren of the Shenandoah anything she wanted.[10]

In addition to collecting military data herself, Boyd acted as a courier for information that others brought to her. Two of her slaves also served as couriers. One was her personal maid, who throughout her life, even as an old woman and no longer a slave, continued to write to her former mistress.[11] After the first battle at Manassas in July 1861, Belle Boyd was appointed a courier for Generals P.G.T. Beauregard and Stonewall Jackson. She quickly increased her activities to include passing information to the Confederate forces in the Shenandoah Valley. Boyd also stole weapons, ammunition, sabers, and medical supplies, especially quinine, that were desperately needed by Confederate troops. Boyd was not only a spy and courier, but a land blockade runner.

In May 1862, Boyd acquired crucial information about a Union plan to trap Stonewall Jackson, who was heading north through the Shenandoah Valley. The plan called for five different federal forces to combine against him: General Nathaniel Banks with 4,000 men in Strasburg, a small force at Winchester, General Julius White's troops at Harpers Ferry, Generals James Shields and John W. Geary near Front Royal, and General John C. Fremont, west of the Shenandoah Valley. Boyd realized that Jackson had to act before the Union forces could unite. It was important that she get this information to Jackson as soon as possible.[12] In doing so, Boyd was to become a Confederate hero at the Battle of Front Royal.

Front Royal was a critical position for both the Union and Confederate armies. With the valuable military information gleaned from an unsuspecting member of Shields's staff, Boyd ran across the field of battle with gunfire exploding all about her to deliver her message. When she arrived, her dress was full of bullet holes, but not one shot hit her.[13] Major Henry Kyd Douglas later recalled Boyd's daring act: "Boyd was dressed in white as she hurried in his [Jackson's] direction and she seemed, when I saw her, to heed neither weeds nor fences, but waved a bonnet as she came on." Douglas rode out to meet her. Boyd was nearly breathless as she spoke: "Go back quickly and tell him that the Yankee force is very small — one regiment of Maryland infantry, several pieces of artillery, and several companies of cavalry. Tell him I know, for I went through the camps and got it out of an officer. Tell him to charge right down and he will catch them all." Douglas quickly conveyed the message to Jackson. As a result of her foresight, courage, and determination, the Confederates won a decisive victory on May 23.[14] After the battle, Boyd received thanks from Stonewall Jackson himself: "I thank you, for my self and for the army, for the immense service that you have rendered your country today."[15]

Boyd returned to Front Royal during the time Confederate troops occupied the town. A Mrs. Annie Jones was taken into custody, claiming to be the wife of a soldier from the Michigan cavalry. Boyd, who was sympathetic to her plight, provided her with clothing and tried to comfort her. When the Union forces returned with numbers in their favor, Jackson was forced to evacuate the town. The Union army quickly reoccupied the town. Annie Jones, now freed, reported Boyd to General Nathan Kimball as a "most dangerous rebel, and a malignant enemy of the Federal government."[16] Kimball placed Boyd under arrest. Within a few hours of the arrest, General Shields, senior of General Kimball, arrived in Front Royal. Boyd approached Shields with a smile. She was quickly released.

By the summer of 1862, Belle Boyd's reputation as a spy was well established. At the same time, word of her actions was spreading, and federal officers were growing weary of her interference with their plans. On July 30, 1862, Boyd was arrested under orders from Secretary of War Edwin Stanton, who ordered her brought to Washington. Boyd was stunned and feared what her treatment would be, but her spirits remained high. While en route to Washington, she waved a Confederate flag from the window of the train at every whistle stop.

Boyd was taken to the Old Capitol Prison, a three-story structure that had once been the United States Capitol building. When Congress moved to its new location, the old building became a boarding house, and then a makeshift jail. No effort was made to restore the structure or to adapt it to its new function. In addition to its broken window panes, decayed walls, cracked floors, and a dark, gloomy interior, its bedrooms were infested with lice and bedbugs. The food was poor, but some prisoners had special privileges and were able to receive food and gifts from friends outside. The prison was originally intended to house political prisoners and prisoners of war but soon became crowded with spies, smugglers, and blockade runners.[17]

Despite the prison's sorry condition, Boyd was able to withstand her imprisonment there. General William Doster, provost marshal of the District of Columbia, described Boyd in prison: "It was her dashing manner . . . and air of joyous recklessness. . . . During the whole stay she was never, to my knowledge, found in ill-humor, but bravely endured a tedious and companionless imprisonment." Boyd was greeted as a celebrity by the superintendent: "I am very glad to see you, and will endeavor to make you as comfortable as possible; so whatever you wish for, ask for it, and you shall have it. I am glad to have so distinguished a person for my guest. Come, let me show you to your room."[18]

Chief of Detectives, Lafayette Baker, visited Boyd in prison on behalf of Secretary of War Stanton. Baker hoped to have her confess and be repentant, telling her he had plenty of proof against her. Boyd's reply was simple: "Sir, I have nothing to say." Baker thrust a copy of the Oath of Allegiance at her, reminding her that Mr. Stanton would be informed of her response. This time Boyd was defiant: "Tell Mr. Stanton from me, I hope that when I commence the oath of allegiance to the United States Government, my tongue may cleave to the roof of my mouth; and that if I ever sign one line ..., I hope my arm may fall paralyzed to my side." With that Baker departed.[19]

During her imprisonment, Boyd continued her defiant attitude toward the Yankees. She sang the anthem "Maryland, My Maryland," the words of which raised the morale of those imprisoned there, and led cheers for Jefferson Davis and Stonewall Jackson. But Boyd unwitting assisted Joseph Kerbey, a Union spy, who had been mistakenly imprisoned with her. Thinking he was a Confederate operative and of value to the South, she devised a plan to help him escape and told him of all the safe houses along the route to freedom. Kerbey willingly went along with her plans. On the day that the escape was to take place, Kerbey was released from prison; apparently Stanton had realized his mistake. Belle Boyd never realized what had happened and that all the information she had supplied him had fallen into federal hands.[20]

Boyd remained in the Old Capitol Prison until August 1862. Lafayette Baker finally gave up trying to get Boyd to confess and ordered her returned to Confederate lines, with the provision that she remain there until the war was over. Should she be caught in land occupied by federal troops, she would be arrested again. By the time she left Old Capitol, she had won over many of her enemies as well as the other prisoners. In Richmond, Boyd received a hero's welcome and General Jackson appointed her an honorary aide-de-camp with the rank of captain.[21] Determined not to let the enemy restrict her movements, Boyd went to Martinsburg. In the summer of 1863 she was arrested again for being within federal lines in contempt of the orders related to her release.

Boyd was returned to Washington and this time imprisoned at the Carroll Prison, an annex of the Old Capitol. After three months, her health began to fail and she again was released. When the doctors in Richmond advised her to

Washington's Old Capitol Prison, where Belle was imprisoned. She annoyed Union guards by leading the prisoners in Confederate songs and cheers.
(Library of Congress)

take time out to improve her health, she conceived another way to serve the Confederacy: Boyd became a courier of dispatches from the Confederacy to its supporters in England. In May 1864, Boyd sailed for England on the *Greyhound*, a blockade runner. But the *Greyhound* was captured off the coast and forced to return. Boyd, however, charmed Lieutenant Samuel Hardinge, an officer on the federal ship that captured the *Greyhound*, and with his help was able to gain her release. This time she was banished to Canada, from which she made her way to England. Because of Hardinge's involvement with Boyd, he was suspected of consorting with the enemy. As a result, he was court-martialed and discharged from the navy.[23]

The smitten Hardinge followed Boyd to England, where the two were married on August 25, 1864. Boyd convinced him to return to the United States and spy for the South, but he was caught and died in prison. Boyd was still in

England at the time of her husband's death. A widow at the age of twenty-one, Boyd remained in England until the end of the war. During that time she wrote and began to market her memoirs, *Belle Boyd in Camp and Prison*. Although they embellished her espionage activities with undocumented stories, she was able to capitalize on them. Utilizing her new found popularity, Boyd converted the theatrical nature of her memoirs into a career on the stage.[24]

When Boyd returned to the United States, she continued her appearances, billing herself as the "Cleopatra of Secession." She continued to capitalize on her glamour and fame, appearing on the stage for more than a decade. Boyd supplemented her income from the stage by giving lectures at veterans' meetings. Always sensitive to the latest trends of the time, initially her theme was one of reconciliation and national unity. But by the 1880s, she had tailored her presentations to rewriting the defeat of the Confederacy into a Lost Cause victory.[25]

Boyd married two more times and bore three children. Her second marriage was to a former officer of the British army named John Hammond. It ended in divorce in 1884. Her third marriage was to Nathaniel High, the son of a clergyman. The two lived together until her death.[26]

Boyd died of a heart attack in 1900 at the age of sixty-seven in Kilbourne, Wisconsin. In 1929 the Daughters of the Confederacy moved her remains from the cemetery in Kilbourne to the town of her birth.[27] Belle Boyd loved the Confederacy, sacrificing much for its cause, more than most would dare to do. Southerners realized this and took pride in her accomplishments just as they did in their generals. Belle Boyd, like others from the Civil War, has become a Southern legend.

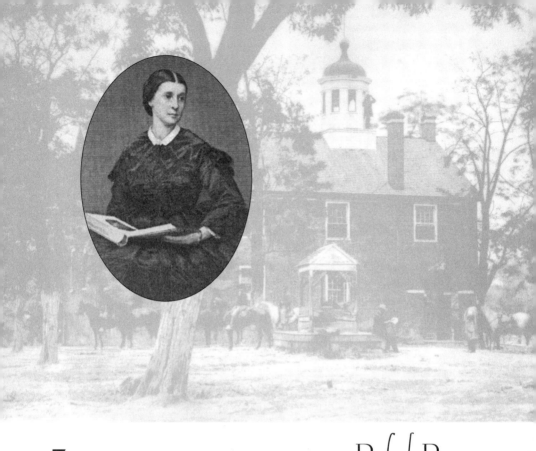

5   Rebel Rose

ROSE O'NEAL GREENHOW

OF ALL the Confederate spies during the Civil War, Rose O'Neal Greenhow was the most spectacular. She was beautiful, seductive, and in her own words was not reluctant to use her feminine powers to acquire what she wanted: "I employed every capacity with which God has endowed me, and the result was far more successful than my hopes could have flattered me to expect."[1] Courted by important politicians of Washington and befriended by a future president, she became well established in Washington's society. Her high social position gave her access to the country's most influential men and the secret information they possessed. Greenhow's role in providing information to Confederate generals helped them to win many of the early battles of the war. She willingly entered the world of espionage before the war began, and her contributions to the Confederate efforts are legendary.

Greenhow was born Rose O'Neal in 1817 in Montgomery County, Maryland. Although the O'Neal family was of modest means, she was raised in the genteel tradition of the Old South, practicing the social etiquette required of Southern aristocrats. When she was a young girl, her father was murdered by a slave. This event, it is believed, influenced her anti-abolitionist position on slavery.

By the time Greenhow was in her teens, she had developed into a breathtaking beauty. She and her sister Ellen moved to Washington in the 1830s to live with an aunt who ran a boarding house in the Old Capitol Building. Many of her aunt's tenants were men who would later hold high political office during the war. Soon Rose O'Neal became the center of attention, and the source of endless gossip. Fair-skinned, tall, and graceful, she had jet-black hair, dark eyes, strong facial features, and a pleasing personality, always knowing what to say and when to say it. She quickly developed a taste for an active social life and associating with people in power.[2]

One of her most ardent admirers was Cave Johnson, who later became postmaster general under the Polk administration. He and many others deluged Rose O'Neal with flowers, dinners, carriage rides and endless attention. But it was a quiet physician and historian who won her hand. In 1835, at the age of twenty-six, the belle of Washington married forty-three-year-old Dr. Robert Greenhow, a wealthy and socially prominent Virginian. Through her husband, she got to know virtually everyone of importance in Washington. Marriage to Dr. Greenhow allowed her to continue the association with the social world she enjoyed and had grown accustomed to at her aunt's boarding house.[3] When one of Dr. Greenhow's friends, John C. Calhoun, the Senator from South Carolina, became ill in 1850, Greenhow nursed him back to health. Their common view on states' rights and slavery helped to solidify their friendship.

By the time Greenhow was in her mid-thirties, she was the mother of four

Previous page:
Rose O'Neal Greenhow was considered the most beautiful of the female spies. Her practice of trading sex for information was most effective.
(National Portrait Gallery, Smithsonian Institution)

daughters and had not only established strong connections with the political elite of Washington but had become socially prominent herself. In addition to the advantages her prestigious husband provided her, Greenhow became known for "her beauty, the brilliance of her conversation, her aptitude for intrigue, the royal dignity of her manners, and the unscrupulous perseverance with which she accomplished whatever she set her heart upon."[4]

In 1850 Greenhow and her husband left Washington for San Francisco where Dr. Greenhow hoped to strike it rich; instead an injury caused his death. Greenhow returned to Washington four years later with her daughters and moved into a small house near the White House. Living off her inheritance, she resumed all the important contacts that she had established before her trip out west.[5]

Greenhow was no longer a young woman. Men, however, still found her attractive and irresistible. James Buchanan, the nation's only bachelor president, was a frequent visitor to her house. She loved to entertain and often had dinner parties. Invitations to her affairs were highly sought after. Although Greenhow's sentiments about the South were well known, even after the war began, Union army officers and high-ranking political officials in Washington continued to frequent her house.[6] In the 1860s, Greenhow enhanced her position as a Washington hostess and socialite, as well as her reputation as a woman of great influence. As a result of her status, she was able to influence members of Congress and gain favors for her friends.[7]

Before the war began, Greenhow was approached by Captain Thomas Jordan of Virginia, serving as assistant quartermaster in the United States Army, but secretly the man responsible for recruiting spies for the Confederacy. He knew of Greenhow's Southern sympathies and was able to recruit her; she enthusiastically accepted not only the position of spy, but that of the spymaster for an entire ring. Greenhow soon had a well-established spy ring operating in Washington.[8] With Jordan's help, Greenhow learned how to use a simple twenty-six symbol cipher for passing written notes. An elaborate system of communication also was developed so that Greenhow could transmit information to Jordan by raising and lowering the shades of the windows on one side of her house.[9] Greenhow's network was well in place when hostilities commenced in April 1861, and her efforts had immediate implications for the war. Her first success is the one most remembered, occurring just before the First Battle of Manassas.

Two of Washington's most important officials were captivated by Greenhow's charm and beauty. They were the United States Senator from Massachusetts, Henry Wilson, and Colonel Erasmus D. Keys, secretary to General-in-Chief Winfield Scott. Wilson also held the important position of chairman of the Senate's military affairs committee. When Greenhow was eventually arrested, a packet of love letters written on Senate stationery and signed with the initial H were found. Although the name of her lover was never discovered, there seems to be little doubt that the "H" letters belonged to Senator Wilson. They indicate that the writer was interested in the Pacific Railroad bill, as was Wilson, and the handwriting was similar to his. In the letters, H poured out his love: "You know how I love you — and will sacrifice anything.... You know that I do love you. I am suffering this morning ... and know that nothing would soothe me as an hour with you.... I will be with you tonight, and then I will tell you again and again that I love you." The passion of H's letters indicated that Greenhow had little trouble getting whatever information she wanted from him.[10] Along with the letters was a notation by Greenhow: "letters from H. Not to be opened — but burnt in case of accident or death."[11] No official accusations were ever made against Wilson and he continued to serve on the military affairs committee. In 1872 Wilson became vice president of the United States.

In a position to possess vital military information as General Scott's secretary, Colonel Keys claimed that he had never been compromised by Greenhow's charm. Greenhow was the "most persuasive woman that was ever known in Washington," he stated. Often he "had been lured to the brink of the precipice," he said, "but always resisted temptation."[12]

From either Colonel Keys or Senator Wilson, Greenhow was able to provide General P.G.T. Beauregard with vital information about Union troop size and movements. Greenhow's account of the event indicated that she had a copy of the map used by the Senate committee on military affairs showing the Union's planned route to Manassas. She also provided a copy of Major General Irvin McDowell's actual order to his troops. When Beauregard received Greenhow's message, he immediately notified President Davis of McDowell's planned movement of 55,000 troops to Manassas from Arlington Heights and Alexandria. He requested that General Joseph Johnston's 12,000 troops, who were sixty miles away in the Shenandoah Valley, be sent to him as reinforcements. To Greenhow, General Beauregard sent a note: "Let them come: We are ready for them."[13]

Secretary of State William Seward reported the outcome of the battle to

Lincoln: "General McDowell's army [is] in full retreat through Centreville. The day is lost. Save Washington and remnants of the army." Before the battle, picnickers had gathered outside of Washington to watch, anticipating a Union victory and a quick end to the war. Now McDowell's defeated army was stumbling over these picnickers, whose carriages blocked the roads and bridges back to the capital.[14]

Delighted with her success, Greenhow became even more active in her spying activities. She also ministered to Confederate prisoners captured during the battle and raised money to feed and clothe them. An agent involved in spying usually tried to keep a low profile, but such behavior was not a part of Rose Greenhow's personality. Before long, she was barred from visiting Confederate prisoners.[15]

Greenhow continued to gather and transmit information to her Confederate contacts: "I was urged to leave the city more than once," she later wrote, "and an escort offered to be furnished me if I desired; but, at what peril, I resolved to remain, conscious of the great service I could render my country, my position giving me remarkable facilities for obtaining information."[16] On August 11, 1861, Greenhow sent Confederate agent Jordan a detailed report of Washington's defense system. She described every fort in detail, including the number of guns, their caliber and range, weak spots in the earthworks, the strength of regiments, the amount of ammunition issued to each soldier, and an itemized list of wagons, ambulances, and stores. It was the kind of information that helped to win battles.[17]

After the First Battle of Manassas, McDowell was replaced by General George McClellan, known for his organizational ability. He built the Army of the Potomac into a huge fighting force but soon realized that information about his army was being leaked from Washington to the Confederates. He intended to put a stop to Confederate espionage by employing Allan Pinkerton of the Pinkerton Detective Agency.[18] Greenhow continued to move about in Washington with apparent impunity, but the Federals were becoming more suspicious of her. Pinkerton ordered a close surveillance of the Greenhow home, this in spite of his concern about angering her most powerful friends in Washington. He also ordered the arrest of all persons entering or leaving the house.[19]

During the early months of counterintelligence operations, the procedures were often unsophisticated. Pinkerton's surveillance of Greenhow was a good example of this. He and three of his men stationed themselves outside Greenhow's house. When they observed one visitor entering, Pinkerton stood on the shoulders of the other men and peered into the window. He watched as the man gave Greenhow a copy of a map and explained to her details of the strength of each fortification on the map. Then Greenhow led the man into another room. An hour later the two returned "arm in arm." There was no doubt in Pinkerton's mind that the information she had received had been paid for with sex. The man was escorted to the door by Greenhow. Pinkerton later stated that he heard what he believed to be a kiss.[20]

After the man left, Pinkerton followed him for a few blocks; then something went wrong. Pinkerton was suddenly arrested, thrown into a guard house, and later interrogated by the man he had been following. When Pinkerton refused to answer questions, he was returned to his cell. Later he was able to get a message to one of his contacts in the War Department. The next day he was taken to the office of Thomas A. Scott, assistant secretary of war, where he reported what he had discovered about Rose Greenhow. The conspiring man was now identified as Captain John Elwood of the 5th Infantry and arrested.[21]

Pinkerton continued his surveillance of Rebel Rose. Greenhow knew she was being watched but was far from being fazed; in fact, she seemed to enjoy the attention she was receiving. But piece by piece, Pinkerton accumulated evidence until he was ready to make his move. Finally on August 23, Pinkerton believed he had gathered sufficient evidence to charge Greenhow with treason and place her under arrest. As she was returning to her home from a walk, he confronted her. "I've come to arrest you," Pinkerton said. Greenhow asked to see his warrant, but Pinkerton had failed to obtain one. However, this was war, and Pinkerton would do his duty, warrant or not.[22]

When Greenhow was finally arrested, Pinkerton made the mistake of doing so in front of her house and then taking her inside for questioning. It is considered a bad procedure to do this. It not only alerts other agents who might be in the area, but it provides the agent the opportunity to destroy incriminating evidence. Greenhow had the chance to do both.[23]

Upon seeing her mother arrested, her daughter "Little Rose" went outside, climbed a tree, and shouted, "My mother's been arrested," a great way of alerting agents to stay away from her house. Inside, Greenhow pretended to be having an attack of heat stroke and asked to go to her room to change her clothing; while there, she destroyed some of the evidence in the house. But Greenhow was not able to destroy all the evidence. Pinkerton's search uncovered a wealth of incriminating evidence, including the love letters from H, a letter in cipher from Greenhow to Jordan, other notes, and shredded correspondence. Despite the efforts of Greenhow's daughter to warn members of the spy ring, several Confederate sympathizers called at the house later that day and were arrested as spies.[24]

Greenhow's experience after being arrested was not a pleasant one. It was not until 4 o'clock the next morning that she was finally allowed to get some sleep. She later described the situation as a "most trying day." Instead of being jailed, Greenhow was placed under house arrest with around-the-clock surveillance by male guards. When her treatment became known, it raised indignation throughout the South. Mary Boykin Chesnut, the South Carolina diarist, described Greenhow's plight: "For eight days she was kept in full sight of men, her room wide open, and sleepless sentinels watching by day and night. Beautiful as she is, even at her time of life, few women like all the mysteries of their toilette laid bare to the public eye."[25]

At the end of August, Greenhow's house was converted to a prison. Female prisoners were now confined to "Fort Greenhow," as her house was now called. Pinkerton's detectives were replaced by McClellan's personal bodyguards, known as the Sturgis Rifles. The men of the Sturgis Rifles were more considerate of her feelings than the Pinkerton operatives had been. As a result, Greenhow was again able to use her beauty to gain favors. In her memoirs, *My Imprisonments and the First Year of Abolition Rule in Washington*, Greenhow tells how the commanding officer of the Sturgis Rifles, Lieutenant N. E. Sheldon, allowed her to send notes to her Confederate friends. Throughout her stay at Fort Greenhow, Greenhow continued to communicate with the Confederacy — and not just by means of Sheldon. She devised a way of sending messages through her tapestry work, which was hung across the windows from time to time.[26]

During this time, War Department employees went through the documents and scraps of paper found in Greenhow's home. She had destroyed the key to Thomas Jordan's cipher, but because of its simplicity, dispatches written using it were easy to decipher. The most damaging of these messages proved that Rose Greenhow controlled more than fifty spies in five states. Information was found describing Union military installations and the disposition and deployment of troops.[27]

Confinement in Fort Greenhow was unpleasant for Greenhow because of the other women imprisoned there. Although they shared a common cause,

Greenhow was unwilling to adjust to class differences. She refused to talk with some of the inmates, saying that they were "generally of the lowest class."[28] As the weeks dragged by, however, Greenhow became a celebrity. Northern newspapers praised her wit and beauty. The *National Republican* called her "the beautiful Rebel of Sixteenth Street . . . the fascinating female spy." Because of the large number of admirers that gathered outside the Greenhow residence, additional guards were needed to control the crowds.[29]

Greenhow tried to make good use of both her political connections and her celebrity status. She wrote to Secretary of State William Seward complaining of the conditions of her imprisonment, but the letter failed to gain her release. When guards learned of a Confederate plot to free Greenhow, she and her eight-year-old daughter were moved from Fort Greenhow to the Old Capitol Prison, the same building in which her aunt had maintained a boarding house. Greenhow's new place of confinement was anything but comfortable. She was imprisoned with Confederate soldiers, spies, suspicious persons, Union deserters, and indigent freed slaves who had no other place to go. The Old Capitol Prison was in great disrepair. Where window panes were broken, wooden boards were nailed across windows. The food consisted of fatty pork, moldy beans, and half-cooked rice.[30]

Rebel Rose and her daughter were placed in a small room on the second floor. The room had a single window that overlooked the courtyard. Secretary of State Seward personally selected the room so she could not send messages to anyone in the street. Curiously, Greenhow was allowed to keep an unloaded pistol in her room. The reason for this was never explained, but it was assumed that should she be sexually attacked, she would have, at least, the empty pistol to fight off the molester.[31]

Near the end of March 1862, Greenhow was given a hearing in the office of the military governor. Judge Edward Pierrepont read the charges of espionage against her. Greenhow responded: "If I gave the information that you say I have, I must have got it from sources that were in the confidence of the government. . . . If Mr. Lincoln's friends will pour into my ear such important information, am I to be held responsible for all that?" Her argument did not convince the judge that she should be released. Judge Pierrepont asked her if she would be willing to take an oath of allegiance if she were released, but Greenhow refused. Pierrepont, frustrated with her rebuff at his attempt to let

Rose and her daughter, "Little Rose," were both imprisoned in the Old Capitol Prison.
(Library of Congress)

her off easy, declared that she was more guilty of mischief than of treason. Greenhow, however, was not acquitted, nor was she released.[32]

While Greenhow and her daughter continued in prison, friends sent petitions to Seward and Stanton requesting that she be freed. Although they were ignored, her spirit was not broken. Finally, despite General McClellan's insistence that she be detained until the end of the war, officials in Washington agreed that Greenhow should be released; she was paroled to the South on her promise not to return to the North for the duration of the war. On June 6, 1862, Mrs. Greenhow and her daughter arrived in Richmond amid a wildly cheering crowd. Drawing a Confederate flag from under her clothing, she displayed it throughout the parade. Later she dined with President Davis. Davis's words of thanks lifted her spirits as much as her release from prison had: "But for you there would have been no battle of Bull Run." Later she claimed that these words of praise from Davis "repaid me for all that I had endured."[33]

Greenhow continued her activities on behalf of the South. President Davis sent her and Little Rose to England and France to solicit their support for the Confederacy. She remained in Europe for more than two years, acting as an unofficial ambassador for the Confederate government. While in France, she had an audience with Napoleon III; he was courteous, but noncommittal. In England she met Queen Victoria, who was delighted with Greenhow's grace and wit, but Greenhow was unsuccessful in getting England's support in the war.

As the months passed, Greenhow was anxious to return to America, where she still owned property and where she could be closer to the fighting. In September 1864, with $2,000 in gold in her possession, she boarded a blockade runner, the *Condor*, bound for North Carolina. On the night of September 30, the *Condor* attempted to run the Union blockade off the coast of Wilmington, North Carolina. Hoping to avoid a confrontation with Union ships, the captain raced up the Cape Fear River. Instead of escaping, he ran his ship aground a sandbar. Fearing she would be captured again and placed in prison, Greenhow insisted on trying to reach shore. Despite the stormy weather and against the captain's wishes and advice, Greenhow and two other passengers boarded a lifeboat and headed for shore. Waves quickly swamped the small boat and overturned it. While the other two passengers were able to cling to the boat, Greenhow was weighed down by the gold sewn into her dress. Greenhow's body was first discovered by a Confederate soldier, who took the gold and pushed her corpse back into the water. Later her body was found again and identified as that of Rose Greenhow. When the soldier learned whom he had robbed, he turned the gold over to the Confederate government. Even in death, Rebel Rose worked her magic on another man.[34]

Rose Greenhow's body was draped in a Confederate flag and placed in the state capitol for public viewing. On the afternoon of October 1, her body was carried in a long funeral procession through the streets of Wilmington, a guard of honor accompanying her horse-drawn casket to the Oakdale Cemetery. Each year on the anniversary of her death the Daughters of the Confederacy place a wreath on her grave.[35] Rose O'Neal Greenhow dedicated herself to the Confederacy, serving it well by gathering and transmitting valuable military information. The whole South grieved the loss of a woman whose beauty was legendary and whose spirit remained unconquered.

6   The Death of a President

JOHN WILKES BOOTH

AT 9:30 on the evening of April 14, 1865, John Wilkes Booth dismounted his horse at the rear of Ford's Theater on 10th Street in Washington D.C., and handed the reins of his horse to Edman Spangler, a stagehand. Once inside the theater, Booth made his way to the adjoining Star Saloon. There he chatted with the bartender and other customers as he drank. On several occasions he walked from the bar into the lobby of the theater and back again. Finally, at a little after ten o'clock, he walked up to the ticket taker, borrowed a chew of tobacco, and made his way to the vestibule outside President Lincoln's box.[1]

Ford's Theatre, where President Lincoln was assassinated. (Library of Congress)

John Parker, Lincoln's bodyguard, had wandered away to watch the performance, leaving the president completely unprotected. Because Booth was such a well-known stage actor, having performed numerous times at the theater, he had a free run of the theater and was not challenged. Earlier that day Booth had drilled a peephole in the door of Lincoln's box and placed a piece of wood in the vestibule outside to bar the hall door. Now peering through the peephole, he made certain that Lincoln was in the box. Lincoln, his wife, and a young couple, Major Henry Rathbone and his fiancee, Clara Harris, were enjoying the popular play *Our American Cousin*.[2]

On the stage, a lone actor was delivering a humorous soliloquy: "Well I guess I know enough to turn you inside out, old gal — you sock-dologizing

Opposite:
Through a most foul and treacherous deed, John Wilkes Booth achieved the notoriety for which he had hoped. (National Archives and Records Administration)

old man-trap. Heh, heh, heh." This aroused the audience as Booth knew it would. Amid the laughter, the assailant pushed open the door to the president's box and fired a single shot to the back of Lincoln's head; the president slumped forward in his rocking chair. Rathbone sprang to his feet in an attempt to get hold of the assassin, but Booth broke free. Puzzled theatergoers looked on in amazement as Booth leaped to the stage, more than ten feet below. One of Booth's spurs caught in the flag that had been draped below the box, causing him to land off balance and break a bone in his left leg. Rising to his feet he shouted, "Sic semper tyrannus!" (thus always to tyrants), the motto of the commonwealth of Virginia. Then he hobbled across the stage and out the back door to the alley. Once outside, Booth mounted his horse and rode away. Some members of the audience still did not realize what had happened.[3]

Dr. Charles Leale, a young army assistant surgeon, was the first to come to Lincoln's aid. Leale found the president slumped in the rocker, with Mrs. Lincoln supporting his head; Lincoln had no pulse. Leale was soon joined by a second doctor, Dr. Charles Taft. Leale removed a clot of blood from the wound, hoping this would relieve the pressure on the brain. Lincoln recovered slightly when he was given mouth-to-mouth respiration. Leale later wrote: "Then a feeble action of the heart and irregular breathing followed." Lincoln was carried across the street to the home of William Petersen, where he was placed on a bed. Lincoln's personal physician, Dr. Robert King, was sent for at Mrs. Lincoln's request. Someone was sent to notify Secretary of War Edwin Stanton of the tragedy.[4]

At about the same time Lewis Paine, a former Confederate soldier, rode up to Secretary of State William Seward's house on Lafayette Square. Seward lay in his bedroom, his fractured jaw and shoulder encased in a metal and leather brace, the result of an accident earlier in the week. His daughter and soldier-nurse were in the room and his two sons and a servant elsewhere in the house. When Paine rang, Seward's servant answered the door. Paine claimed he had medicine for Seward and insisted on personally delivering the package to him. Pushing aside the servant, Paine ran up the stairs and attacked Seward's son Frederick, beating him with his revolver and fracturing his skull. Bursting into Seward's room, Paine savagely attacked him with his knife. Although Seward was cut severely, his brace prevented the attack from being fatal. Seward's other son, Augustus, rushed to his father's aid. Fighting like a madman, Paine was able to inflict a long gash across Augustus's scalp and stab Seward's nurse in the chest and shoulder. Paine then ran out of the house, leaving four badly wounded persons behind.[5]

In the parlor of the Petersen house, Stanton took charge of the situation. Throughout the night, he interrogated eyewitnesses and gathered information. Frantic with grief, Mary Lincoln rested as best she could, returning frequently to check on the condition of her husband. On one of these visits she sobbed bitterly, "Oh, that my little Taddy might see his father before he died." The physicians thought this would not be wise and advised her against it. Finally when Mary became hysterical, Stanton ordered her out of the room, shouting loudly, "Take that woman out and do not let her in again."[6]

At 7:22 A.M. on April 15, Lincoln breathed his last breath. Surgeon General Joseph Barnes crossed Lincoln's hands over his motionless chest. The Reverend Dr. Phineas Gurley stepped forward and offered a prayer. Stanton raised his head, the tears streaming down his face. Then, as a look of peace settled on Lincoln's face, he whispered, "Now he belongs to the ages."[7]

The president lay dead, the secretary of state seriously wounded, and later it was discovered that the plan also had intended the assassination of Vice President Johnson and General Ulysses Grant. All of this was believed to be a plan developed by John Wilkes Booth. Almost immediately after Lincoln's death, the assumption was that the assassination was the result of a grand conspiracy of Confederates and Copperheads. In February 1861, the *Cincinnati Commercial* published a letter to Lincoln which threatened him with assassination. This was just one of the many threats against the president. Lincoln kept in his desk at the White House eighty or more letters threatening his life. In 1863, federal intelligence agents obtained evidence that a group of Virginians were offering a reward for Lincoln's assassination. At about the same time, the secret service discovered a group of fanatics, the Knights of the Golden Circle, and other Copperheads were signing blood-oaths to kill the president. In August 1864, a shot was fired through Lincoln's hat by a sniper. There were also schemes to kidnap Lincoln. Various conspirators were waiting for the opportunity to abduct or kill the president. The Capital was flooded with Union troops and an army of government workers, but there were also secession partisans, subversive agents, and Confederate spies. As early as January 1865, the War Department received word that John Wilkes Booth and his gang were meeting at a boarding house on H Street, an establishment run by Mary Surratt. Booth, a Confederate operative and courier, had already set in motion a series of events that would eventually lead to the president's death.[8]

At the age of twenty-six, John Wilkes Booth was a highly successful actor, commanding as much as $500 to $1,000 a week, an excellent sum for the time. He was one of ten children born to the famous Shakespearean actor Junius Brutus Booth and his common-law wife. The Booths lived at Bel Air, a town just outside of Baltimore, during the summer and shifted to Baltimore during the wintertime. The family had a home on Exeter Street. Young John attended St. Timothy's Hall in Catonsville, a school with a military program. As a child, John was playful and lighthearted but was subject to fits of temper. He was consumed by a desire for fame. His older brothers, Junius Brutus Jr. and Edwin, who followed their father on the stage, were being acclaimed, and Booth's desire to surpass his father and brothers on the stage became an obsession. A childhood friend recalled a prediction of his: "My name would descend to posterity and never be forgotten, for it would be in all histories of the times, and be read thousands of years after we are dead."[9]

As an actor, Booth soon became one of America's most popular performers, especially in Richmond and other Southern cities. His appeal as an actor was enhanced by his good looks and charming personality. Lacking conceit, Booth enjoyed associations not only with his theatrical peers, but with bit players, stagehands, hotel clerks, and men who hung out at the bars with him. He was free with his money and always good for a round of drinks. His close association and popularity with lower-class citizens would prove very helpful.[10]

When the Civil War began, Booth made little effort to conceal his strong sympathies for the South, but he did not rush to join the Confederate army. As an excuse for not enlisting, he claimed he had promised his mother that he would never go to war. Others, however, insisted that Booth had a fear of being wounded and disfiguring his body or face. Although not serving in the military, Booth became an operative in the Confederate secret service. The extent of his involvement is not known; however, he helped to smuggle medical supplies and acted as a courier, delivering messages back and forth across Southern lines. He was allowed to travel freely to the South and made trips to Canada to consult with Confederate operatives there.[11]

In March 1864, explosive news broke in Richmond. Union Colonel Ulric Dahlgren was killed while leading an aborted raid on Richmond. In his pocket were papers indicating that his orders were to burn the Confederate capital and kill President Jefferson Davis. Northern opponents of Lincoln and Southerners were outraged. Secretly the Confederate high command planned to retaliate.[12] Near the end of 1864, the Union's large manpower pool gave it an insurmountable advantage over the Confederacy; approximately 50,000 Southerners were being held captive by the Union. There was a desperate need to fill the depleted Confederate ranks. In order to aid the Southern cause, Booth planned to abduct President Lincoln and hold him hostage for the release of Confederate prisoners.[13]

The idea of abducting Lincoln was not new. Such schemes appeared in Southern papers from time to time and were considered fair by the rules of war. The Confederate government had encouraged such attempts to capture Lincoln. The first provided for Maryland cavalrymen under Brigadier General Bradley Johnson to abduct Lincoln as part of Lieutenant General Jubal Early's drive on Washington. The effort failed when Early's troops were repulsed at Fort Stevens. The second plot originated with Confederate agent Thomas Conrad and had the approval of the Confederate secretary of war, James Seddon. Conrad planned to abduct the president in Washington, but with the election of 1864 approaching, Lincoln was assigned more guards; Conrad was forced to give up his plan.[14] Whether Booth's plan had the approval of the Confederate government is not known.

To carry out his scheme, Booth gathered an eclectic group of conspirators together. They consisted mostly of boyhood friends, vagrants, and ne'er-do-wells. The charismatic Booth had little trouble enlisting his band of Southern sympathizers. One of Booth's first recruits was twenty-three-year-old David Herold, a former Washington drugstore clerk who was unemployed. Because Herold was familiar with the backroads and waterways of southern Maryland, he could act as a guide for the escaping conspirators.[15] In addition, there was twenty-eight-year-old Samuel Arnold and twenty-seven-year-old Michael O'Laughlin, both of whom were Booth's old school friends and former Confederate soldiers. Arnold was drifting aimlessly around Baltimore. O'Laughlin was working for his brother in the feed and produce business. At first O'Laughlin was delighted to join Booth in his scheme, but as time progressed and plans changed, he had second thoughts.[16]

During the fall, posing as a prospective buyer of farms and horses, Booth made several trips into southern Maryland to scout roads, relay stations, and ferries across the Potomac. It was here that Booth was introduced to Dr. Samuel Mudd, a Charles County physician. Mudd had given up much of his medical practice to devote time to his farm and was known to have strong Southern sympathies. Whether Booth's meeting with Mudd was accidental or arranged is uncertain. During his visit, Dr. Mudd invited Booth to stay overnight at his home.[17]

Booth also recruited longtime associate Edman Spangler, who had worked as a carpenter on his father's Bel Air home and was now an assistant stage carpenter and scene changer at Ford's Theater. Booth and Spangler were often seen drinking together. It is doubtful Spangler fully understood that Booth's plans were to abduct or assassinate the president, but he was so enthralled with the popular actor that he would do whatever Booth wanted him to do.[18]

Booth also sought out John Surratt, a Confederate courier familiar with the underground routes from Washington through southern Maryland to Virginia. Surratt who had attended divinity school at one time, held a position as postmaster at Surrattsville until November 1863, when his Southern sympathies became known. Then he was replaced by someone more sympathetic to the Union cause. In 1864, young Surratt made a secret trip to Richmond; from then on he operated as a spy and courier between Richmond, Washington, and Canada. By the time Mrs. Surratt established her boarding house in Washington, her son John had become an operative in the Confederate secret service. At first the twenty-year-old Surratt was skeptical of Booth's plan to kidnap the president, but he soon joined the group and helped to get the services of George Atzerodt.[19]

George Atzerodt, a thirty-three-year-old carriage painter, lived in Port Tobacco, Maryland. Early in the war, Atzerodt was involved in rowing his secessionist friends back and forth across the Potomac and in blockade-running. Of Booth's co-conspirators, Atzerodt was the coarsest; he was extremely conspicuous in a restaurant or hotel parlor. Booth probably selected Atzerodt to be used as a decoy, planted to divert counterintelligence from the real objective.[20]

The last of Booth's conspirators to be recruited was Lewis Powell, alias Lewis Paine, a twenty-year-old former Confederate private. Booth's charismatic personality quickly convinced Powell to join his band; thereafter, he displayed an unwavering allegiance to Booth and a readiness to carry out whatever Booth requested. Powell, the son of a Baptist minister, had enlisted in the Confederate army at the age of sixteen and fought until he was taken prisoner at Gettysburg. Assigned by his captors to help with the wounded Union soldiers, he soon escaped. After returning to Virginia, Powell is believed to have enlisted in Mosby's Rangers. In 1865 he turned himself in to federal authorities and signed an oath of allegiance to the Union.[21]

Booth's conspirators met several times at Mary Surratt's boarding house in Washington. Until her husband's death in July 1862, Mrs. Surratt had managed a tavern in Surrattsville, Maryland. In the fall of 1864, she rented her farm and tavern and moved to Washington. Did Mrs. Surratt participate in the conspiracy? The federal government would contend that she did. The conspirators met at her house; her son John had operated for months as a Confederate spy and courier; one of the conspirators was caught at her house. To the day of her death, however, she would deny any complicity in Lincoln's assassination.[22]

Booth's plan at first was to kidnap Lincoln. He had an opportunity to shoot the president on several occasions before April 14. At Lincoln's second inaugural on March 4, 1865, Booth stood only a few feet from him, but at that time his interest was in kidnaping rather than murder. Booth proposed three different plans for seizing Lincoln. The first involved taking Lincoln at the theater, but his fellow conspirators quickly rejected that. Another plan was to take the president while he was visiting an army hospital, but there would likely be soldiers in the area. The most workable of the three plans seemed to be to intercept Lincoln's carriage along a deserted stretch of road, abduct the president, and take him into the countryside.

During the fall and winter of 1864, while Booth was recruiting his gang of conspirators, he spent time studying maps and exploring the roads in Charles County, Maryland. Sometime later the word was sent to Confederate operatives along the way to be prepared to move a captured high official to the South.[23] The whole plan, despite its seriousness, had a theatrical quality about it.

The conspirators' first opportunity to kidnap Lincoln came on January 18. The president was scheduled to attend a performance at Ford's Theater, but when the night was stormy, he stayed home. It was not until March 17 that they were ready for another attempt.[24] With time running out for the Confederacy, Booth received word that Lincoln was scheduled to visit the Campbell Hospital in Washington. The members of the gang took their assigned places along the road and waited for the carriage. As it approached, Booth rode alongside to see if its passenger was the one they wanted. To his surprise and dismay, he found that the occupant was not the president, but Chief Justice Salmon Chase. At the last moment, Lincoln had decided to review an Indiana regiment instead. Again their plan had to be aborted.[25]

Although Louis Weichmann, a friend of John Surratt and boarder at Mrs. Surratt's house, was keeping the War Department informed of Booth's plan to kidnap the president, no formal action was taken. With the war so near an end, the responsible persons in the War Department probably thought the danger was over.

On April 2, Richmond fell to General Grant. Now there was no place to take a captive Lincoln, and the conspiracy to abduct the president seemed to be at an end. On April 9, the news of Lee's surrender at Appomattox reached Washington. While the Union celebrated, John Wilkes Booth sulked and grew more bitter. There were still Confederates fighting under General Joseph Johnston in the Carolinas; the South still had a chance, Booth thought. By April 11, the conspiracy to kidnap Lincoln had reached a turning point; Booth now planned to disrupt the government by assassinating the president and other key officials.[26]

April 14, 1865, Abraham Lincoln's last full day of life, was also Good Friday for the Christian religion. It was solemnly observed by many Americans through prayer, fasting, and meditation. For Lincoln it was another day of work, but he planned to relax that evening by attending the theater, his favorite form of entertainment. The newspapers carried the announcement that General Grant, President Lincoln, and their wives would be attending the comedy *Our American Cousin* at Ford's Theater.[27]

Lincoln was happy about the news that General Sherman was about to negotiate the surrender of General Joseph Johnston's army in North Carolina. This, for all practical purposes, would end the war. In planning for the peace that would follow, Lincoln had said that he had no plans to hang or kill the Confederate leaders, "even the worst of them." The best course of action, he said, would be to allow them to leave the country. "Enough lives have been sacrificed; we must extinguish our resentment if we expect harmony and union."[28]

This was proving to be the usual exhausting day for Lincoln, but it didn't seem to bother him. Now that the long ordeal of the war was nearly over, Lincoln seemed to have renewed energy, and he handled his duties expeditiously and with enthusiasm. His whole appearance seemed to change. Senator James

Harlan recalled: "He seemed the very personification of supreme satisfaction. His conversation was, of course, correspondingly exhilarating."[29]

At three o'clock, Lincoln broke away from his work to take his wife Mary for a ride in an open carriage. Lincoln discussed the prospect of returning to his law practice after his term was up. "I never felt so happy in my life," he said. Mrs. Lincoln's reply was morbid but, unfortunately, almost prophetic. "Don't you remember feeling just so before our little boy died?" she asked. Mrs. Lincoln had never recovered from the loss of their thirteen-year-old son in 1862.[30]

That evening Lincoln had dinner earlier than usual because he had promised to attend the show at Ford's Theater. By this time Mary had developed a headache and wanted to stay at home, but Lincoln insisted on going, saying that he had committed himself to attend. Tickets, he said, were being sold with the expectation that he would be in attendance. Earlier Lincoln had extended an invitation to General Grant and his wife to attend the performance with them. Grant had happily accepted but later had to cancel at the insistence of his wife, giving the excuse that they were going to New Jersey to see their son. The Lincolns were able to get another couple, Major Henry Rathbone and his fiancee, Clara Harris, to join them at the theater.[31]

Lincoln's advisers urged him to stay away from crowds and to avoid the theater. One of Lincoln's friends and sometimes bodyguard, Ward Lamon, also advised him not to go to the theater. Before he left on a mission to Richmond, he had begged Lincoln: "Promise me you will not go out at night while I am gone, particularly to the theater." Lincoln would only promise to do the best he could. Stanton, too, warned Lincoln about mingling with crowds at the theater. His appearance and General Grant's had been announced in the newspapers; someone planning to do him harm would know where to find him. Lincoln requested that Major Thomas Eckert, chief of the Telegraph Bureau, be assigned as his bodyguard for the evening. Eckert was a man of great strength and was believed to be capable of protecting the president. But Stanton said that Eckert's services were needed elsewhere, so John Parker, a metropolitan policeman, was assigned instead.[32]

Lincoln and his party arrived at the theater at about 8:30 P.M.; the performance had already started. When he entered the theater, the orchestra interrupted the performance and played "Hail to the Chief." The audience stood and cheered.

Reaching his box, Lincoln stepped to the rail and acknowledged the applause with bows and smiles and sat down in his rocker. Mrs. Lincoln curtsied and took the seat beside him.[33]

The president seemed to be enjoying the play, laughing heartily at various times. The theater was a relief for him from the drudgery and pressure of the presidential office. As Lincoln watched the performance, the door of his box was closed but unlocked. Parker had left his post to watch the play from the audience. Later, one of the president's guards, William Crook, revealed: "It was the custom of the guard who accompanied the President to the theater to remain in the little passageway outside the box ... he [Parker] confessed to me the next day that he went to a seat at the front of the first gallery so that he could see the play. The door to the President's box was shut; probably Mr. Lincoln never knew that the guard had left his post."[34] Parker was charged with "neglect of duty," but the charge was later dismissed. He continued to serve on the White House staff for a month after the assassination and on the police department for an additional three years. It is not known why he was exonerated.[35]

In the box, Mary Lincoln sat close to her husband and whispered, "What will Miss Harris think of my hanging on to you so?" With a smile, he replied, "She won't think anything about it." These were Lincoln's last words.[36] During the second scene of the third act, it happened. The laughter and the applause drowned out the sound of a shot in the presidential box.

In anticipation of what would happen that night, Booth wrote a letter for publication, explaining and defending his actions. Unfortunately the friend to whom he had given the letter destroyed it and remembered only the closing words: "The world may censure me for what I am about to do, but I am sure that posterity will justify me." Booth also tried to justify his actions in his diary, which was uncovered when he was captured. In it he wrote that the country owed all of its trouble to Lincoln, "and God simply made me the instrument of his punishment."[37]

Because the telegraph lines from the War Department to the South were not working, the search for Booth was slow getting started. Stanton ordered Lafayette Baker to take charge of the manhunt. Baker had a reputation for being ruthless and making wholesale arrests. In his effort to discover all those involved in the conspiracy, Baker acted true to his reputation. Members of the cast of *Our American Cousin,* the Fords, and anyone believed to be a friend or associate of Booth were taken in for questioning. A reward of $100,000 was offered for the apprehension of the conspirators.[38]

Five hours after the shooting, the police went to Mrs. Surratt's house looking for her son John. She told them that he had left for Canada on April 13. Later that day the informant Louis Weichmann, one of Mrs. Surratt's boarders, was taken into custody. On April 17, Lewis Powell (Paine) was arrested when he returned to Surratt's house after hiding in the woods for more than two days. On the same day, Samuel Arnold and Michael O'Laughlin were arrested, Arnold at Fort Monroe and O'Laughlin in Baltimore. Although the two had been involved in the plot to abduct the president, they played no part in the plan to assassinate Lincoln. That night detectives went back to Mrs. Surratt's house and arrested her, her daughter, and some of the boarders. Three days later George Atzerodt was apprehended in western Maryland. The last of the conspirators to be arrested, other than Booth and Herold, was Edman Spangler.[39]

On April 24, Dr. Samuel Mudd was arrested. Booth had visited Dr. Mudd after the assassination to have his broken leg treated. Mudd told officials that he had not recognized Booth when he stopped at his house or while setting his leg, but later became suspicious after the injured man and his friend left and he learned that Lincoln had been killed. He did not immediately report his suspicions to the troops in Bryantown, he said, because he feared reprisals from Confederate sympathizers living in the area. Later Mudd told his cousin, Dr. George Mudd, what had transpired and asked him to pass the information along to the federal troops searching the area. Mudd's delay in reporting the two men who had stopped at his house provided more time for Booth to escape and was a strong point used against Mudd at his trial.[40]

Leaving confusion and hysteria behind him at Ford's Theater, Booth had headed toward the Navy Yard Bridge at the end of 11th Street in southeast Washington. Guarding the bridge were three soldiers, Sergeant Silas T. Cobb and two privates. Wartime security was still in effect, but it had been relaxed somewhat after Lee's surrender. However, passage in and out of Washington still required a pass. Booth had no pass, but he gave his correct name and was able to convince Sergeant Cobb to let him through. The guards did not know that an attempt had been made on the president's life. Not long afterward a second rider, believed to be David Herold, was able to persuade the sentries to allow him to cross the bridge also. The two met up somewhere outside of

Washington. Herold claimed the meeting was accidental, but in his trial the War Department contended that their meeting had been planned.[41]

The pair next stopped at a tavern in Surrattsville, now operated by John Lloyd, to pick up a package left there for Booth by Mary Surratt. Before leaving Washington on April 14, Booth had visited with her, leaving a package which later was found to contain a pair of field glasses and asking her to take it to Lloyd. Lloyd would later tell authorities that Mary Surratt and Louis Weichmann had delivered the package to him. At her trial, Lloyd testified that Mary Surratt told him to have the "shooting irons ready" and that they would be picked up later that evening by persons unnamed. A month earlier David Herold had delivered them to the tavern in anticipation of the abduction of the president. John Lloyd's testimony and the independent corroboration of the details by Weichmann played an important part in Mary Surratt's conviction and would put a noose around her neck. At the trial, the defense was not able to show that either Lloyd or Weichmann had lied. Since both witnesses had turned state's evidence, no charges were placed against them.[42]

Booth and Herold arrived at the tavern about midnight, finding Lloyd asleep and intoxicated. Once roused, Lloyd got two carbines, some ammunition, and the field glasses for the men. Herold took one of the carbines, but Booth refused, saying he could not carry it with his injured leg. After taking several swigs of whiskey, Booth told Lloyd what they had done. Then the two fugitives mounted their horses and headed south. A steady rain was falling when they arrived at Mudd's farm; it was about 4:00 A.M.[43]

Waking Dr. Mudd, David Herold appealed to him for help. Mudd set Booth's leg and put him to bed in the guest room. Dr. Mudd later swore that he had not recognized Booth because he was wearing a shawl and a false beard. Yet it was discovered that Booth had been in Mudd's home at least twice the previous fall, and the two had been seen together in Washington in December.[44]

At mid-morning, Dr. Mudd rode into Bryantown, hoping to borrow a carriage for Booth. Mudd was surprised to find Union soldiers searching the town. The manhunt was now in full-swing. Mudd soon realized that the subject of their search was the assassin of the president, believed to be John Wilkes Booth, the famous actor. Mudd immediately turned his horse around and galloped home, reaching his farm at 4:30 P.M.[45]

Mudd claimed that when he reached home, the fugitives were in the process of leaving. Later in 1877, Mudd confided in a friend that when he learned that

Booth was responsible for Lincoln's death, he asked him to leave rather than inform the soldiers in Bryantown. Today Dr. Mudd's involvement in the plot to assassinate the president is still an unanswered question. Some historians have concluded that Mudd was no more than an innocent doctor who became a victim of a vengeful government. Others say the evidence clearly points to his involvement.[46]

Leaving Mudd's house, Booth and Herold headed west along the murky edges of the Zekiah Swamp. They emerged from the swamp after dark, arriving at Samuel Cox's home in Rich Hill. Cox fed them but was afraid to let them stay; he later denied that the two ever entered his house. Booth and Herold spent the night in a pine thicket nearby. The following morning Cox sent for Thomas Jones, a Confederate operative who lived near the Potomac. Aware that the area was swarming with soldiers, Jones told the fugitives to remain in the thicket until it was safe to cross the Potomac River. For five days and four cold nights, Booth and Herold remained in the woods, hidden in the bush. Cox made daily trips to bring food, drinks, and newspapers to them. During his wait, Booth wrote in a pocket diary and read newspaper reports about the death of the president and the search for his assassin. He was dismayed to learn that he was not viewed as a hero, but rather as a villian.[47]

On Tuesday, April 18, Lincoln's body was placed in the East Room of the White House. On that day 25,000 people passed by the open coffin. On April 21, one week after that tragic Good Friday, Lincoln's body was placed on a seven-car funeral train which would take him home to Springfield, Illinois. It is estimated that 7 million people either saw the train pass by or filed by the open casket as the body lay in state at various cities along the way. This trip was essentially the reverse of the one Lincoln had taken just four years earlier when he came to Washington as the president-elect.[48]

On the same day Lincoln's body left Washington, the federal troops withdrew from the area where Booth and Herold were hiding. The two fugitives were ready to attempt to cross the Potomac. That evening, in the darkness, a strong incoming tide carried them up the river rather than across it. As a result they were still on the Maryland side when morning came. On the following night they made another attempt and were able to successfully cross the river.[49]

By then the countryside was alive with pursuers. Many military units and posses were searching for the fugitives; the reward for their capture had grown to $200,000. At last Booth had made good his flight to the Confederacy. His welcome, however, was far from enthusiastic. Virginia was now occupied by federal troops; Southern loyalists were not foolhardy enough to harbor Lincoln's assassin. Virginians were willing to give them food but were unwilling to take them into their homes. Dr. Richard Stuart, who had been active in the Confederate underground, fed the fugitives and passed them along to a nearby cabin of a free black man named William Lucus. The next day, Lucus's son drove them to Port Conway, Virginia. With the assistance of three ex-Confederate soldiers, they were able to cross the river to Port Royal. In the process Booth revealed his true identity and told the Confederates that he was the man who had killed the president. Despite the great risk to himself, one of the Confederates, William Jett, found refuge for Booth and Herold at the farm of his friend, Richard Garrett.[50]

Jett introduced Booth to Garrett as a Confederate soldier named Boyd who had been wounded at Petersburg. Garrett offered Booth a bed for the night. The next day, Herold arrived at the Garrett farm pretending to be Davey Boyd, Booth's brother. Later, when the fugitives learned that federal troops were approaching, they fled into the woods. By now Garrett had become suspicious of the Boyds. Booth asked him if he could furnish them horses so they could ride to Guinea Station; they could pay well, Booth said. Garrett, stalling for time, promised to do it in the morning. Garrett became even more suspicious when Booth asked if he and his brother could sleep in the barn that night. Fearing the two men might be planning to steal his horses, Garrett had his son lock the barn door and sleep in the corn crib nearby.[51]

By morning federal troops, led by Lieutenant E. P. Doherty, had picked up Booth's trail and had Jett in custody. With his help, the troops made their way to Garrett's farm. They surrounded the barn and ordered Booth and Herold to surrender. Once the fugitives realized they had no way out, Booth yelled out, "Cap, there is a man in here who wants to surrender mighty bad." As Herold gave himself up, Booth shouted once more: "I declare before my Maker that this man [Herold] here is innocent of any crime whatever."[52]

When Booth failed to come out with his hands up, the soldiers set the barn on fire. Booth dropped one crutch and moved toward the door with a carbine on his hip. Before he could reach the door, a shot rang out, and Booth fell forward on his face. The bullet went through the right ear, passing out of his neck on the other side. At first it appeared that Booth had shot himself, but Ser-

geant Boston Corbett admitted to having fired the shot. Asked why he had dis-
obeyed orders not to shoot Booth, Corbett replied: "Providence directed me."[53]

The soldiers laughed at Corbett's remark. Corbett was a religious fanatic
and considered an eccentric. Nevertheless, he was arrested for disobeying
orders, and the episode was reported to Stanton, who proclaimed Boston Corbett a hero: "The rebel is dead. The patriot lives. He has saved us continued
excitement, delay, and expense ... the patriot is released." Corbett's share of the
reward was $1,653.85.[54]

Booth was carried to the porch of the Garrett house and placed on a mat-
tress. Booth was paralyzed from the neck down. He made an effort to speak,
but it was difficult for him to manage only a whisper. When Booth asked for
water, he found he couldn't swallow, so they soaked a rag and placed it in his
mouth. "Tell my mother that I died for my country," he said. Several times he
begged the soldiers to kill him. Just before he died, Booth asked to see his
hands. When they held up his hands for him, he murmured, "Useless, useless."
He died two hours after he was shot.[55]

Treatment of the conspirators was harsh by any standard. Kept in the holds
of two ironclads in the Potomac, the principal male prisoners were manacled
with cuffs connected with iron rods. Their ankles were shackled and linked by
chains to a seventy-five-pound iron ball. A canvas hood, padded with cotton,
with small holes for eating and breathing but none for seeing or hearing, was
placed over their heads and tied around their necks. The hoods were worn day
and night. Mary Surratt was treated more humanely; she was spared the smoth-
ering effect of a hood, and her hands were left free; only a chain bound her
ankles. On April 27, the male prisoners were moved to the Old Capitol Prison
in Washington.[56]

Finally, on the recommendation of surgeon George Porter, the canvas hoods
were removed. Stanton moved ahead with plans for a military trial. In a military court, the laws of evidence were less demanding than in a civilian court;
thus, the chance of conviction was much greater. In addition, the punishment
and sentences in a military court were usually more severe. Stanton felt it was
necessary for swift and stern punishment of the conspirators. Nine military officers were named to form a commission that would try the accused. Presiding
over the court was Major General David Hunter, who had been a personal
friend of Lincoln.[57]

The commission met on May 9 and adjourned for one day to allow the prisoners to speak to their attorneys. This was the first opportunity they had to do so. The next day, with less than twenty-four hours for the defense counsel to prepare their case, the trial began. Although the charges placed against the conspirators were somewhat different, in general they were accused of having "traitorously conspired to kill and murder Abraham Lincoln, Andrew Johnson, William Seward, and Ulysses Grant."[58]

When the trial began, the accused were only able to confer with their lawyers while they were in court. The prosecution began by presenting their witnesses, 198 in all. In calling their witnesses, the defense was at a great disadvantage. They were required to present to the judge advocate general a list of witnesses they planned to call. The prosecuting attorneys did not have to do this, allowing them to produce surprise witnesses for which the defense was not prepared.[59]

There was no reason to place the defense at such a disadvantage. There was already ample evidence to connect the accused to either the kidnaping, murder plots, or both. Lewis Powell had attacked the Sewards, and Herold had helped Booth escape, and George Atzerodt had accepted the assignment to kill Johnson. Although Michael O'Laughlin and Samuel Arnold had not taken part in the murder plot, they were involved in the plan to kidnap the president. Edman Spangler was connected to the crime by being the man who held Booth's horse for him at Ford's Theater. Mrs. Surratt's house had been used as a meeting place for the conspirators; the question of how much she knew about Booth's plans to murder the president still remains. Dr. Mudd admitted that Booth and Herold stopped at his house. John Surratt, however, had fled to Canada and was not captured until well after the trial.[60]

On June 29 the trial ended. All eight defendants were found guilty. Mrs. Surratt, Powell, Herold, and Atzerodt were sentenced to be hanged. O'Laughlin, Arnold, and Mudd were given life sentences. Spangler was sentenced to six years at hard labor. The four condemned prisoners were scheduled to be hanged on July 7. A last-minute attempt by Mrs. Surratt's daughter to see President Johnson for a commutation of her mother's sentence failed. As scheduled, eight days after being sentenced, the trap doors were dropped, and the four prisoners fell through. Their bodies swung for fifteen minutes and then were pronounced dead by the attending physician.[61]

With five of the conspirators dead and all but John Surratt in prison, Stan-

While eight people were convicted of conspiracy, only four were hanged.
(Library of Congress)

ton was content to close the door on the Lincoln murder case. In 1867, when John Surratt was finally captured, he was tried before a civil court. He admitted to having taken part in the plot to kidnap Lincoln but denied any part in his murder. After two months, a jury could not agree on the guilt or innocence of John Surratt. The desire for retribution had lessened, and there was a general feeling that Surratt's mother had paid the price for both of them. He was never retried.[62] One of the last acts of President Johnson before he left office was to pardon three of the surviving conspirators, Samuel Arnold, Dr. Samuel Mudd, and Edman Spangler. Michael O'Laughin died in prison before he could be pardoned.

Immediately after the death of John Wilkes Booth, the investigation turned its attention to determining whether or not the Confederate government had been involved in the plot to assassinate the president. The first evidence collected by the War Department seemed to support the viewpoint that they had. On May 2, 1865, President Johnson declared the assassination had been "incited, concerted, and procured" by Confederate President Jefferson Davis and five rebel officials in Canada.[63]

In their haste to satisfy the North's demand for vengeance, the Union prosecutors tried to link the conspirators to Confederate government officials; however, they were unable to prove their case. Confederate records had either been destroyed or were in such chaotic condition that no definite evidence could be found. As a result of the weakness of the case against the Confederate government, other theories were presented.[64]

Shortly after the trial of the conspirators, the case against Jefferson Davis was abandoned. The public came to believe that the crime was an act by an individual, with the support of a few ne'er-do-wells, rather than an act of war perpetrated by the Confederate government.[65] Those who believed that John Wilkes Booth was responsible developed rationales to explain his actions. Some explanations contended that Booth was insane; only an unbalanced person could commit such a crime. Others concluded that Booth hated his father and had killed Lincoln as a substitute for him. Still another theory stated that in 1864, when Booth was performing less because of a failing voice, he seemed to have a greater sense of guilt over keeping himself in comfort and safety while other Southerners were sacrificing so much. He would perform an act, saving the Southern cause, and at the same time give the world a dramatic performance which would forever inscribe his name in history. There is a lack of sufficient evidence to support with certainty any of these theories.[66]

In 1870, new evidence came forth to support the involvement of the Confederate government. The *New York Times* reported a speech given by John Surratt, who said the kidnaping conspiracy had been "instigated by certain Confederates in order to bring about a fair exchange of prisoners." There had been other plans to abduct Lincoln supported by the Confederate government earlier in the war. Brigadier General Bradley Johnson, commander of a cavalry brigade, and Thomas Conrad, a Confederate agent, both published their accounts of plans to kidnap the president. Both plans had to be abandoned before the attempt could be made.[67] Today the question of the Confederate government's part in the assassination of Lincoln is still strictly speculation. No documentary evidence directly proves its involvement. There is some personal testimony, much of it by persons either under arrest or with obvious biases. The only evidence of Confederate government involvement in Lincoln's murder is mostly circumstantial.[68]

Whether or not Booth acted on his own or with the consent of the Confederate government, the result of his actions was a tragedy for both North and South. Had Lincoln lived beyond the war and had the opportunity to implement his more conciliatory Reconstruction plan, the years of pain suffered by the South might have been reduced. The effects of Lincoln's premature death linger still.

Part 2   Warriors Behind the Lines

THE RAIDERS

For the first two years of the Civil War, Confederate cavalry proved to be superior to their Union counterpart. From the outset of the war, the South had an advantage at raiding. Many of the Southerners, bred in gentlemanly traditions, were experienced horsemen and quickly adapted to the duties in the cavalry. Since the majority of the purebred horses came from the South, this too gave them an early advantage. Noted cavalry leaders such as J.E.B. Stuart, John Hunt Morgan, Turner Ashby, and John Singleton Mosby took the initiative at mounted raids. They were able to infiltrate Union lines, inflict great damage, and then quickly slip away. It took several years before the Federals were able to develop cavalrymen of that quality.[1]

Without proper training and quality horses, the federal horsemen proved to be inferior and were often humiliated when they encountered Confederate cavalry. During the spring of 1863, Major General Joseph Hooker ordered Major General George Stoneman and his cavalry corps of 10,000 troops on a raid against the supply and communication lines of Lee's Army of Northern Virginia. This was to take place before Hooker's main body attacked Lee. Stoneman was two weeks late in crossing the Rappahannock because a heavy storm had flooded the river. Although the raiding party destroyed some railroad tracks and other property, their efforts had no lasting effect. Furthermore, the detachment of the cavalry deprived Hooker of their service during the Battle of Chancellorsville, a factor that led to a decisive defeat of the Union.[2]

In February 1864, Union Brigadier General Hugh Judson Kilpatrick, with 4,000 mounted horsemen, attempted a raid on Richmond; their objective was to capture the city and liberate the prisoners confined there. A portion of his command became separated and were ambushed. Many were killed or captured. Kilpatrick's main raiding party was repulsed outside of Richmond and was forced to withdraw across the Chickahominy River. The raid failed, but it might have been successful had the Confederates not intercepted a dispatch containing the plan of attack.[3]

Hugh Judson Kilpatrick earned his nickname, "Kill-Cavalry," by carelessly risking the lives of his men.
(U.S. Army Military History Institute)

At the beginning of the war, Union cavalry did not enjoy a favorable reputation within the army. According to one Pennsylvania trooper: "for the most part [they are] scattered about and used as escorts ... and orderlies for all the generals and their numerous staff officers." For the most part this was true. It took hard work and outstanding leadership to raise the performance of the federal cavalry to the level where it was respected and could challenge the mounted Confederate troopers.[4]

By 1863, the Union army had developed its share of experienced and capable cavalrymen and was making strikes into Confederate territory. Once Union riders had tasted victory in battle and acquired better horses and equipment, they were ready to challenge Stuart and Morgan. Some degree of uncertainty remained, however, on the part of federal cavalry leaders when they encountered their opponents. During his campaign in the Shenandoah Valley, Major General Philip Sheridan noted: "I knew I was strong, yet I deemed it necessary to be cautious."[5]

A year later, resourceful Union cavalry leaders such as George Custer, Alfred Pleasonton, and Wesley Merritt were making a name for themselves. Although not noted for leading raids behind enemy lines, they nevertheless contributed to the growth and improvement of the Union cavalry and were instrumental in encouraging others who did.[6]

As early as June 1862, Confederate leader J.E.B. Stuart had demonstrated the possibilities of an independent raid by mounted cavalry when, with 1,200 troopers, he rode around the Union army on the Virginia peninsula. Again in October, with the Pennsylvania raid, Stuart proved that the cavalry could move through hostile country with impunity. His raids were instrumental in drawing federal troops from the front to protect important targets and did much to raise the morale of the South.[7]

In the spring, Union Major General Sheridan's cavalry had grown to 12,000 men. He launched a raid on Richmond hoping to draw J.E.B. Stuart out into the open. Although the raiders never reached Richmond, in a battle at Yellow Tavern, Stuart, the pride of Lee's cavalry, was mortally wounded. His death prompted Sheridan to report: "Under him [Stuart], the cavalry of Lee's army had been nurtured but had acquired such prestige that it thought itself well nigh invincible. Indeed, in the early years of the war, it had proved to be so. This was now dispelled." The death of Stuart was a blow to the Confederacy from which they would never recover, and it did much to enhance the reputation of the federal cavalry.[8]

On October 19, 1864, the Battle of Cedar Creek proved to be the shining moment for the federal cavalry. At dawn, five Confederate divisions launched a massive attack against Sheridan's Army of the Shenandoah, catching them by complete surprise and causing great damage to two of his three corps. Sheridan was twelve miles away in Winchester when he learned of the attack. Quickly he rode to the site of the battle only to find a steady stream of his retreating army. To inspire his troops, Sheridan took his personal battle flag and crossed between the Union and Confederate troops, galloping the full length of his line. Cajoling the army, he inspired his men, restoring their broken ranks. By noon, his troops had rallied and were on the offensive, his cavalry attacking the Confederate flanks and causing them to scatter.[9]

Through attrition, the ranks of the Confederate cavalry would be depleted. Over time, great Southern cavalry leaders and raiders such as Stuart, Morgan, and Ashby would be killed. The availability and quality of Confederate horses would also decline. By the war's end, the federal cavalry at last dominated.

One of the most important and dangerous assignments of the cavalry during

Turner Ashby's death contributed to the declining strength of the Confederate cavalry.
(The Virginia Historical Society)

the Civil War was raiding. Quite often, cavalry made raids en masse deep behind enemy lines to destroy supply and communication lines and to harass the enemy's rear. Reflecting upon the use of Confederate raiding activities during the 1862–63 winter, President Lincoln remarked, "In no other way does the enemy give us so much trouble, at so little expense to himself, as by the raids of rapidly moving small bodies of troops harassing, and discouraging loyal residents, supplying themselves with provisions, clothing, horses, and the like, surprising and capturing small detachments of our forces, and breaking our communications."[10]

General Sheridan shared Lincoln's assessment and wrote, "During the entire campaign, I have been annoyed by guerrilla bands under such partisan chiefs as Mosby, White, Gilmor, McNeill, and others, and this had considerably depleted my line-of-battle strength, necessitating as it did large escorts for my supply-train." At first, despite their strong support of the Southern cause, Confederate partisans had to operate without official sanction. The Confederate government was reluctant to sponsor armed groups over which they could have little control. In March 1862, the Commonwealth of Virginia was the first to authorize the formation of ten companies of rangers who were trained for close-combat raids and scouting. These irregular horsemen would operate primarily behind enemy lines. One month later the Confederate government passed a Partisan Ranger Act, which provided for the organization of companies of partisans. Unlike the lawless guerrilla bands that roamed Missouri and Kansas, these partisans would receive the same uniforms, pay, and rations as other Confederate soldiers. Under this law, raiders were to be paid for any weapons or ammunition that they captured. Enlistment in partisan outfits was flooded with recruits at the expense of the regular army.[11]

Partisan units were raised in the same way as regiments for the regular army. A local citizen, usually someone with military training and prominence, would gather a group of volunteers and obtain a colonel's commission from Richmond. Other lower ranking officers were elected by the men. Under the colonel's leadership, drilling and preparation for fighting would take place. Partisans often fought on their own and usually were not supported by other military units, but they often enjoyed the help of local citizens.[12]

One of the myths that persisted from the Civil War is that the cavalryman's role was one of privilege, that he rode to battle while his comrades in the infantry trudged along rough roads. He was perceived as an aristocrat who had an easy life, free of a boring existence and hardships. The truth of the matter is that the horse soldier, because of his speed and mobility, saw combat more frequently than the foot soldier. While the infantry remained in camp for long periods of time during lulls in campaigns and when operations were suspended during winter months or bad weather, the opportunities for long periods of inactivity for cavalrymen were few and far between. When not involved in battles or skirmishes, they scouted, reconnoitered, and made raids behind enemy lines.[13]

An effective cavalry raid was one that surprised the enemy at predetermined targets and avoided battle with enemy forces of equal or larger size when possible. The object of the raid was to gather information about the enemy's position and troop strength and to destroy as many resources as possible. Then the raiding party would attempt to return to their home base as quickly as they could and with as few casualties as possible. The most frequent targets of the Civil War raiders included lines of communication, supply bases, railroads, and wagon trains. Often, raiding parties attacked undefended cities or were used as diversionary actions to distract from the real movement of the main army. Usu-

A typical raid, captured for Harper's Weekly, *as were many Civil War activities, by Alfred Waud.*

(Library of Congress, *Harper's Weekly,* October 24, 1863)

ally the raiding parties had to be small enough to facilitate speed and maneu-
verability but, at the same time, large enough to carry out their assigned mission. Confederate raider John Mosby often operated with less than two dozen
men.[14]

The leader of the raid had to be daring and capable of exercising strict control of his men. He had to be prepared for the unexpected and able to make
split-second decisions. The leader, or his scouts, had to have a knowledge of
the land to be traversed, including back roads to be used in the case of emer-
gencies. Since most of the Civil War was fought in the South, Confederate
raiders enjoyed the advantage of being familiar with the terrain.[15]

A cavalry raid required endurance and sacrifice on the part of the partici-
pants. Often the horsemen were required to remain in the saddle as much as
twenty hours a day. They often were hungry for extended periods of time, especially in regions that had been depleted by months of war. Since raiders were
often in hostile territory, there was always the fear that a sniper would be hiding behind a tree, waiting to take a shot at them.[16]

A raiding party often contained two or more regiments, and in some
instances, as many as several brigades. Scouts who were familiar with the area
rode in front of the main body to point the way. In order to go unnoticed,
they sometimes dressed as civilians or in the uniform of the enemy. This was
dangerous; if caught they could be executed as spies. Some Confederate raiders
sent their scouts into an area well in advance of the raid in order to gain information and to plan the best route for the raiders. John Hunt Morgan and John
Singleton Mosby were among the Confederate raiders who often used this tactic with great success. Behind the scouts came the vanguard of the raiding party,
consisting of about one hundred men. The size of the advance guard depended on the size of the enemy force they were expecting to encounter. The main
column, consisting of several regiments, followed about a half a mile behind; a
narrow gap was left between each of the regiments. The raiding commander
usually rode among or in the rear of his troops. Aides and couriers communicated orders to other officers in his command. Several companies of flankers
rode on both sides of the main body. A guard of several companies protected
the rear of the main column. The rear guard was also responsible for rounding
up stragglers and completing the destruction of bridges, rail lines, and supply
depots not completed by the main body.[17]

Being militarily weaker than their enemy, the Confederate army's strategy included frequent use of raids. This involved fewer troops with a greater pay-off than the same number used in conventional warfare. Much like terrorist operations, raids left the enemy off balance and with the fear of repeated attacks. The effects of a raid were often felt long after it ended. The possibility of an attack at any time meant that the defender had to guard all potential targets all the time. This required the deployment of enormous numbers of troops at the expense of those available on the front. The raiders had a definite advantage; they only had to maneuver a small band of fast-moving cavalry to be effective. They also enjoyed the privilege of selecting from any number of targets the one least defended. The element of surprise and the hit-and-run tactics all played to their advantage.[18]

The frequency and destructive nature of Confederate raids caused the Union to divert large numbers of troops from the front to protect positions behind their lines. When the Union took the offensive and moved into the South, they had to protect their supply and communication lines from Confederate raiding parties. In January 1863, when rebel raiders menaced Mississippi and Tennessee, the Union deployed over 50,000 troops to protect railroad and supply lines against only 13,000 Confederates. As the occupied Southern territory increased and supply and communication lines lengthened, the conditions became even more aggravated. The Confederates were aware of this and were willing to dedicate a sizable portion of their cavalry to harassing Union communication and upsetting political conditions.[19]

In 1862, Brigadier General John Hunt Morgan wreaked havoc in Kentucky, destroying bridges, telegraph lines, and supply depots and capturing horses and prisoners. Morgan, who became known as the "Thunderbolt of the Confederacy," was daring and willing to take great risks, and until his luck ran out, he proved an effective rebel raider. In Virginia the "Gray Ghost," John Singleton Mosby, became a painful thorn in the side of the Union army, particularly in the region that became known as "Mosby's Confederacy." Long rides, sudden attacks, and rapid withdrawals became the signature of Mosby's Rangers as they sabotaged the Union's lines of communication. It is estimated that Mosby was able to divert and keep at least 30,000 troops away from the front.

Confederate raiders were particularly adept at destroying railroad tracks, causing untold problems for Union supply officers. Cavalry raids to destroy railroad tracks in hostile territory were dangerous and had to be conducted with dispatch. With the proper tools, four men could remove a rail in three minutes. Then a chain or iron rod was driven into the ground to serve as a ful-crum so the rail could be bent and finally broken. In some cases Confederate raiders tried to warp rails by laying them on top of piles of burning ties until they sagged of their own weight. This proved to be an ineffective method of destroying rails; the burning took too much time, and it was a rather simple matter to rebend the rail back into shape. To destroy tracks beyond repair, the Union developed a technique of their own. It consisted of a steel hook that could be inserted under the rail. By applying leverage, the steel hook was able to tear the rail from the ties. Then it was twisted in a spiral motion similar to a corkscrew. To repair the twisted rail was almost impossible.[20]

As the war progressed, the Union developed construction corps to repair the damage done by Confederate raids on rail lines and bridges. By the end of the war, the corps had grown to 10,000 workmen. The crew became proficient in righting and repairing derailed locomotives. They seemed able to rebuild damaged bridges and stretches of tracks almost overnight. It took them fewer than five days to rebuild a 780-foot span over the Chattahoochee River in Geor-gia. In 1864 the construction corps was able to restore thirty-five miles of track in Georgia to full operation in only thirteen days.[21]

One of the most unusual raids of the Civil War involved an attack on a railroad believed to be important to the defense of Chattanooga. It was "the deepest scheme that ever emanated from the brains of Yankees," declared the April 11, 1862, issue of the *Southern Confederacy*. The plan was proposed by James J. Andrews, a part-time Union spy who had made a number of trips into the Confederate territory and was familiar with the area to be raided. It called for federal raiders to enter Georgia, seize a locomotive on the Western and Atlantic Railroad, and then head north, destroying bridges on the line between Atlanta and Chattanooga. Once the Confederate supply route from Atlanta was cut off, Chattanooga would fall to the Union forces attacking from the west.[22]

Volunteers for the raid were recruited from the Ohio Brigade in Tennessee. Dressed in civilian clothes, sixteen men boarded the northbound passenger train. Since they were traveling in civilian clothes behind enemy lines, they could be hanged by Confederate authorities if caught. When the passengers and crew got off the train for breakfast, Andrews and his men uncoupled all but three cars behind the locomotive. The raiders fired up the engine and sped north-ward, stopping to cut telegraph lines and attempting to destroy some of the track behind them.[23]

Having cut the communication lines and destroyed parts of the track behind him, Andrews reasoned that pursuit would be unlikely, if not impossible. What Andrews hadn't counted on was the courage and persistence of William Fuller and Jeff Cain. When the two railroad men realized that their train had been hijacked, they found a handcar and, with a small group of men, used it to follow the stolen train until they found a locomotive on a siding. Using the locomotive, the men continued the pursuit until they encountered a break in the line. The men abandoned the locomotive and ran the next three miles on foot; after finding another train and firing it up, they continued their chase. Still later the pursuers found another break in the line. Undaunted, they set out on foot again until encountering a southbound train. Commandeering it, Fuller and his party ran the locomotive in reverse and renewed the chase. Farther down the tracks, ten soldiers from the 1st Georgia joined Fuller in his pursuit.[24]

Forced into a siding by other southbound traffic on a single-line track, the Union raiders lost valuable time and saw their lead dwindle. Because they were so closely pursued, the raiders did not have time to burn bridges and destroy large sections of track as they had planned. The fleeing raiders dropped crossties on the tracks and uncoupled the three boxcars they were pulling to slow down Fuller. The Confederate locomotive merely pushed the cars ahead of them and continued their pursuit. Two miles north of Ringgold, Georgia, and just five miles from the Tennessee border, the raiders ran out of water and wood and were forced to abandon the train and flee into the woods. "When the orders were given by Andrews," said one raider, "the boys lit out like a flock of quail." Within a few days all of the raiders were captured. Andrews and seven of his men, selected at random, were hanged; eight of the men escaped from prison; the rest of the original party remained in prison until exchanged in March 1863. Later, the survivors were awarded the newly authorized Congressional Medal of Honor.[25]

The raid was well conceived and probably would have served as a model for future raids had it not been for the valiant efforts of William Fuller and his men, who, because of their tenacity, were able to thwart it. It was the last time the Union would attempt another raid of that type.

Operations against railroads and supply depots continued. One of the most effective federal raids occurred in the mountains of West Virginia in December 1863, just after the region had entered the Union as a free state. After the Battle of Gettysburg, Confederate Lieutenant General James Longstreet and his corps were detached to Tennessee to oppose Major General Ambrose Burnside at Knoxville. Longstreet's main line of supply was the Virginia and Tennessee Railroad. The federal leadership felt a raid against this important supply line would relieve some of the pressure on Burnside.[26]

Brigadier General William Averell and a brigade of mounted infantry were directed to interrupt the transport of troops and supplies between Richmond and Knoxville. Because the situation in Knoxville was quickly becoming critical for Burnside, a midwinter raid against the Confederate railroad was imperative. The plan called for Union forces to feint attacks at Lewisburg from the north and Staunton from the south in an attempt to have the Confederates concentrate their forces. This would open a hole in the line through which Averell's troops could slip, disrupt the lines of transportation, and then return, hopefully, without a fight. On December 8, Averell and his mounted infantry left their post at New Creek, Virginia. As planned, Union forces moved toward Staunton and Lewisburg, fooling the Confederates into thinking they were the points of attack. Traveling over infrequently used roads, Averell's column was able to penetrate deeply into Confederate territory without being detected.[27]

Averell's success in not being detected was due in part to the work of his scouts. Dressed in Confederate uniforms, they were often able to capture enemy couriers and their dispatches, thus discovering rebel troop movements and preventing information about their location from reaching Confederate lines. Without this information, their pursuit was hampered. Averell was able to reach Salem, Virginia, and his target, the Virginia and Tennessee Railroad, without detection. On December 16, Averell's advance guard rode into Salem just before the arrival of a train carrying reinforcements from Lynchburg. The raiders cut telegraph lines and destroyed railroad tracks, forcing the train to return. When the rest of his men arrived, they continued to destroy railroad tracks and burn the depot and its contents. Before leaving, Averell's men planted false information about their movement among the townspeople, hoping to confuse the Confederate pursuers.[28]

As Averell's command made their way back, the Confederate noose was beginning to close around him. On one night they were forced to leave their campfires burning in order to escape from a Confederate trap. Nearly trapped on several other occasions, Averell nevertheless was able to lead his men to safety; the raid ended at Beverly, West Virginia, on Christmas Eve. Averell's raid across the entire state of West Virginia, with relatively few losses, had been a success. Through Averell's skillful planning and leadership, his raiders had infiltrated enemy lines, moving deeply into rebel territory and disrupting valuable supply and troop movements. But the raid had accomplished more than just this; it had proved that Union raiders could make successful raids behind Confederate lines.[29]

Over the four years of the war, federal cavalrymen developed from rank beginners to accomplished dragoons. At the same time, Confederate cavalry was diminishing in strength. Grant's war of attrition had worked against the Confederate mounted commands just as it had against the infantry. Those horsemen who remained fought bravely to the end of the war. There would be more raids, both Confederate and Union. Some of the leaders would make names for themselves, and their episodes would become legend; some would die in their effort. Their stories are told in the chapters that follow.

7 Gray Ghost of the Confederacy

JOHN SINGLETON MOSBY

IT WAS the opportunity of a lifetime; within three blocks of each other were the headquarters of Union Brigadier General Edwin Stoughton and Colonel Percy Wyndham, protected only by a few guards. Although risky, the prize was enticing. Other than the guards there were no troops in town, but for Mosby's Rangers to reach their destination, they would have to avoid 2,500 Union troops in the vicinity. The challenge was to pass through Union lines at Chantilly and at Germantown. The telegraph line between Centreville and Fairfax Court House would have to be cut. The time frame for carrying

Fairfax Court House, Virginia, where Mosby captured General Stoughton.
(National Archives and Records Administration)

out this raid was narrow. Mosby needed to pass through enemy lines under darkness while most of the troops were asleep. If an alarm was sounded, Mosby ran the risk of being captured; it would be the end of his career as a Confederate raider. For John Singleton Mosby it was a challenge such as this and the excitement that he loved.[1]

The raiders, twenty-nine in all, set out with Mosby for Fairfax Court House. There was a mist in the air, and it began to rain after dark. It was a perfect night for raiding, dark and cold; the enemy sentries would probably not be out in force. The raid came as a complete surprise. Some of the Federals captured were so surprised that they thought it was a practical joke. When they finally realized what was happening, it was too late to do anything about it.[2]

Opposite:
John Singleton Mosby, seen here without his trademark cap and ostrich feather plume.
(*Dictionary of American Portraits*, Library of Congress, Brady–Handy Collection)

At 2:00 A.M. they reached the town without a single challenge. At Colonel Wyndham's headquarters, Mosby discovered that he was in Washington. Then, with a small party, Mosby went to General Stoughton's headquarters. Saying that he had a message for the general, Mosby convinced the aide to tell him where Stoughton was sleeping. In Stoughton's room, Mosby pulled down the bedclothes and slapped Stoughton on the rear end with his sword. "Get up, General, and come with me," Mosby said. Stoughton, waking up and seeing the men in his room, inquired what they wanted. "Did you ever hear of Mosby?" Mosby asked. "Yes, have you caught him?" Stoughton asked. "No," replied Mosby, "but he has caught you." While Stoughton dressed, Mosby went to the fireplace, took a piece of coal, and wrote on the wall "Mosby." This was part of Mosby's psychological campaign against the enemy. Less than an hour after arriving in town, Mosby and his men left. With them they had a general, thirty-three other prisoners, and fifty-eight horses.[3]

Mosby's exploit delighted Robert E. Lee, who wrote: "Hurrah for Mosby!" When President Lincoln was told that Mosby had captured one of his brigadier generals and fifty-eight horses, the president commented: "Well, I'm sorry for that. I can make a new brigadier general, but I can't make horses."[4]

Mosby's Rangers were an elite partisan unit that operated with unusual success in northern Virginia and Maryland. John Singleton Mosby was twenty-seven years old when he joined the Confederate cavalry. Within a short time his daring and ingenuity brought him to the attention of J.E.B. Stuart, and with his approval, Mosby was authorized to raise a company of his own. Mosby rarely acted with more than a few dozen men at a time, but with this small force he attacked supply wagons and railroads and harassed Union troops often in greater numbers than his own. Mosby's Rangers were able to collect valuable information for General Lee and J.E.B. Stuart. General Grant became so infuriated with the raiders that he ordered the immediate execution of any Ranger that was captured. Some called Mosby the "Gray Ghost," others the "Devil Incarnate." To his own men he was an inspirational leader and hero.

John Singleton Mosby was born to Alfred and Virginia McLaurine Mosby in Powhatan County, Virginia, on December 6, 1833. The family moved to Charlottesville, where his father earned enough to see that his eight children were all educated. Mosby's first education took place in a one-room schoolhouse, but at the age of ten he transferred to a school in Charlottesville. He was an avid learner, and even though he had to walk four miles to school, he rarely missed a day. He was not like most boys of his age; he disliked physical activities and preferred to read. "I always had a literary taste," he later wrote. In October 1850, Mosby became a student at the University of Virginia in Charlottesville. He excelled in Latin, Greek, and English but did poorly in mathematics.[5]

While at the university, Mosby encountered the town bully, George Turpin. In a conversation with some of Mosby's friends, Turpin insulted him. When he learned of Turpin's statements, Mosby sent him a note asking him to explain himself. A note from the nineteen-year-old Mosby angered Turpin, who went to Mosby's boardinghouse. As Turpin approached, Mosby confronted him with a pistol. Without saying a word, Mosby squeezed the trigger. Turpin collapsed, a bullet having entered his mouth and lodged in his neck. Mosby was arrested and charged with the "malicious and unlawful shooting" of an unarmed man. Few townsfolk liked Turpin and knew he had a record of prior assaults, but Mosby had nearly killed him. A jury found Mosby not guilty of "malicious shooting," but guilty of "unlawful shooting." He was sentenced to one year in the local jail and required to pay a fine of $500. Mosby served nearly seven months of his one-year sentence until he was pardoned by the governor. During his incarceration, Mosby began the study of law, borrowing law books from his prosecutor, William Robertson. When released from jail, Mosby continued his study of law and training in Robertson's law office. Several months later he was admitted to the bar, and he opened his own practice in Howardsville.[6]

In 1857, Mosby married Pauline Clarke, daughter of Beverly Clarke, a former United States congressman. The newlyweds moved to Bristol, Virginia, where Mosby opened a law office. He did well with his practice, and they began a family.

In 1860, when Abraham Lincoln was elected president, talk of secession was prevalent in Virginia. Mosby opposed secession, but when Virginia left the Union, he joined a cavalry militia company, the Washington Rifles. "Virginia is my mother, God bless her!" Mosby explained. "I can't fight against my mother, can I?" Weighing only 125 pounds and not an experienced horseman, Mosby was not a likely candidate for the cavalry, but he soon found that a weapon was a great equalizer. "I was glad to see," he said later, "that little men were a match for big men through being armed."[7]

Mosby's first six months of service were under Colonel William "Grumble" Jones. During that time he did not impress his superiors. A member of J.E.B.

Stuart's staff recalled: "He was rather a slouchy rider, and did not seem to take an interest in military duties.... [W]e all thought he was rather an indifferent soldier."[8] Soon Mosby became more acclimated to military life. He did not care for routine camp life, but he preferred assignment to the outposts. From the middle of 1861 to the spring of 1862 he served along the picket line and also scouted. Jones was impressed with Mosby and appointed him to the position of staff adjutant. When his scouting abilities were noticed by General Stuart, he was promoted from private to lieutenant.

When Colonel Fitzhugh Lee assumed command of the 1st Virginia Cavalry, Mosby resigned his commission and requested to be assigned as a scout to General Stuart. In June 1862, during Stuart's famous ride around General McClellan's army in the Peninsula Campaign, Mosby's exploits were cited by Stuart as "a shining record of daring and usefulness."[9] Mosby brought Stuart a report that changed the course of the war. He scouted and found the entire Union army, telling Stuart that he believed that all 100,000 troops could be circled in a matter of days. With Lee's approval, Stuart made the spectacular raid with Mosby leading the way. Mosby's enthusiasm for the military was greatly increased after this episode. To his wife he wrote: "My dearest Pauline, I returned yesterday with General Stuart from the grandest scout of the war.... Everyone said it was the grandest feat of the war. I never enjoyed myself so much in my life."[10]

Mosby had a keen intellect and enjoyed reading. He carried volumes by Shakespeare, Plutarch, Byron, and others in his saddlebag. John Cooke, a member of Stuart's staff, said that Mosby had "one of the most active, daring and penetrating minds." As a partisan commander, Mosby left nothing to chance. He carefully planned and calculated for each raid. When in action, he seldom talked but concentrated on the raid as he plotted his next move.[11]

During the winter of 1862, Mosby asked Stuart to allow him to organize a small, independent force to operate behind enemy lines. Stuart agreed, leaving him with nine men while he and his cavalry went to winter quarters near Fredericksburg. Originally Mosby had not planned to organize a partisan command, but the nine-man detail proved so successful that it continued to grow until his command reached battalion size. It was the beginning of two years of raids, ambushes, and attacks against any Union invader that dared enter a small area that became known as "Mosby's Confederacy," the Virginia counties of Fauquier, Loudoun, Fairfax, and Prince William.[12]

Mosby's Rangers were authorized by the Confederate government and operated under their authority. Because they wore standard Confederate uniforms, the laws of war accorded them full belligerent rights. This meant if captured while in uniform, they should be treated as prisoners of war.[13]

When Mosby was spotted by the enemy, there was no question about who he was. His dress was a sure giveaway. He wore a fine Confederate uniform brightened with gold braid. His cap was lined with scarlet, while his broad-brimmed felt hat, like that of his hero, J.E.B. Stuart, was decorated with an ostrich plume. His men usually were not armed with sabers or carbines but relied on at least two and sometimes as many as six Colt revolvers. Each man had at least two mounts and many had more. In fighting the enemy, Mosby and his men employed deception and speed as well as audacity and surprise. In Mosby's Confederacy, they could count on its inhabitants to give them food and shelter and to protect their identities and whereabouts. Attacking in the dark or at dusk, they were able to penetrate federal lines almost at will. After each surprise attack, they would scatter and vanish into the countryside.[14]

When Mosby's chance at independent command came, he made the most of it. Within a few days, Union officers in the area began reporting a series of nighttime raids against their outposts. By the middle of January, Mosby had taken twenty-two prisoners. He and his men were welcomed by the residents of the area, enjoying the hospitality of many families. One resident noted in her diary: "The arrival of Mosby's men is like bright sunshine after dark clouds." Men were anxious to join Mosby's Rangers. During the course of the war, more than a thousand men served with him at one time or another. Most were young, rode well, and were willing to follow orders. Although daring, they had to be discreet, guarding what they said. Above all else, they had to follow orders because Mosby would not permit any other behavior.[15]

Mosby's Confederacy contained hundreds of square miles of forested mountains and woodlands, interspersed with farmlands. An individual sentry, positioned on a knoll, could observe miles of territory, looking for enemy troops. Hidden trails provided easy movement without detection for his Rangers. The homes of planters and farmers in the area provided secure hiding places and a willing group of informants.[16]

Mosby's effectiveness as a raider was expressed by Union Lieutenant Colonel Henry Gansevoort, commander of the 13th New York, when he wrote: "In fact, the whole country, in our rear, front and flanks is full of guerrillas. The chaps murder, steal and disperse. . . . They fight with desperation when attacked, but principally confine themselves to dashes here and there, and long pursuits of small bodies of our forces. The night does not know what morning may disclose." Mosby's Rangers continued to frustrate the Union's efforts to capture them. It was as though they were shadows; the night always brought the unknown. Despite federal reprisals against civilians, killing and arresting them and burning their buildings, the Rangers were always welcomed back. Union patrols made daily searches. Their efforts yielded few rewards — only a handful of rangers were ever captured.[17]

The news of Mosby's escapades reached the office of the Union general-in-chief, Major General Henry Halleck. "Most of the difficulties are caused," Halleck wrote, "by the conduct of the pretended non-combatant inhabitants of the country. They pretend to act the part of neutrals, but do not. They give aid, shelter, and concealment to guerrilla and robber bands like that of Mosby.... If these men carried on a legitimate warfare no complaint would be made." Those that supported the Rangers, Halleck said, "forfeited their lives by their actions when captured within Union lines." The Union command believed that Mosby's Rangers could not continue to exist without the assistance of the residents of Mosby's Confederacy.[18]

Despite the danger to their lives and property, the people in Mosby's Confederacy continued to support his efforts. Many of the people had a personal stake in their success and safety. One young woman wrote, "We all had brothers, cousins, and lovers with Mosby, and each one thought of her loved one" when they heard of fighting in the area. Many of the residents had an open-door policy for Mosby's men. Rangers often stayed with civilian families or stayed at their own homes whenever it was safe to do so. "Safe houses," as the Rangers called them, were located throughout the area. Each "safe house" had a secret hiding place for the Rangers when they were on the run. Some contained underground passageways leading to the outside; others had a false wall behind which one could hide. The residents also maintained a network of spies, who provided useful information about Union troop movements and size.[19]

Mosby expected his Rangers to be model citizens. He accepted no breach of proper conduct. When he learned of a violation, he either reprimanded the offender or returned him to the regular army. By keeping his men under control, Mosby gained the respect and trust of all those in the region. Mosby's authority extended beyond that which he exerted on his men. He enforced the civil laws in the region after the war had destroyed the governments and court systems. With his legal background, Mosby was able to fill the void. He believed his powers to be a "trust." He acted as both judge and jury, settling disputes between neighbors, ruling on complaints made against his command, and punishing those who broke the law. Mosby's justice was swift, allowing no appeal. His word was law. The vast majority of the residents approved of his exercise of both military and civil power. As a result of Mosby's actions, the civilians were able to avoid many of the scourges that plagued Southerners in other parts of the country.[20]

On one occasion when Mosby and his wife were visiting with James and Elizabeth Hathaway, they had unexpected Yankee visitors. The Union cavalrymen entered the house and began to search for Mosby, going from room to room. Mosby slipped through a window and climbed onto a limb of a nearby tree. There he clung while the Federals searched his room and questioned his wife. When the Yankees left, Mosby crawled back into the house.[21]

After his narrow escape, Mosby stayed undercover. In June 1863, when Lee moved through the Shenandoah Valley toward Pennsylvania, Stuart called Mosby to scout for him. It was Mosby's information that convinced Stuart to get permission from Lee to ride around the Union army during the Gettysburg Campaign. Mosby advised Stuart of what he thought was the best route to Pennsylvania. Unfortunately, his intelligence was dated, forcing Stuart to detour around the Union flank and causing him to arrive at Gettysburg late. While many criticized Stuart for his late arrival, Mosby believed he himself was partially at fault. He would defend Stuart's action at Gettysburg for the rest of his life, even to his grave.[22]

Union wagon trains were regular targets for Mosby's Rangers. In July, Mosby reported to Stuart that he had captured a fleet of sutler's wagons, along with prisoners and horses. Sutlers were civilian businessmen who sold a variety of supplies. The wagons were loaded with food, tobacco, alcohol, newspapers, and books. Instead of destroying the wagons, Mosby decided to take them with him. Union cavalry pursued the Rangers and were able to overtake the slower-moving convoy. The outnumbered Rangers were forced to abandon the wagons and flee. One of the Rangers groaned that with the wagons, they could have opened the first department store in Mosby's Confederacy.[23]

In August 1863 Mosby was wounded in the thigh and groin and disabled for nearly a month. During that time he turned his command over to subordinates, and discipline suffered while he was away. It was clear that it was his presence and leadership that held the command together. By the beginning of 1864 Mosby was back in the saddle again. In January he suffered a defeat at Loudoun Heights, the mountains above Harpers Ferry, Virginia. It was one of only a few such setbacks he would suffer during the war. Mosby lost several men and two of his most efficient officers. It was a devastating loss for Mosby and his men and ended all of their romantic notions of the war. For Mosby and the Confederate army, it was a preview of the long, bloody, and bitter events that would follow.[24]

In May, there was more bad news: the death of Stuart at Yellow Tavern. Lee had lost the eyes of his army, and Mosby had lost his good friend. After Stuart's death, Mosby would report directly to Lee, the only commander of a unit below corps level to do so.[25]

In 1864 the Army of the Potomac fought three bloody battles in Virginia at the Wilderness, Spotsylvania, and Cold Harbor, but had little to show for it. Confederate General Jubal Early was active in the Shenandoah Valley and threatening the capital. In order to ensure Washington's continued safety, General Ulysses Grant dispatched Sheridan. In August, Sheridan arrived in the Valley hoping to clear it of all Southern forces and to eliminate it as a food source for the Confederacy. He soon realized he had a problem to face — John Singleton Mosby. Mosby threw all his men and resources into an effort to harass and frustrate his effort.[26] Sheridan jokingly commented that Mosby's Rangers were "substantially a benefit to me as they prevented straggling and kept my trains well closed up."[27]

As Mosby's raids continued, they became more of a problem for Sheridan. He decided to form an elite unit of "independent scouts" under the command of Captain Richard Blazer to combat it. Blazer's first encounter with Rangers occurred in September. Catching a group of Mosby's Rangers by surprise, Blazer inflicted heavy casualties on them. When Mosby learned of their defeat, he was furious, mocking those who escaped. "You let those Yankees whip you," he thundered. "Why, I ought to get hoop skirts for you! I'll send you all into the first Yankee regiment we come across!"[28]

By November, Blazer's scouts had begun to take their toll on Mosby's operations. He had paid little attention to them at first, concentrating more on the harassment of Sheridan's army and the disruption of the Manassas Gap Railroad. But after the defeat of one of his squadrons, Mosby's patience was exhausted and he dispatched the 1st Squadron to put an end to Blazer's scouts. Within a few weeks, Blazer was captured and his threat to Mosby's Rangers ended.[29]

Mosby continued to be a thorn in the Union's side. He was promoted to the rank of lieutenant colonel and finally to colonel. In October, Mosby and his Rangers derailed a Baltimore and Ohio train outside of Harpers Ferry. The loot was divided among the Rangers, each receiving $2,100, although Mosby took none. Again he had embarrassed Sheridan. On that same day one of Mosby's men was hanged. The Rangers were now declared to be outlaws, since they had seized private as well as nonmilitary Union property. At the express orders of General Grant, several captured Rangers were hanged without a trial.[30]

When Mosby learned that George Custer was responsible for the executions, he instructed his men to withhold any of Custer's command who were captured from those sent to Richmond. Mosby informed Lee of his plan for retaliation: "It is my purpose to hang an equal number of Custer's men whenever I capture them." Lee and Secretary of War James Seddon both gave their approval. From a group of twenty-seven federal prisoners, seven were selected for execution. Mosby ordered that four of the condemned men be shot and the other three hanged. Two of the men to be shot were able to escape. The Rangers placed a note on the body of one of the three men who had been hung: "These men have been hung in retaliation for an equal number of Colonel Mosby's men hung by order of General Custer at Front Royal. Measure for measure."[31]

Mosby later commented on the escape of the two prisoners: "If my motive had been revenge, I would have ordered others to be executed in their place and I did not. I was really glad they got away as they carried the story to Sheridan's army." His objective, he said, "was to prevent the war from degenerating into a massacre. . . . It was really an act of mercy." Mosby also wrote a note to Sheridan explaining that he would hereafter treat any prisoner falling into his hands with kindness "unless new acts of barbarity shall compel me to adopt a course of policy repulsive to humanity."[32]

Mosby had many close calls during the war, but perhaps the narrowest escape came in December 1864 at the home of a friend, Ludwell Lake. He had stopped there for the night and was having dinner when a noise was heard in the yard. Looking out the door, Mosby saw Union cavalrymen approaching. Quickly he extinguished the lamp and started for the bedroom, hoping to escape through a rear window. Several shots were fired as the Union troops entered the house, one hitting Mosby in the abdomen. Mosby lay on the floor, bloody saliva running from his mouth. When approached by Union soldiers, Mosby pretended to be dying, claiming to be Lieutenant Johnson of the 6th Virginia Cavalry. The Federals never realized that Mosby was in their grasp, and not wishing to bother with a dying Confederate, they left. Mosby was moved to his father's house in Lynchburg, where he recovered. At the end of January he appeared, pale and thin, in Richmond, where he was given a hero's welcome. By the end of February, he was back with his command.[33]

On April 9, 1865, the Army of Northern Virginia surrendered at Appomattox Court House. Mosby, however, never surrendered his command formally. Instead, he called his men together and officially disbanded the 43rd Battalion of the Virginia Cavalry: "Soldiers! I have summoned you together for the last time. The vision we have cherished of a free and independent country has vanished, and the country is now in the spoil of a conqueror. I disband your organization in preference to surrendering it to our enemies. I am now no longer your commander. After association of more than two eventful years, I part from you with a just pride, in the fame of your achievements, and grateful recollections of your generous kindness to myself. And now at this moment of bidding you a final adieu accept the assurance of my unchanging confidence and regard. Farewell!" Mosby went south in hopes of joining up with Joseph Johnston's army. When Johnston surrendered to Sherman, he abandoned any thought of continuing to fight. With a $5,000 reward for his capture, Mosby went into hiding until he was paroled two months later by Grant.[34]

Mosby moved to Warrenton and opened a law practice. He was soon joined by his wife and children, and with his home once more organized, he turned to making a serious living. Mosby took up civilian life with the same fervor he had shown in the military. He stayed clear of the political field and added successful cases to his practice, enhancing his legal reputation.

In 1870, Mosby had a chance meeting with General Lee in Richmond. Shortly afterward, Mosby met George Pickett, who was still bitter over Gettysburg. Pickett spoke bitterly of Lee and referred to him as "that old man," adding that he "had my division massacred at Gettysburg." Mosby, very supportive of Lee, replied, "Well, it made you immortal."[35]

After the war, living in the South was not easy. Gradually the shackles of military control were eased, and the Southern states were granted some political independence. During his first term as president, Grant had shown marked leniency and consideration toward the South. The president's behavior was able to win the hearts of some Southerners but failed to convince the die-hards. Defeat had removed the social order from the South, but not its party loyalties. Mosby went to see President Grant, who was informal and friendly. They spoke of the close escape Grant had had from being captured by Mosby while returning to the Army of the Potomac during the spring of 1864. "If I had captured you," Mosby said, "things might have changed — I might have been in the White House and you might be calling on me." Grant agreed. Mosby was convinced that Grant wanted to help the people in the South. After their meeting, he was determined to support Grant, believing this to be the best way to aid the crippled South.[36]

The South turned against Mosby when he took Grant's side. In 1872, with the country still bitter and feeling the effects of the war, it was political and social suicide to support the political party of Lincoln. Mosby was denounced by the press and public alike, by people who had been close to him, and by those who knew him only by reputation. Even some of his old command spoke out against him. Mosby accepted this condemnation with the same indifference with which he had accepted the hatred of the North during the war.[37]

When Grant was nominated to run for a second term, Mosby began campaigning in his behalf. Regardless of their own political views, many of his old comrades rallied to his side, making certain that he had the opportunity to speak. As early as August, Mosby promised Grant that he could count on Virginia's votes. When the final ballots were counted in November, Mosby wired Grant: "Virginia casts her vote for Grant, peace and reconciliation." It was the first time that a Republican had carried the state of Virginia.[38] Grant wanted to reward Mosby with a political appointment, but Mosby refused, explaining that he could be more influential by taking nothing for himself. He refused to share in the election spoils just as he had refused to take part in the rich loot from the Union army raid during the war.

In 1876, Mosby supported Rutherford Hayes, Grant's choice for president. His political views still continued to be controversial, sometimes placing him in danger. One night as Mosby stepped off the train at Warrenton, someone took a shot at him. When Grant learned of this, he was concerned for Mosby's safety. He asked President Hayes to help Mosby. It was soon announced that John Singleton Mosby would be the next consul to Hong Kong. For the next

Mosby's raiders capture a sutler's carriage. (Library of Congress, *Harper's Weekly*, September 5, 1863)

seven years, Mosby made his home in the British crown colony. When his appointment was scheduled to end with the inauguration of the new president, Grover Cleveland, Mosby wrote to Grant asking him to help him locate employment. July came and Mosby prepared to return to the United States, but he still had not heard from Grant. The day before Mosby left for America, a message arrived for him — Grant was dead.[39]

Despite his life-ending illness, Grant had not forgotten the man who had supported him in the South in his run for president. One of the last pieces of correspondence that Grant wrote before his death was a note to railroad executive Leland Stanford. When Mosby arrived in America, he was notified by Stanford that a position was awaiting him with the Southern Pacific Railroad. Mosby augmented his income with a series of lectures that were published in the *Boston Herald* and compiled into a book called *Mosby's War Reminiscences*. Other books followed. He gave a defense of J.E.B. Stuart in *Stuart's Cavalry Campaigns* and in *Stuart's Cavalry in the Gettysburg Campaign*, a dissertation that caused other military leaders to sharply challenge him. Other efforts included *The Dawn of the Real South* and finally, his *Mosby's Memoirs*.[40]

Throughout the years there would be many Ranger reunions, but Mosby attended only one. In January 1895, he went to the 43rd Battalion's reunion at Alexandria. More than 150 Rangers were present. This is the first time some had seen him since their final meeting at Salem. The reunion reached its climax at a banquet, an affair that left few dry eyes. Mosby's speech started the tears: "Your presence here this evening recalls our last parting. I see the last line drawn up to hear read the last order I ever gave you. I see moistened eyes and quivering lips. I hear the command to break ranks. I feel the grasp of hands and see the tears on the cheeks of men who had dared death so long it had lost its terror. And I know now as I knew then, that each heart suffered with mine the agony of the Titan in his resignation to fate."[41] He continued saying: "Life cannot afford a more bitter cup than the one I drained when we parted at Salem, nor any higher reward of ambition than that I received as commander of the 43rd Virginia Battalion of Cavalry."[42]

On a summer day in 1896, Mosby would have one more narrow escape with death. While driving a buggy, the horse became frightened and struck out with one of its hoofs, giving Mosby a hard blow to the face. He was rushed to the University of Virginia hospital, where he lay unconscious for days. The diagnosis revealed that he had fractured his skull and that he would be blind in his left eye. One of the best known surgeons, Dr. Hunter McGuire, Stonewall Jackson's army physician, was called to consult on the treatments.[43]

The period of danger passed and Mosby soon began to recover, but he would never again look the same. His physical appearance was marred by an eye that would no longer function. His energy dissipated, and he became dependent on naps every afternoon.[44]

In February 1898, the battleship *Maine* was sunk in Havana Harbor, killing 260 American sailors. Although there was no real evidence of sabotage or the involvement of the Spanish government in the catastrophe, America went to war. The words "Remember the Maine" were headlines in many newspapers. Mosby, now in his sixties and blind in one eye, did not altogether approve of the war. Nevertheless, he offered his services to the government. When Mosby was rejected by the army and told senatorial support would be needed in order to be considered, he fired back: "I have no influence except my military record." Pressed by a newspaper, he said: "I was surprised to hear that congressional influence was required to secure the privilege of fighting the battles of the country. . . . I cannot imagine what any congressman could say that would add anything to the endorsement I have received from General Grant and General Robert E. Lee."[45]

Mosby formed his own unit, calling them the "Hussars." Mosby drilled his troops, "instilling the same enthusiasm that he showed when at the head of his raiders." By early August, the war was nearly over, and Mosby's Hussars were disbanded without having seen any action.[46]

Through the years, Mosby maintained a personal and paternal interest in his men. When he learned that one of them was in financial difficulty, he took it upon himself to find the man's son a responsible job, reminding the young man that he must send a part of his salary to his father. He frequently shared with others, even though he himself needed more. As the years passed, Mosby felt more separated from his battalion. "I am beginning to feel very lonely in the world now," he once remembered. "Nearly all my friends are gone and I have made no new ones."[47]

By the close of 1915, Mosby was confined to his home because his health had deteriorated. Six months later he died at the age of eighty-two. Mosby was conscious almost to the last. As the end drew near, one of his daughters poured the water of baptism over her dying father's head. Two days later Mosby's body, escorted by a uniformed guard, was taken by train to Warrenton to lie in state.

The governor sent a wreath, and three thousand people attended the funeral. He was buried in Warrenton, surrounded by the graves of his wife Pauline and two sons who died as infants.[48]

When John Singleton Mosby's career as a raider is evaluated, it is clear that he emerges as the outstanding partisan fighter of the war. Grant wrote of Mosby's feats in his memoirs: "There were probably few men in the South who could have commanded successfully a separate detachment in the rear of an opposing army, and so near the border of hostilities, as long as he did without losing his entire command."[49] On the Confederate side, J.E.B. Stuart and Robert E. Lee believed there was no better scout in the Confederate army.

8

Bold Cavalier

J.E.B. STUART

ON May 2, 1863, during the Chancellorsville Campaign, Confederate troops fired at what they thought were federal cavalrymen approaching their position. The result was one of the greatest tragedies for the Army of Northern Virginia. One of the men they shot and wounded was Confederate General Stonewall Jackson, who was returning from a reconnaissance. Several days later he would be dead. Moments later, Jackson's senior commander, Major General Ambrose P. Hill, was wounded by artillery fire. Although remaining on the field for a time, Hill was unable to continue in command. Jackson's orders to Hill before being wounded had been: "Press them, Hill!"[1]

Jackson's corps was at the brink of either a glorious victory or a disastrous defeat. Lee had divided his smaller force in the face of the enemy. All Major General Joseph Hooker had to do was to realize this, and he would have the chance to destroy either part of Lee's army. Someone had to restore Jackson's assault and reunite the separate parts. J.E.B. Stuart was sent for. He was the senior officer and the only major general in the area. Although Brigadier General Robert Rodes was next in command under Hill, he yielded to Stuart for the sake of morale among the troops. "General Stuart's name was well and very favorably known to the army, and would tend, I hoped, to re-establish confidence," Rodes later said.[2]

Stuart faced one of his greatest challenges as he took over for the wounded Stonewall Jackson at Chancellorsville. Now he had to think in terms of infantry; all of his past experience had been with the cavalry. Stuart was aware of Lee's strategy for attacking Hooker, but the battle was only half won. He was responsible for continuing the attack the next day. It was a formidable task, even for someone as confident as Stuart.[3]

By 1863 Stuart had risen to command all the cavalry of the Army of Northern Virginia. Lee had learned to rely on him for swift and accurate information, often obtained from daring raids behind enemy lines. Others also recognized his capability. General Joseph Johnston had written to President Davis of Stuart: "He is a rare man, wonderfully endowed by nature with the qualities necessary for an officer of light cavalry. Calm, firm, acute, active and enterprising, I know of no one more competent than he to estimate the occurrences before him in their true value." Stuart was also a superb fighter. After the war one of Stuart's staff wrote: "I have spoken of his reckless exposure in battle. It would convey a better idea of his demeanor under fire to say that he seemed unaware of the presence of danger. This air of indifference was unmistakable." Thus, Stuart brought to his new challenge experience in assessing tactical situations and bravery on the battlefield. For the first time he had the command

---

Opposite:

J.E.B. Stuart had a penchant for fine dress, often wearing gold fringe, plumed hats, and high boots. (Valentine Museum, Richmond, Virginia)

of a large force of infantry already involved in a major battle. Stuart had been preparing for just such a situation all his life.[4]

James Ewell Brown Stuart, called Jeb by his friends, was born into a prominent Virginia family on February 6, 1833, at Laurel Hill in Patrick County. Laurel Hill was a large rambling house in an oak grove with a view of the Blue Ridge. Slaves did most of the work on the plantation.[5] Stuart was the seventh child and youngest son of Elizabeth and Archibald Stuart in a family that eventually included ten children. Archibald Stuart was a popular lawyer and was well known politically. Elizabeth is said to have "no special patience with nonsense" and insisted that her sons take an oath never to drink liquor. James began his education at home with his mother, but at the age of twelve he attended a succession of schools in southwest Virginia.[6]

At the age of fifteen Jeb attended nearby Emory and Henry College. Early in his school days he gained the reputation of one who was quick to fight in order to preserve his honor. So frequent were his encounters that he took pride when he wrote home one year, "Contrary to the expectations of all I have been so fortunate as not to have a single fight since I have been going to school ... but not from cowardice." Even though there were times when James enjoyed peace, fighting was a habit difficult to break. While at Emory and Henry College, he blamed his poor performance on a history examination on a bloody nose he had received in a fight and which had required him to spend the first half-hour of the test period taking care of his injury.[7]

Fight he would, but there was also a sensitive side to Stuart. He displayed it in his concern for the feelings of others, interest in writing poetry, and appreciation of beauty in nature. There was a tenderness which he hid behind his manly posturing. In a rural, mountain environment, refinement was rare; toughness was demanded and rewarded. As a result, Stuart placed great importance in physical courage and looked for opportunities to show his manhood even as a boy.[8]

The first half of the nineteenth century was an age when religion played an important part in almost all of life's activities. The Stuarts were Presbyterian, the prominent religion throughout the Virginia Valley. Stuart's mother, however, like many of the great Virginia families, was Episcopalian. Religion was important to Stuart all his life, and the training he received from his mother was simple, sincere, and pious.[9] During his freshman year at Emory and Henry, he joined the Methodist Church. During the war he seldom wrote a personal

letter or issued a general order without invoking "Divine Providence" or including a prayer to God.[10]

Emory and Henry College provided young James with excellent preparation
for his entrance to the U.S. Military Academy at West Point. The only problem keeping Stuart from the Academy was the lack of an appointment. His
father had been a U.S. congressman, but when he failed to win re-election it
looked as though he had missed the opportunity to appoint his son. Fortunately, Archibald's opponent made the appointment his first official act as congressman, and Stuart entered the Academy in June 1850.[11]

Ironically, he was called "Beauty Stuart" by his friends at West Point because
of his plain appearance. He was about five feet nine inches tall, with broad
shoulders and a "sturdy" body frame. Because of his erect posture, many believed
he was actually taller than he was. Later, when Stuart grew a beard, one of his
friends said that he was "the only man he ever saw that a beard improved."[12]

Stuart did well at West Point, excelling in his studies and gaining confidence. He was enormously impressed with the place. "So far as I know of no
profession is more desirable than that of the soldier," he wrote. His class standing improved each year, and in 1854 he graduated thirteen in a class of forty-
six. He became a friend of Custis Lee, son of Robert E. Lee, who was superintendent of the Academy during Stuart's last two years there. Stuart was a
frequent guest at the superintendent's home, and as a result, his social skills
improved greatly.[13]

Stuart became as distinguished for his fighting around the barracks as for
his finesse on the parade ground. But the rough-and-tumble young man had
another side; he wrote sensitive letters to young ladies. In a letter to his cousin,
he wrote: "Myriads of flowers leaned forth, laughing with joy." Despite Stuart's
delight in feminine beauty, he was uncomfortable in the presence of attractive
young women. He was much more at ease with older women. Two he had
charmed were Mrs. Robert E. Lee and Mrs. Winfield Scott. Both women were
like mothers to him.[14]

With graduation in sight, Stuart realized that his high grades would place
him in the elite corps of engineers, a branch he considered dull. He deliberately let up on his work to make poorer grades.[15] Stuart was drawn to the dash
and color of the mounted service during practice charges at West Point. He
was overjoyed when he received his orders to join the Mounted Rifles to put
down a Comanche uprising in west Texas.

In the spring of 1855, after his brief tour with the Mounted Rifles, Stuart moved to Kansas for service with the 1st Cavalry. There, at Fort Leavenworth, he met and fell in love with Flora Cooke, daughter of the fort's commander, Colonel Philip St. George Cooke. Flora came from an old Virginia family and graduated from a private school in Detroit. Although not pretty, she had a charming personality. They were married on November 14 at Fort Riley and traveled the next day to Leavenworth, where they began their life together on the raw post. There was soon good news for Stuart — promotion to first lieutenant.[16]

Army life on the Western frontier, even in the cavalry, was generally boring and uneventful. Lieutenant Stuart was involved in two encounters with Indians during his seven years of service there. The first of these was a major engagement with the Cheyenne. It was one of the few Indian battles in which a cavalry charge with sabers was successful. During the pursuit, Stuart encountered three officers being held at bay by a Cheyenne warrior with a gun. Attacking with his saber, Stuart was shot in the chest. It was a painful wound, but not dangerous. This was the only time he was wounded until the fatal shot in the battle at Yellow Tavern.[17] Stuart's other encounter was against the Kiowa at Blackwater Springs, Nebraska Territory. He was in command of the detachment in pursuit of the Kiowa Chief, Sotanko. The chase continued for a long time until the horses could run no more. Several Indians were killed and fifteen captured.[18]

With little activity on the frontier, Stuart found other things to occupy his time. Since his evenings at West Point, when he had spent hours reading after lights out, he had enjoyed good literature. His letters contained allusions to Shakespeare as well as Byron, Scott, and Irving. Stuart's letters revealed his keen eye for detail, a skill he would put to good use during the war. They also reflected Stuart's dual personality. He complained of the lack of opportunities for combat and chances to prove himself; at the same time, he was deeply moved by the sight of "a beautiful flower on the roadside." "Fond as I am of flowers," he wrote, "I did not pull it, but left it as an ornament to the solitude."[19]

In 1859, fanatical abolitionist John Brown raided the little town of Harpers Ferry and took prisoners. Then he seized the brick building where the village fire engine was kept. Colonel Robert E. Lee was ordered to lead a force of U.S. marines to Harpers Ferry to capture John Brown and restore order. Stuart, in Washington on business at the time, was assigned as Lee's aide.[20]

After surrounding the engine house, Lee wrote a message to Brown demanding immediate surrender, assuring Brown that escape was impossible and promising to protect him and his companions if they surrendered; if they didn't, Lee said, he couldn't be responsible for their safety. Lee ordered Stuart to deliver the message under a white flag of truce and to make it clear that he would not accept anything but immediate surrender. If Brown rejected the demand, Stuart was to signal by waving his hat, and Lee would launch an attack.

At 7 o'clock in the morning, Stuart delivered Lee's message to the door of the engine house. Calling to Brown, he informed him that he had a message from Colonel Lee. As soon as the door opened, Stuart faced a cocked carbine. Stuart read the message, and Brown began to bargain. From behind the door, Stuart could hear pleas from the hostages inside that he intercede for their safety. Amid the clamor, one of the prisoners shouted, "Never mind us, fire!" At that point, Stuart broke off the conversation, waved his hat, and jumped out of the line of fire. The marines made short work of their task, killing two of Brown's men and capturing two others. All thirteen of Brown's hostages survived unharmed. Lee acknowledged Stuart's skill and service in the capture of John Brown in his report to the War Department. "Everyone involved witnessed his courage before the door of the engine house," Lee reported.[22]

During the winter of 1860–61, when the discontented Southern states began to leave the Union, Stuart was at Fort Wise in what is now Colorado. He followed the crisis as best he could. Stuart's solution to the prospect of disunion was simple: "I go with Virginia." When Virginia seceded on April 17, 1861, Stuart was on leave of absence. He immediately headed eastward with his family. Although he had just been promoted to captain of the 1st Cavalry, he resigned and obtained a commission as lieutenant colonel in the Provisional Army of Virginia.[23]

When Virginia left the Union and joined the Confederacy, most of the Cooke family sided with the South, but Philip St. George Cooke remained loyal to the Union. In anger over what he believed to be betrayal, Stuart demanded that Flora pick a new name for their third son, who bore his grandfather's name. Stuart wrote about Cooke's decision: "He will regret it but once, and that will be continually."[24]

Most of the young men of Virginia answered the call to arms and, like Stuart, had been superb horsemen from early childhood. The Confederate War Department, however, was slow in organizing cavalry units. Experienced cavalrymen such as Lee and Joe Johnston were put into positions of high command and charged with building a conventional army — infantry and artillery. Even Stuart's initial commission was as colonel of infantry.[25]

Once again the impending struggle between North and South carried Stuart to Harpers Ferry, this time as second in command to Stonewall Jackson. They soon became friends, and Stuart received permission to organize a cavalry troop. Later when Joseph Johnston assumed command, Jackson withdrew his unit to Winchester. With orders to pull the unit together, Stuart imposed strict army discipline. Most of the men were volunteers, and this was their first experience with a West Point–trained officer who tried to make them into cavalrymen. They quickly learned that life in the 1st Virginia consisted of long hours of training. Despite Stuart's strict discipline and hard training, the men under his command soon began to respect and admire him. George Eggleston, a member of the 1st Cavalry, noted: "We learned to hold in high regard our colonel's masterly skill in getting into and out of perilous positions. He seemed to blunder into them in sheer recklessness, but in getting out he showed us the quality of his genius. And before we reached Manassas, we had learned, among other things, to entertain a feeling close akin to worship for our brilliant and daring leader."[26]

Stuart was fond of military pageantry, which he demonstrated in his own dress. He was always mounted on a superb horse, projecting a swashbuckling appearance. The true value of Stuart as a cavalry leader, however, should not be overlooked because of his dress — the scarlet-lined cape, the rose in his lapel, the upturned hat with the plumed feather flowing behind. His appearance left one of the most striking physical impressions of any leader on either side. When Stuart was in the area, everyone knew it. He was a fun-loving character, full of energy and always optimistic. His confidence was contagious. Despite his flamboyant decorum, Stuart still emerges as an outstanding cavalry commander. He was imaginative and daring. As a leader, he was quick to earn the total support and respect of all who served him.[27]

The cavalry's mission was to control the ground between their army and the enemy's, to discover the enemy's location, strength, and intentions, and to prevent the enemy from doing the same to them. It was also used to guard the flanks when armies met in battle, as well as for reconnaissance. Stuart saw another important function of the cavalry: to raid the enemy's rear and disrupt its movement of supplies and communication. It was here that Stuart would gain his greatest fame.[28]

In July 1861, Stuart had his first opportunity to prove himself. He and his 1st Cavalry were asked to screen the movement of Johnston's Army of the Shenandoah from Winchester, south to the Manassas Gap Railroad. There they joined Confederate forces at Bull Run. At the First Battle of Manassas on July 21, Stuart led his troops in a charge on the New York Zouaves. With his saber drawn, he slashed through their ranks, creating confusion and panic. His action contributed to the Confederate rout of the Union army in the first important battle of the war. Stuart's strict discipline and training of his men had paid off. They behaved well under fire. Stuart's reward for his role at First Manassas was promotion to brigadier general and the command of more troops.[29]

In the spring of 1862, General McClellan began his Peninsula Campaign against General Johnston and the Confederate capital at Richmond. For months Stuart screened the Confederate withdrawals and fought rear-guard actions as Johnston retreated up the peninsula. On May 31, the armies engaged in combat on the very outskirts of the capital in the Battle of Seven Pines. During the battle, Johnston was severely wounded and was replaced by Robert E. Lee. When Lee assumed command of the army, Stuart emerged as his cavalry commander. One of Lee's first orders to Stuart was to carry out a reconnaissance to find out where the Union right flank was north of the Chickahominy River. So began Stuart's famous "Ride Around McClellan." In three days he led 1,200 cavalrymen around the Union army. In the process he determined the weakness on McClellan's right flank and destroyed railroad bridges, supply trains, and wagons.[30]

General Cooke, Stuart's father-in-law, commanded the Union cavalry force that was responsible for maintaining security in the rear of McClellan's army. Cooke was slow to react; when he did, he sent out infantry troops to pursue Stuart. All they were able to find was the destruction left behind after Stuart's raid. It was a sweet revenge for Stuart, who still harbored ill feeling for his father-in-law because he sided with the Union. Finally, after his hundred-mile circuit around McClellan's army, Stuart returned to Richmond.[31]

Stuart reported immediately to Robert E. Lee and received his personal congratulations for his "brilliant exploit," and for the "courage and skill so conspicuously exhibited throughout by the general and the officers and men under his command." Lee put the information gathered by Stuart into immediate use to plan a counteroffensive against McClellan.[32] All along a three-mile front, Lee's army moved forward. The price was heavy; 8,000 Confederates were killed or wounded. Union losses were extensive also. But Lee's victory was great. He won the battle on sheer nerve and intelligence from Stuart. McClellan commenced a full-scale withdrawal that would not stop until he reached the James River. Lee had saved Richmond and changed the direction of the war.[33]

Stuart's ride around the Army of the Potomac did more to unsettle McClellan than any other event during the early stages of the Seven Days' Campaign. Lieutenant John Cooke, a member of Stuart's staff, said, "It was the conception of a bold and brilliant mind, and the execution was as fearless." The *Richmond Daily Dispatch* reported: "History cannot show such another exploit as this of Stuart's! The whole country is astonished and applauds. McClellan is disgraced. Stuart and his troops are now forever in history."[34]

Stuart's daring and his cavalier attitude were not all that were involved in his success. He worked hard and planned carefully, his efforts often concealed by his easy manner. On July 25, Stuart was promoted to major general and given command of all cavalry in the Army of Northern Virginia. Stuart commanded three brigades of seasoned troops but was obligated to remain in close proximity to Lee and to coordinate the operations of his detachments. Fortunately he was blessed with excellent subordinate leaders — Wade Hampton, Beverly Robertson, and Fitzhugh Lee, General Lee's nephew.[35]

The new major general had a humbling experience in August 1862. Federal horsemen slipped through Southern lines where Stuart was napping. In the process of making good his escape, Stuart lost his plumed hat and cloak. No event of the war so humiliated Stuart; the Yankees had made off with the very symbol of the Confederacy's "Bold Cavalier." The rest of the day Stuart was forced to ride with his head wrapped in a bandanna, and he had to face the teasing of his friends and from the ranks: "Where's your hat?"[36]

On the rainy night of August 22, Stuart rode to get revenge. With 1,500 cavalry, he swept through the Union line and descended on the headquarters of Major General John Pope, commander of the Union Army of Virginia. The Confederates destroyed what they could and took trophies, including money, gold, Pope's dispatch book, and his personal baggage, which contained his best uniform. Stuart sent this last item to Governor Letcher in Richmond as a prize of war. Letcher had it hung in the state library for all to see, and for the next several weeks it was a great attraction. Before sending the coat away, Stuart could not resist one last opportunity to display his sense of humor. He sent a message through the lines to General Pope: "You have my hat and plume. I have your best coat. I have the honor to propose a cartel for the fair exchange of the prisoners." Pope never responded.[37]

In late summer 1862, Lee began the Second Manassas Campaign. Stuart and his cavalry accompanied Stonewall Jackson's corps through northern Virginia during the early part of the campaign. While the battle raged, Stuart scouted a route for General Longstreet's corps so they could join Jackson. Pope's preoccupation with Jackson allowed Longstreet to attack his flank. The result was a Confederate victory, very similar to the Union defeat at First Manassas.[38]

Wanting to keep the momentum of the Army of Northern Virginia's advance, Lee sent his men northward into Maryland behind Stuart's cavalry screen. At Frederick, Stuart was welcomed and invited to dine at the home of one of the residents. The celebration was a gala one, with dashing cavalry officers escorting local young ladies and music filling the air. Near midnight, when federal troops approached, Stuart and his men excused themselves to face the enemy. After a skirmish, the Confederates rode back to the ball, and the gaiety resumed as though nothing had happened.[39]

On September 17, 1862, Lee's army met McClellan's at Antietam. The fighting began at dawn and raged all day among the fields and forests near Sharpsburg. Lee's army of 40,000 troops faced a superior force of 75,000 Federals. By day's end, the battle had been the war's bloodiest day. When the numbers were finally counted, the cost of a single day of battle would be more than 24,000 casualties. Despite his heavy losses and inferior numbers, Lee elected to face the enemy again the next day. When dawn came on the 18th, the Army of Northern Virginia was in place to receive another Union attack. Mercifully, the Union Army of the Potomac was equally battered, and McClellan chose to avoid further engagement. After sundown, Lee ordered his army to withdraw from the field. Lee's attempt to invade the North had been repulsed and his army severely damaged, but he would fight again.

During the withdrawal, Stuart spent a night with a family in Frederick and enjoyed dancing with the host's lively daughters. Stuart reported the instance to his wife in a letter. "The ladies of Maryland," he said, "make a great fuss over your husband — loading me with bouquets — begging for autographs, buttons, etc. What shall I do?"[40]

In early October, Lee ordered Stuart to destroy a railroad bridge near Chambersburg, Pennsylvania, and to gather information about federal troops in the area. Lee also wanted him to capture civilian hostages who might be used in exchange for Virginians the Yankees were holding.[41] Although it was dark and raining, Stuart reached Chambersburg at about seven in the evening. He sent a message to the town's officials, demanding their surrender and threatening to open fire on the town if they refused; however, there was no one on hand with the authority to surrender the town. The next morning Stuart's men woke to find no one to challenge their presence, allowing them to secure arms and ammunition as well as military clothing. After helping themselves to all they could carry, they destroyed what was left. They were, however, unable to destroy the bridge because it was built of iron.[42]

Stuart's column left Chambersburg in the morning, returning through Maryland. Stuart's entire trip covered 126 miles. They rode the final eighty miles nonstop in less than thirty-six hours. For the second time he had ridden around McClellan's Army of the Potomac, destroying enemy property and wreaking havoc. In addition, his troops had captured 1,200 horses and made federal cavalry look foolish.[43]

Such feats were always enthusiastically received by the South, having an immediate, positive influence on its morale. Major Channing Price noted, "General Lee was excessively gratified at the result of the expedition, and expressed warmly his thanks to the cavalry, and their gallant and noble leader." Stuart believed the credit belonged elsewhere, saying, "the hand of God was clearly manifested in the deliverance of my command from danger, and the crowning success attending it, I ascribe to Him the praise, the honor and the glory."[44]

After the Chambersburg raid, Stuart's reputation continued to increase, gaining him international attention. The *London Times* of October 28, 1862, wrote, "Anything more daring, more gallant, and more successful than the foray of General Stuart ... has never been recorded."[45]

One of the greatest personal tragedies that Stuart suffered during the war was the death of his five-year-old daughter, Flora. When he learned of her illness, he felt helpless and told his officers, "I shall have to leave my child in the hands of God; my duty requires me here." Little Flora died on November 3, 1862. Learning of her death, he broke into tears. His grief was genuine, more so because he had been unable to be with his child during her suffering. Stuart sent a telegram to his wife, asking her to come to Culpeper so they could share their grief together. General Lee visited Stuart and his wife to express his sympathy.[46]

On November 7, 1862, Lincoln replaced McClellan with Major General

*On his deathbed, Stonewall Jackson request-
ed that Stuart command his troops. Though
denied, Stuart could not have been more
proud.*

(Dictionary of American Portraits,
Alexander H. Ritchie)

Ambrose Burnside, and the huge Union army moved eastward toward Fredericksburg. Based on Stuart's intelligence, Lee moved to face the Union threat,
placing Longstreet on the high ground overlooking the town. Later, Lee brought
Jackson from the valley to occupy the low hills which extended southward from
Marye's Heights; for Lee, Fredericksburg was to be a defensive battle. Burnside's army crossed the Rappahannock on December 13 and moved against
Longstreet on Marye's Heights. During the long day's battle, Stuart operated
from the right flank, directing his artillery batteries. Although the Confederate
army absorbed 5,000 casualties, the federal losses were twice as great. On the
following day, neither army renewed the fight, and on December 15, a truce
permitted the two sides to bury their dead. During the night, Burnside recrossed
the Rappahannock.[47]

A few days after the battle at Fredericksburg, Lee sent Stuart on another
raid into Union-held territory. Both armies had gone into winter quarters; the
mission would be conducted amid snow and icy winds. The day after Christmas, Stuart started up the south bank of the Rappahannock. Behind him rode
three full brigades, 1800 strong, and four light cannons. When he discovered
that Dumfries, the objective of the raid, was heavily protected, Stuart decided

to bypass it. After sundown on December 28, the raiders approached Burke's Station. Surrounding the depot, they captured dozens of pickets, hundreds of mules and horses, and a large number of supplies. The strike was so swift that the telegraph operator was not able to give an alarm. For several minutes, Stuart received dispatches from Union General Samuel Heintzelman's headquarters telling of Yankee troop dispositions. Stuart's men were so successful in frightening their enemy that one of the intercepted messages gave instructions to destroy everything in case they were attacked by Stuart's raiders.[48]

During the raid Stuart displayed a little humor. Just before cutting the wire, he sent a message complaining to federal Quartermaster General Montgomery Meigs: "The next time I capture some of your mules, supply better mules. These are kind of worn out." After sacking the depot and burning a nearby railroad bridge, Stuart's force resumed their homeward jaunt, returning to camp on New Year's Day.[49]

On May 1, at the Battle of Chancellorsville, Stuart's cavalry discovered that the right flank of Major General Joseph Hooker's Army of the Potomac was exposed. The next day Stuart and his men led Stonewall Jackson's corps as it marched to attack the weak spot. When Jackson was accidentally wounded by his own men that evening, Stuart took command of his corps. The next day he renewed the attack on Hooker's flank, pressing the assault and seizing control of a crucial ridge. There he placed his artillery to support the Confederate advance. The Union troops were forced to retreat across the Rappahannock.[50]

Stuart had done well in his temporary corps command. Chancellorsville had been a stunning Confederate victory, and he had played a major role in it. In his report to Lee, Stuart did not hesitate to point out that he had been "called to command ... without any knowledge of the ground, the position of our force, or the plans thus far pursued, and without an officer left in the corps above the rank of brigadier general. Under these disadvantages the attack was renewed the next morning and prosecuted to a successful issue." He believed he had proven his ability to lead an infantry corps.[51] Chancellorsville was a great tribute to the military genius of Lee and Jackson, but without Stuart, the battle might have ended far less successfully than it did.

Stuart had hoped to keep command of Jackson's corps, but he was too valuable as a cavalry commander to be assigned to the infantry. Stuart had been told that on his deathbed, Jackson had recommended that he assume the command of his corps. "I would rather know that Jackson had said that," Stuart said, "than to have had the appointment."[52]

A.P. Hill was not badly hurt and was able to return to duty. After Jackson's death, Lee reorganized his army into three corps commanded by Hill, Longstreet, and Richard S. Ewell. By June, Stuart's command had grown to almost 10,000 men.

In early June 1863, Stuart held several reviews of his enlarged force at Brandy Station. Invitations were sent to friends and families as well as General Lee and others in his command. The reviews provided an opportunity for him to display his cavalry and to bring attention to himself. First Stuart rode up and down the ranks of his troops. Then the artillery passed in review, followed by the cavalry. Three bands played while the horses trotted by. All the time Stuart was playing up to the young ladies. That evening there was a ball. While Stuart was parading his horsemen and celebrating at balls, the enemy was riding to battle.[53]

Early in the morning of June 9, 11,000 Union cavalry and infantry troops under Major General Alfred Pleasonton crossed the Rappahannock near Brandy Station and converged on Fleetwood Hill, the site of Stuart's headquarters. Stuart was taken by surprise and was hard pressed by Pleasonton from the very beginning. Only after he had assembled enough troops on Fleetwood Hill was Stuart able to stem the Yankee attack and organize his defense. A timely charge by Wade Hampton's men saved the situation.[54] The battle at Brandy Station raged for ten hours in fierce combat; it was the largest cavalry action ever fought in North America. When Pleasonton saw Confederate infantry approaching, he reluctantly decided to withdraw. Stuart had gained control of the battlefield, but he could not rightfully claim a victory since the Yankees had never intended to occupy the field anyway.[55]

Although Stuart claimed a victory at Brandy Station, the truth has been the subject of debate. Stuart had fought a magnificent battle. Genuinely surprised, he had reacted quickly, concentrating his forces where the danger was the greatest. "Here, there, and everywhere . . . ringing out the words of command," recalled a cavalryman.[56] But the battle had a profound psychological effect on Stuart. He was surprised by the bold Union advance and the strong, determined fight the Yankees had given him. The Union cavalry had finally found parity with the Confederates. After Brandy Station, Stuart struggled more and more with an ever-growing, better equipped Union cavalry. As Union forces grew in number and their skills improved, the Confederate cavalry was growing weaker. The South still had great and inspired leadership, but they lacked supplies, good mounts, and experienced cavalrymen. All of these factors severely weakened the Confederate cavalry. Some scholars see Brandy Station as the point when the tide turned in favor of the Union cavalry in the east.[57]

After Brandy Station, the newspapers were critical of Stuart. Some charged "negligence and bad management." A woman from the Culpeper area wrote to Jefferson Davis to complain that Stuart's behavior had been "perfectly ridiculous, having repeated reviews for the benefit of his lady friends, he riding up and down the line thronged with those ladies ... devoting his whole time to his friends' company." Stuart did pay a lot of attention to women, and his wife began to ask questions. Stuart was indignant, insisting that his friendships were innocent. Furthermore, he believed he should be receiving her encouragement rather than her condemnation. Stuart now seemed to enjoy the attention he received from beautiful young ladies. For him the affections of women were an indication of his military success and a measure of his fame.[58]

During June, Stuart screened Lee's movement as he made his way into Maryland. Once Lee's army was safely in Maryland and on its way into Pennsylvania, Lee ordered Stuart to raid the Union rear. Stuart moved east of the Union army, tearing up railroad tracks and scaring the residents of Washington and Baltimore. These activities, however, were of little help to Lee, because Stuart did not keep the lines of communication open, and Lee had no idea where he was. The only news that Lee received about the Union army was brought by a scout who informed him that Major General George Meade had replaced Hooker as commander of the Army of the Potomac and that Meade was rapidly moving his army northward. Lee quickly began to consolidate his army a few miles west of Gettysburg. In the meantime, Stuart moved through Westminster, Maryland, toward Hanover and York in Pennsylvania, pursued by federal troops. En route he captured a long wagon train and numerous Union prisoners, which he brought with him, greatly slowing down his progress. He would be too late to help Lee in the important battle that followed.[59]

On July 1, Lee engaged Meade's army at Gettysburg. Stuart arrived on the afternoon of July 2. "General Stuart," Lee said, "where have you been? I have not heard a word from you in days, and you are the eyes and ears of my army." Stuart's reply was that he had brought 125 wagons and many prisoners. "Yes, General," Lee responded, "but they are only an impediment to me now." Then

Lee's anger subsided, "We will not discuss this matter longer," he said. "Help me fight these people." The battle had already developed without the intelligence that Lee had relied upon Stuart to provide. It was clear that Lee felt Stuart had let him down. No victor emerged on July 2, and it seemed the battle would be decided in a third day of fighting.[60]

On the morning of July 3, Lee decided to send eleven infantry brigades with Major General George Pickett's division in a frontal assault on the Union center. At the same time Stuart was engaged in a skirmish in a field about a mile behind the federal line. About the time Pickett began his desperate charge, Stuart ordered a charge of his own, attacking the northern flank of Meade's army. His charge was met by an equal number of Union cavalry. The opponents collided in a violent battle. The clashing of sabers and the firing of pistols filled the air. Finally Stuart's men withdrew from the field.[61]

As soon as the Battle of Gettysburg was over, questions and recriminations began. Disappointed Southerners refused to believe that Robert E. Lee could lose a battle. Someone else must be to blame. Lee had accepted full responsibility for the loss when he said, "It is all my fault," but supporters inside and outside the army began to look for a scapegoat; they quickly found one in Stuart. Criticism of Stuart soon appeared on the front pages of Southern newspapers. At issue was Stuart's failure to provide Lee with crucial information about Union troop movements. The lack of accurate intelligence, it was said, had caused Lee to blunder into a battle he did not seek, on ground he did not choose. It was Stuart's fault for going off on a raid around the Union army when Lee needed him close at hand. Stuart's defenders, however, contend that he had followed Lee's orders and was innocent of the accusations made against him.[62]

Stuart didn't help his own cause when he submitted his report of the campaign. In this report, Stuart attempted to justify the virtues of his raid and its strategic soundness. His self-righteous attitude and tendency to blame others for the failure of the campaign caused the report to be questioned and considered unreliable. By questioning the soundness of Lee's strategy, Stuart incurred the wrath of all Lee's defenders.[63] Stuart did not accept failure gracefully. He had failed so infrequently that he never learned how to handle failure. Stuart feared failing more than death, dealing with it as though it never happened. In his report on Brandy Station and Gettysburg, he was unable to acknowledge any blame for the outcome of the battles.[64]

While Lee's army retreated in the rain on July 5, Stuart's cavalry provided a screen until they were out of danger. In the months that followed Gettysburg, Stuart again performed up to the standards by which he had become famous. In May 1864, Stuart served Lee well at gathering information during the Battle of the Wilderness, which was fought in dense woods just west of Chancellorsville. Stuart still continued to maintain a positive attitude and to demonstrate that he was a professional soldier.[65]

After Gettysburg, the war went badly for the Confederacy. While Stuart continued to fight well, he faced serious problems. He was losing dependable men in battle and was unable to find capable replacements. Supplies were low, horses and weapons scarce, and Union forces continued to grow in strength. Stuart was also distracted by occasional criticism and always felt that he had to defend himself.[66]

The Battle of the Wilderness, which ended on May 7, 1864, left Lee marginally the victor, but it was very different from his victory on the same ground a year earlier. Then, the Army of the Potomac, under Major General Hooker, had retreated in disorder. Now, General Grant ignored his tactical defeat and ordered the army under George Meade to advance toward Richmond. Grant's action served notice to the Confederacy that the Union had a leader who was not intimidated by Lee's legendary reputation.[67]

During the Wilderness Campaign, newly appointed Union cavalry leader Philip Sheridan and Meade had disagreed over the use of cavalry. Sheridan thought that his cavalry would be more effective if he had more latitude in their use. In the midst of their disagreement, Stuart's name came up. "Never mind Stuart," Meade remarked. "He will do about us as he pleases anyhow." "Damn Stuart," was Sheridan's reply. "I can trash hell out of him any day." Later when Grant heard of Sheridan's remark, he replied, "Did Sheridan say that? Well, he generally knows what he's talking about. Let him start right out and do it." Grant was confident that Sheridan was not just boasting. They had served together in the West, where Sheridan had earned Grant's respect by his fighting ability. Grant gave Sheridan a free hand to demonstrate that he was able to carry out his boast.[68]

With General Grant's blessings, Sheridan and a force of 10,000 horsemen headed for Richmond. Stuart, with 4,500 cavalrymen, tried to block his path. On May 11, Stuart took up a defensive position at Yellow Tavern, a crossroads just north of Richmond. Stuart had sent a brigade to harass Sheridan's rear, leaving him only 3,000 men to meet Sheridan's full force. Sheridan never reached Richmond; Stuart prevented that. During the battle, however, a bullet plunged into Stuart's right side, below his ribs. As he watched his men, disorganized and retreating, he sat up and said: "Go back! Go Back! And do your duty, as I have done mine, and our country will be safe. Go Back! Go Back! I had rather die than be whipped." They went back.[70]

An ambulance carried Stuart to the Richmond home of his brother-in-law, Dr. Charles Brewer. Doctors applied ice to the wound and sent a telegram to his wife to come at once. Flora was nearby, but because of the battle and condition of the roads, she arrived too late to see her husband before he died.[71]

Before Stuart died he heard artillery outside the city and was told that it was Fitz Lee's troops attempting to trap Sheridan. "God grant that they may be successful," said Stuart, "but I must be prepared for another world." When President Davis arrived, he asked how Stuart was doing. "Easy," replied Stuart, "but willing to die, if God and my country think I have fulfilled my destiny and done my duty." As the afternoon passed, Stuart's condition worsened. His intestines, as well as numerous blood vessels, had been severed, and he was suffering from internal hemorrhaging and peritonitis. When Stuart was told that he would not survive the night, he said: "I am resigned if it be God's will, but I would like to see my wife.... But God's will be done." At 7 P.M., the Episcopal Reverend Joshua Peterkin gathered everyone in the house around Stuart's bed and led them in prayer. They then sang Stuart's favorite hymn, "Rock of Ages." Stuart tried to sing along but was too weak. When it was over, Stuart told Brewer, "I am resigned; God's will be done." He died at 7:38 P.M. on May 12, 1864.[72]

When Robert E. Lee was notified of Stuart's death, he was speechless for several minutes. Then he said to his staff, "Gentlemen, we have very bad news. General Stuart has been mortally wounded." He stood silent a few minutes then added, "He never brought me a piece of false information." Later that night, Lee remarked, "I can scarcely think about him without weeping."[73]

On May 13, Stuart was laid to rest in Hollywood Cemetery in Richmond. Later, Lee addressed the army, saying, "The commanding general announces to the army with heartfelt sorrow the death of Major General J.E.B. Stuart. The mysterious hand of an all-wise God has removed him from the scene of his usefulness and fame. To his comrades in arms, he has left the proud recollection of his deeds and the inspiring influence of his example."[74]

Before Stuart died, he said he was resigned to the will of God. He once said that all he ever desired from life was to be killed while leading a cavalry charge. Ironically, he died in bed after hours of pain and agony. Stuart lived by the saber; he hoped to die in the same way.[75]

9

Brief Glory

TURNER ASHBY

O N June 6, 1862, and for the preceding nine days, Major General Stonewall Jackson's army had been retreating up the Shenandoah Valley, just one step ahead of the Union troops of Major General John C. Fremont and Brigadier General James Shields. Earlier in the day, Fremont had attacked the Confederate rear guard, commanded by Brigadier General Turner Ashby, and had been repulsed.[1] Now Jackson was interviewing several prisoners captured during the recent battle. Among them was Sir Percy Wyndham, an English soldier of fortune who had joined forces with the

Union and commanded the 1st New Jersey Cavalry in the Shenandoah Valley. Wyndham had frequently boasted that he would capture or kill the daring Confederate cavalry leader, Turner Ashby. Instead, he had been captured by Ashby and now was exchanging pleasantries with Jackson; at that point in the war it was still a "gentleman's" conflict, and it was not unusual for officers of similar rank to socialize with each other.[2]

Their meeting was interrupted by a courier from the cavalry camp, bringing shocking news — General Ashby had been killed leading a charge against Fremont's infantry just outside Harrisonburg, Virginia. Jackson quickly completed his interview with Wyndham and withdrew to his bedroom, where for the next few hours he paced the floor, meditating and mourning his slain cavalry chief.[3] Later Jackson wrote a short note to Colonel John Imboden, notifying him of the disaster: "Poor Ashby is dead. He fell gloriously. . . . I know you will join me in mourning the loss of our friend, one of the noblest of men and soldiers in the Confederate Army." Jackson then rode to the house where Ashby's body lay and paid his respects. Jackson remained alone for some time in the room and then left "with a solemn and elevated countenance."[4]

That night, soldiers of the Valley army went to see their fallen hero, paying their last respects. The sorrow was deep for all of the troops, but for the men who served under him, Ashby's death was a personal tragedy. "Each felt that he had lost one who had honored him with his friendship," Chaplain James Avirett later said, "and affection paid its tribute in scalding tears." The men passed in silence; some held back tears, and some openly wept. One of Ashby's scouts stared at his dead leader for a while and then said: "We shall miss you in camp! We shall miss you as we go out on the scout! But we shall miss you most, General, when we. . . ." He never finished the sentence; sobbing, he left the house.[5]

Even the Union troops respected Ashby. Although the death of this skilled cavalry leader gave them an advantage, one of General Fremont's officers declared: "I have not yet heard an unkind or injurious word by either the officers or soldiers of our force." The next day, when Ashby's funeral cortege moved

---

Previous page:
Though he argued with Ashby throughout the Civil War, Stonewall Jackson grieved over the loss of his noblest cavalier. (The Chicago Historical Society)

toward Charlottesville, Union prisoners along the road removed their hats in silent respect.[6]

Turner Ashby, it has been said, was the first general of heroic reputation to die in the Civil War. In his brief career, Ashby became a legend; now it is difficult to separate the man from the myth. Ashby, like Nathan Bedford Forrest, was a natural born leader without prewar military training.[7] His ancestors had fought in the Revolutionary War and the War of 1812. The third of six children, Turner was born on October 23, 1828, to Colonel Turner and Dorothy Green Ashby at Rose Bank, their Virginia plantation. Ashby had very little formal education. During his early years, he was educated at home, but later he attended a private school operated by a neighbor. He learned to read, write, and use arithmetic, but his scholarship was limited. He did, however, learn the more practical things at which a country boy usually excelled, such as riding and shooting.[8]

As a young boy, Turner became known as an expert horseman, a reputation he would carry all his life. One of his school friends recalled that "whenever a colt was found too wild and vicious to be ridden by anyone else in the neighborhood, it was his pleasure to mount and tame him." When he was twenty-five years old, financial reverses forced his mother to sell her plantation and move in with one of her married daughters. Turner, who had been successful in the mercantile business, was able to purchase property near his old home, an area he had grown to love. He fit with ease into the life of a young planter and businessman; by the beginning of the war he had already amassed a considerable fortune.[9]

Ashby entered local politics, running as a Whig in a district that was predominantly Democratic. As a result he was unsuccessful in his bid for a seat in the Virginia legislature. Although a strong defender of states' rights, he did not favor secession. Ashby was a slave holder, but he would have willingly liberated his slaves if the act would have prevented war. However, he was a Virginian first, and if war came he would defend his state.[10]

Ashby began his cavalry career in the mid-1850s, when the Manassas Gap Railroad was being built. The laborers on the road often caused trouble in the community, especially on paydays. Ashby organized a small company of mounted vigilantes to keep peace in town. When the railroad was complete and the troublemakers gone, the cavalry company later became a part of the Virginia militia.[11]

For Turner Ashby, the Civil War began on October 16, 1859, with John Brown's raid on the sleepy mountain town of Harpers Ferry in western Virginia. Ashby organized his troops, rode to Harpers Ferry, and offered his services to Colonel Robert E. Lee. Lee assigned Ashby's company to guard the Baltimore and Ohio Railroad bridges around the town; Ashby remained until after Brown was hanged in Charlestown. During that time, he became familiar with the local terrain, a familiarity that would be of great use to him later when the war began. In a few weeks the fear of a slave rebellion subsided, and by January 1860, Ashby and his men returned to their normal routines, at least for a while.[12]

Turner Ashby frequently entertained at his home. One occasion illustrates the feelings and temper of the man. While giving a reception, he invited a neighboring family and their guest, a young man from the North who was courting their daughter. A rejected suitor of the young woman, who was also a guest, took the opportunity to insult the young Northerner: "Isn't it a sublime piece of impudence for a Yankee and a Black Republican [political affiliation] to come down here now and accept the hospitality of a Virginia gentleman after all that has happened?" In just a moment a challenge was given and accepted and arrangements were made for an immediate settlement. When Ashby heard of the incident, he immediately took action, stating to the rebuked suitor that the young Northerner had come to his house as his guest. "When I invited him to come, the invitation was Turner Ashby's word of honor that he should be treated here as a gentleman," he said; "I am sorry to have to explain these points of good breeding to you . . . but you have shown your ignorance of them by insulting my guest. The insult is mine, not his to resent. . . . If you are not prepared to make proper and satisfactory apology at once, both to my guest and me, you must fight Turner Ashby. . . . What do you say, sir?" Taken by surprise, the young man stammered an excuse and signed two apologies that Ashby had written.[13]

With the election of Abraham Lincoln on November 6, 1860, secession became a reality. South Carolina was the first of the Southern states to leave the Union, on December 20. By February 4, 1861, six other states had joined to form the Confederate States of America. The majority of Virginia opposed secession and desired a peaceful solution, but after President Lincoln called upon the states for 75,000 volunteers to put down the rebellion, sentiment in Virginia changed. When Virginia passed its ordinance of secession on April 17,

1861, Ashby and his company were ready to go into action. Ashby received orders directing him and his men to Harpers Ferry.[14]

Ashby was of slight, graceful physique, with swarthy skin, jet-black hair, and one of the army's most imposing beards. He wore a plain, gray uniform which did not reveal his rank. His head was covered with a black plumed hat; he wore long buckskin gauntlets and large boots with sparkling steel spurs; saber, pistol, and bowie knife dangled from his belt. He had astonishing strength for a man of only 135 pounds and was a fearless and spirited leader. Like J.E.B. Stuart, Ashby always rode a splendid mount and appeared unconscious of danger, but he lacked Stuart's cheerful personality. Admirers often remembered his appearance but seldom could recall what he said. Ashby was not a man of words, preferring his actions to speak for him.[15]

Ashby was a tough, proud fighter. His reputation attracted many of Virginia's best horsemen to his command. Ashby's success was due largely to his courage in action and his ability to inspire his men to acts that bordered on impossible. His courage in battle and his quiet, gentle character gained him the loyalty of his men. Ashby's appetite for adventure and his reckless manner, however, sometimes resulted in costly losses. When asked about the extent of military instruction given to his men, one of Ashby's lieutenants remarked: "I do not recollect that during my service under General Ashby we ever had any time to drill except during the five days at Conrad's Store. It was one continued 'Go! Go!' — and Ashby always went!" Although Ashby was disciplined himself, his greatest weakness as a commander was his inability to discipline his men. This impeded his ability to have all his men ready for action when needed, and it contributed to the difficulty he would have with his commanding officer, Stonewall Jackson.[16]

In June 1861, Ashby rode to Winchester, where his company of Mountain Rangers were mustered into a newly formed regiment commanded by Colonel Angus McDonald. Ashby was promoted to lieutenant colonel and his brother Richard assumed command of the Rangers, now designated Company A, 7th Virginia Cavalry.[17] Colonel McDonald moved the new regiment to Romney. From there they were to make raids on the Union, burning bridges and disrupting railroads to help slow down General McClellan's advance. This type of duty appealed to Ashby and his freewheeling troops far more than picket duty. He and his men pictured themselves as dashing raiders, free to strike the enemy in whatever fashion suited their whim at the time. For a while they were moderately successful despite this short-sighted, disorganized strategy.[18] But the harsh realities of war soon dampened their enthusiasm.

On June 26, Ashby sent his brother Richard and eleven men to arrest a Northern sympathizer, but the patrol was ambushed by Colonel Lew Wallace's 11th Indiana Infantry. When Ashby arrived on the scene, his brother was still alive, but his body had been riddled with bullets and then stabbed; he died eight days later. From then on, Ashby was determined to make the enemy pay.[19]

From August to November 1861, Ashby was detached from McDonald's command, acting independently of him. Ashby now commanded over 500 men. With this force, he attacked Union troops under Colonel John Geary and forced them to evacuate Harpers Ferry. Shortly thereafter, McDonald was attacked at Romney, but because of McDonald's inept leadership, the garrison was crushed by Union troops. When McDonald tried to reorganize the shattered remnants of his regiment in Winchester, the men refused to follow him, so he took the problem to the new commander of the Valley district, Stonewall Jackson, who placed McDonald's mutinous companies under Ashby. The rejuvenated 7th Virginia Cavalry, now containing a battery of horse artillery, became known as "Ashby's Cavalry."[20]

Ashby was both fascinating and inspiring. The rougher the battle, the more Ashby seemed to like it, but he didn't behave like a typical cavalry commander. Ashby liked to ride into battle like a gentleman. His typical battle uniform included a spyglass, gauntlets, and a fox-hunting horn, making him quite a spectacle. "Riding his black stallion, he looked like a knight of the olden time," Lieutenant Henry Kyd Douglas remarked.[21]

Stonewall Jackson's arrival in the Valley and Ashby's subsequent promotion marked a turning point in Ashby's short military career. Jackson was a man of action who carried the war to the enemy. As commander of Jackson's cavalry, Ashby's duties increased accordingly. From the outset, Jackson turned to Ashby for much of his needs.

On Christmas day, 1861, the first incident occurred to suggest that Ashby did not have complete control of his cavalry. It was the beginning of a series of situations during Ashby's career that concerned Jackson and other Confederate officers about his ability as a disciplinarian and an administrator. One of Ashby's men, Private Harry Gilmor, was in Shepherdtown, Virginia, and was obviously bored. Drunk, Gilmor set off some fireworks and, not content with the commotion created by them, fired some shots at Union pickets stationed along the opposite shore of the Potomac. In reply, the Federals bombarded the town with artillery. Jackson was very much agitated by the incident and directed Ashby to take steps to keep his men in line.[22]

Then there was the incident on New Year's Day. Deceived by the warm weather on that morning, many of Jackson's infantry left their blankets and baggage by the wayside, and Ashby unwisely allowed his troops to send their winter gear back to Winchester. Shortly after, the weather changed, driving the temperature down, and by nightfall the Confederates were forced to camp during a snowstorm. As conditions grew increasingly worse, the men began to blame Jackson for their plight. Some of the men swore that he had gone mad and openly expressed disapproval of the expedition. Ashby did not defend Jackson's actions, nor did he acknowledge his part in the fiasco, but let Jackson take all the blame for poor judgment.[23]

Throughout the early part of 1862, Ashby was in the saddle more than not, scouting for information, patrolling, or riding the picket line. The end of February marked the beginning of a struggle described as "Hide and Seek in the Valley." Ashby's scouts reported that Major General Nathaniel Banks crossed the Potomac at Harpers Ferry with an army of 38,000 men. On March 11, when Banks moved on Jackson's small force, Jackson realized he had to march or else he would be overwhelmed by the superior Union army. Ashby's cavalry covered the withdrawal from Winchester.

John Esten Cooke, a Confederate soldier, wrote of Ashby's departure. By the morning of March 12, the only Confederate to be seen in Winchester was Ashby. He sat defiantly on his stallion until the enemy column entered the town. The single horseman was clearly visible to Union officers, who instantly sent two mounted troopers to get him. What happened then became the subject of a popular tale. Ashby's escape route was blocked by the two Union riders, who moved down the street to cut him off. Their approach did not seem to frighten him. He rode between them, shooting one dead and dragging the other off his horse by the throat before carrying him back to the rebel lines. Although Cooke did not personally witness this scene, he claimed that it "was witnessed by hundreds of the Confederate and Federal armies." Unfortunately, none of the "hundreds" of witnesses ever substantiated Cooke's story. This illustrates how legends grew up about Turner Ashby.[24]

During the middle of March, Major General George McClellan began his campaign against Richmond. Late in the evening of March 21, Ashby informed Jackson that Banks was moving to reinforce McClellan on the Peninsula. Jackson's orders to Ashby were to prevent McClellan from being reinforced. Ashby attacked Union troops near Kernstown, driving them back into Winchester. There his scouts received information that most of Banks's army had left Winchester. All that remained, according to the information gathered from residents of Winchester, were four infantry regiments, and those were planning to leave for Harpers Ferry the next day. Ashby quickly passed the information to Jackson. Early on the afternoon of March 23, Jackson's lead columns entered Kernstown. The Stonewall Brigade had just completed a thirty-six-mile forced march, and straggling had reduced its size to just a few more than 3,000 men. Lack of rest and forage had also reduced Ashby's strength to less than 300 cavalrymen. Jackson and Ashby, unknowingly, were about to attack Shields's entire division of 9,000 men, most of whom had been concealed north of town.[25]

Ashby had made a grievous error in his intelligence report, but that day, he was magnificent. It was almost as if he was trying to redeem himself for his mistake. R. P. Chew, who later commanded the Army of Northern Virginia's cavalry, believed that Ashby's gallant actions and audacity had "saved General Jackson's army from total destruction." Although Jackson's infantry was forced to leave the field after three hours of bloody fighting, he did not criticize Ashby. The attack at Kernstown, although not successful, had accomplished the greater goal. Lincoln reacted to the battle by ordering two heavy divisions, scheduled to leave the Valley and join McClellan, to remain where they were. In addition, he sent a third division to the Valley to join Banks. Thus a total of 35,000 Union troops were dispatched to the northern end of the Valley to face Jackson's force of 3,600. Two weeks later, President Lincoln detached McDowell's 1st Corps of 38,000 men from McClellan to shield Washington.[26]

For the next three weeks, Jackson retreated up the Valley, pursued by Banks. During that time, Ashby's rear guard fought more than a dozen skirmishes that helped to slow down the pursuit. Finally Jackson took his exhausted army into the Blue Ridge Mountains and Banks withdrew to Strasburg.

During the following weeks, Jackson's concern about Ashby's ability to lead increased. Jackson was disturbed by what he saw as the unacceptable actions of Ashby's free-wheeling troopers. Since the death of his brother, wrote a soldier, Turner Ashby would "quit a meal at anytime for a chance at a Yankee," and had "perhaps killed more of them with his own hands than any one man in the State." On several occasions when their service was needed, however, Ashby could only field a portion of his command. In the discipline demanded for coordinated action with the rest of the army, this was unsatisfactory. The fault clearly lay with Ashby.[27]

Ashby and his troopers had few peers in their partisan operations and rear-guard fighting. But they had never been under the control of a regular army officer, and although they were good in a fight, their lack of discipline made them erratic and undependable.[28] It was common knowledge that Turner Ashby was no disciplinarian. Brigadier General Dick Taylor, who admired his daring, courage, and superior horsemanship, concluded that "he was without capacity or disposition to enforce discipline on his men." Ashby's defenders argued that with his command spread over a great distance on picket or patrol duty, and with almost constant action with the enemy, he had little time for drill and discipline.[29]

Major Kyd Douglas, who admired Ashby for his courage, gave his view of Ashby's discipline: "His idea of the superior patriotism of the volunteer and that he should not be subjected to very much starch and drill, made him a poor disciplinarian and caused the only failure he ever made. . . . His service to the army was invaluable, but had he been as full of discipline as he was of leadership his success would have been more fruitful and his reputation still greater."[30]

In the Kernstown battle, Ashby had been able to field only about half his men. The remainder had been left free to frolic about the countryside on their own business because Ashby thought the action would not begin until the following day. Since then, the situation had deteriorated even more, and Jackson could no longer abide by the inaction of his cavalry leader. Near the end of April, Jackson brought the matter to a head. He ordered ten of Ashby's twenty-one companies attached to General Winder's brigade; the rest went to a brigade under Brigadier General William Taliaferro. Ashby would still remain in charge of either the advance or rear guard, but he could only obtain the men needed for carrying out his assignment by applying to Taliaferro and Winder for troops. Jackson's orders had stripped Ashby of his command.[31]

Ashby reacted as expected. When he received the order, he was furious. Had he and Jackson been equal in rank, Ashby probably would have challenged Jackson to a duel. Instead he took other action; Ashby and his second-in-command, Major Oliver Funsten, decided to resign.[32] Ashby wrote to Alexander Boteler, his congressman, threatening to resign and declaring that Jackson had regularly humiliated him despite the fact that "for the last two months I have saved the Army of the Valley from being utterly destroyed. . . . This I have done without the aid of General Jackson's command." If his men lacked discipline, Ashby continued, they were not alone: "I deem General Jackson's army in the worst condition it had been in since it came into the Valley." This was not the outcome Jackson desired. He did not believe the cavalry's performance would improve without Ashby. Jackson valued Ashby for his fighting spirit and inspirational leadership. Jackson had hoped to change Ashby, not to have him resign.[33]

Help came in the form of General Winder, who negotiated back and forth between the two and arranged for their meeting. On April 24, Ashby called upon Jackson at his headquarters. To lose Ashby would be a catastrophe to morale as well as the fighting ability of the Confederate forces. The two officers talked with each other for a long time. Exactly what transpired was never disclosed. Jackson's quartermaster wrote that the dispute had been resolved "by General Jackson backing square down." The general effect was a compromise. Ashby agreed to tighten discipline. Jackson agreed that the cavalry companies would remain technically under the infantry brigade commanders, but they in fact were "detailed" back to Ashby. Ashby was satisfied, and he and Major Funsten withdrew their resignations. Jackson was not pleased, but at least he had managed to avoid the risk of losing his cavalry in the early stages of what he intended to be a major campaign.[34]

In a letter to General Lee's adjutant on May 5, Jackson gave all the details of his controversy with Colonel Ashby and the reasons for restoring his command. The next day Jackson wrote to Congressman Boteler, who was now supporting Ashby's promotion to the rank of brigadier general. "With regard to Colonel Ashby's promotion I would gladly favor it, if he were a good disciplinarian," he wrote, "but he has such bad discipline and attaches so little importance to drill, that I would regard it as a calamity to see him promoted. I desire so soon as he gives proper attention to these matters to see him promoted."[35]

Jackson's letter had little effect; on May 23, Ashby was promoted to brigadier general. "Sandie" Pendleton of Jackson's staff notified Ashby, adding, "I do this with great pleasure, General Ashby, hoping that as you are soon to command a Brigade, the country may expect less exposure of your life." Ashby smiled, took the paper, and rode off to the front.[36] In less than two weeks he would be dead.

Ashby attacked Union soldiers in Winchester, March 11, 1862. (Library of Congress)

On May 23, a combined force of Ashby, Jackson, and Major General Richard Ewell's 16,000 men moved into action. Banks was surprised by the attack and was forced to retreat from Front Royal, fleeing toward Winchester with Ashby close behind. Finding Banks's wagon train, Ashby attacked. The Union troops did not offer opposition, running for their lives. It was Ashby's finest moment. It was also here that he suffered his worst disgrace. Ashby's command dissolved around him, unable to resist looting wagons that contained large amounts of food, uniforms, blankets, weapons, ammunition, and whiskey. Not even Ashby's personal popularity could prevent this from happening. Many of them loaded their horses with stolen goods and headed for home, not to return for several days. Others just ate and drank until they were drunk. Ashby was left with fewer than one hundred of his 800-man regiment. In the meantime, the Union troops escaped. Jackson finally got Ewell's cavalry to pursue the Federals, but they were out of reach and able to safely cross the Potomac. Jackson could only say, "Oh that my cavalry were in place!"[37]

Despite Ashby's failure, the attack had been successful for the Confederates;

the rebel casualties numbered 400; Union losses were in excess of 3,000. Jackson and Ashby had captured so much equipment that when J.E.B. Stuart heard of it, he laughingly characterized Banks as the best commissary Stonewall Jackson ever had.[38]

When Jackson demanded an explanation of what happened to his cavalry, Ashby was too proud to admit what Jackson already knew, that he had been unable to control his men. He claimed that his command had scattered to round up Federals west of town, and others had been dispatched to keep an eye on Fremont's advance. Jackson accepted Ashby's explanation, but he had already heard rumors of looting. He had seen evidence of it himself when he stopped to take a box of crackers out of one of the captured wagons. Jackson must have had mixed feelings about Ashby's cavalry, which he admired so much for their courage and relied upon for so much but which had now let him down at a critical time. Ashby's inability to organize or discipline his men had cost the army a chance to destroy Banks's army once and for all. Ashby, however, still maintained he could control his men. "My men follow where I lead," he said, "and that is all that matters."[39]

On May 30, Jackson received news that Major General James Shields's division was at Front Royal and that Fremont was moving east toward Strasburg to join him. If they were able to close ranks, as Banks moved southward from Williamsport, Maryland, Jackson's army would be trapped. Jackson's only chance to escape was to withdraw up the Valley through Strasburg ahead of the converging federal armies. On May 31, he began the retreat, with General Ashby in charge of the rear. Near Cedarville, Virginia, Ashby ambushed a portion of Shields's infantry, blocking their advance until Jackson could escape. Because of Ashby's actions, the Union plan to trap Jackson failed.[40]

On June 4, Jackson consolidated all his mounted troops and assigned them to General Ashby's command. As the Confederate forces retreated, they were slowed down by heavy rain. Finally on June 6, the rains ended, and Ashby continued his defense of the Confederate rear. Early in the afternoon the 1st New Jersey Cavalry, led by Colonel Percy Wyndham, was in close pursuit of Ashby. Wyndham had boasted that he intended to capture him. Now it appeared he would have his chance. The two cavalry commanders met head on. For a few minutes the noise of battle raged; then all was quiet. Ashby's sudden frontal attack, along with his attack against both flanks and the rear, was more than the Federals could withstand. After the initial thrust, the Union line broke, and the Yankees left sixty-three prisoners behind, including Wyndham.[41]

As the prisoners were being moved to the rear, more Union cavalry were spotted on the road. Ashby was delighted at the thought of more action. He sent the 2nd Virginia Cavalry out as a decoy and requested that Ewell send the 1st Maryland and 58th Virginia Infantry for support. Ashby was cautioned not to continue the fight by his staff, who felt he should be satisfied with what had been accomplished in the earlier victory, but Ashby persisted in continuing the action. For weeks he had been pressured and harassed by the Union advance; the strain was beginning to tell. "These people have pressed me long enough," he said, "and I will make them stop it today!"[42]

The infantry support on which Ashby was relying was slow in coming up, allowing the federal troops to gain the position where Ashby had hoped to place his infantry. The Confederates were taken by surprise and scattered after the first volley by the enemy. Ashby rode among the panic-stricken troops, shouting and waving his saber, encouraging them to rally behind him. When he led them on a desperate charge, his horse was shot from under him, and he was thrown to the ground.[43] Untangling himself from his dying horse, Ashby jumped to his feet, shouting: "Charge men! For God's sake, charge!" He waved his sword in the direction of the Union line and took a couple of steps. Just then a bullet pierced Ashby's heart, and he fell dead.[44]

With Ashby's last battle, he had bought the time needed for Jackson's army to get their wagons through Port Republic. On June 8, Fremont made a feeble attack but was repulsed. On the 9th, Shields was turned back from Cross Keys. The Valley Campaign was over.[45]

Ashby's body was wrapped in a blanket and carried back to Port Republic. That night a line of mournful soldiers passed by his coffin, giving silent homage to an honored friend. Jackson never revealed the thoughts that must have filled his mind at the loss of his cavalry leader. Ashby had been headstrong, reckless, and a constant frustration when it came to the military discipline that Jackson prized, but he had been one of the most valuable and courageous soldiers Jackson had ever commanded. The force of Ashby's personality seemed to guarantee victory.[46]

In his official report on the campaign, Jackson praised Ashby more than he had anyone before, or ever would again: "The close relations which General Ashby bore to my command for the past 12 months will justify me in saying that as a partisan officer I never knew his superior; his daring was proverbial; his tone of character, and his sagacity almost intuitive in divining the movements and purpose of the enemy."[47]

The legend of Turner Ashby continued to grow after his death. Confederate and Union veterans claimed to have fought with him or against him. Trooper William Wilson provided an appropriate epitaph to describe Ashby's brief glory when he wrote that "Few men like Turner Ashby have graced the annals of any people. Ages will roll away and another like Turner Ashby will not be."[48]

10   *Maryland's Gallant Harry*

HARRY GILMOR

I N THE fall of 1861, a lone rider from Baltimore slipped through Union lines into the shallow Potomac and crossed the river into Virginia. He was Harry Gilmor, the twenty-four-year-old son of a prosperous shipping and mercantile family who had strong Southern sympathies. Gilmor was a member of one of Baltimore's secessionist militia and had already been arrested and held for several weeks by federal authorities before being released. Now Gilmor was determined to serve with Turner Ashby, who was achieving a reputation as the leader of a partisan regiment operating around Winchester, Virginia.[1]

During the early phase of the war, Ashby's reputation and magnetism had attracted daring men like Gilmor. Just north of Winchester, Gilmor found Ashby and some of his men. The outspoken Gilmor bragged of his prowess as a marksman, saying that he could shoot an apple off a man's head. As expected, there were no volunteers to hold the apple, so Gilmor had to demonstrate his expertise by shooting at other targets. Before the day was over, he had become a member of Ashby's raiders.[2]

One of eleven children, the adventurous Harry Gilmor was born on January 24, 1838, to Robert and Ellen Gilmor. His family was one with a heritage of privilege, rank, and honor. His father had attended Harvard College and later served as an attaché in Paris, France. While visiting Scotland, Robert Gilmor was so impressed with the beauty of poet Sir Walter Scott's Abbotsford estate that he had his own Maryland estate built with a similar design. The Gilmor mansion was named Glen Ellen, after his wife Ellen. Lavishly constructed, it contained twenty-five bedrooms, a large library, a circular ballroom, and a gallery surrounding the ballroom for spectators and musicians.[3] Harry Gilmor had the privilege of a good education, being taught by a private tutor from Harvard. But Gilmor moved westward to Wisconsin and Nebraska, where he attempted to homestead, quite a contrast to the elite social life he had enjoyed in Maryland. Gilmor finally returned to Maryland, where he became a gentleman farmer on his father's estate.[3]

When the Confederates attacked Fort Sumter in April 1861, Maryland found itself critically located, separating the Union North and Confederate South. The eastern and southern parts of the state, with their large tobacco plantations, supported the Southern cause. When Maryland did not join with Virginia in secession, the Gilmor family lent their aid to the secessionists in the state. When Lincoln ordered the 6th Massachusetts Regiment to Washington and they attempted to pass through Baltimore, they were rudely greeted by a mob who pelted them with rocks and bricks; the militia fired back. The melee which resulted left twelve Baltimoreans dead and an untold number wounded. The 6th Massachusetts counted four killed and thirty-nine wounded.[4]

Previous page:
Harry Gilmor began his military career as one of Turner Ashby's finest raiders.
(U.S. Army Military History Institute)

As the riots spread throughout Baltimore, Harry Gilmor was drawn into the tempest. As corporal of the Baltimore County Horse Guard, he was dispatched to defend the Maryland Guard armory. When the armory was attacked by a mob of rioters, Gilmor demonstrated his ability to lead. With a small contingent of men, Gilmor quickly forced the mob to disperse.

As the unrest in Baltimore continued, President Lincoln suspended the writ of habeas corpus, the protection against illegal detention or imprisonment, in an area from Philadelphia to Washington. That the Union established with liberty and equality would resort to this breach of the Constitution seemed to be a contradiction. As a result, many chose to leave Maryland and join the Confederacy, preferring "Liberty without Union" to "Union without Liberty."[5]

The scene in Baltimore continued to worsen. On May 13, Union Major General Benjamin Butler sent federal troops to occupy Federal Hill, a strategic position overlooking Baltimore. Immediately, Butler halted supply shipments to the South and ordered that all militia units disband, fearing they might have Southern leanings. Many who served in these units found their way into Confederate ranks. Because of their known Southern sympathies, the Gilmor family was placed under close scrutiny. In a short time, Harry Gilmor was arrested and charged with communicating with the Confederates. He was placed in a cell at Fort McHenry, but after being detained for two weeks, he was released. On August 30, Gilmor crossed the Potomac into Virginia.[6]

Gilmor enlisted in Captain Frank Mason's Company under Lieutenant Colonel Ashby's command. The company was composed exclusively of Maryland men. Shortly after joining the 7th Virginia, he saw his first action at Bolivar Heights, overlooking Harpers Ferry. During the encounter, Gilmor came so close to being hit by a bullet that splinters of lead lodged in his skin. Skirmishes such as this gave Gilmor the opportunity to gain valuable experience as a Confederate raider.[7]

Gilmor saw his first major action in the fall of 1861; again it was at Bolivar Heights. When the tide began to turn against them, Ashby asked for five volunteers to take over an artillery piece that was out of action. Without hesitation, Gilmor went into action. Although the Confederate effort to dislodge the Federals from Harpers Ferry failed, Ashby officially commended Gilmor and his men "for their gallant bearing" during the encounter. In December, Colonel Ashby appointed Gilmor sergeant major of his command, and Gilmor soon found himself at the center of Stonewall Jackson's plan to capture the Union garrison at Romney in western Virginia as Ashby's cavalry formed the vanguard of Jackson's operation. Gilmor was involved in destroying enemy lines of communication and seizing large quantities of Yankee supplies. In Jackson's famous spring campaign, Gilmor also would play a role in its success.[18] In March 1862, Ashby gave Gilmor permission to form a company of cavalry and promoted him to the rank of captain.

In the spring, Union Major General Nathaniel Banks moved his army to Winchester; his objective was to clear the Valley of Jackson's forces. At Kernstown, just outside Winchester, Jackson's outnumbered troops gave battle. Although Jackson was beaten, Lincoln decided to keep General Banks's army in the Shenandoah Valley, thus denying troops to General Irvin McDowell at Fredericksburg and to McClellan as he battled Lee on the Peninsula.

It was in the Shenandoah Valley that Stonewall Jackson's fame grew; his strategic operations are still considered some of the most brilliant in military history. In battle after battle, although outnumbered, he was able to defeat federal forces. By moving rapidly and appearing almost anywhere, Jackson was able to surprise the enemy forces and defeat portions of them at a time. Then he would retreat to fight another day. With only 15,000 men, Jackson was able to outmaneuver and defeat portions of three Union armies with 80,000 men.[9] During this campaign, Gilmor and his scouts played a major role, keeping a constant vigil on the enemy's movements and reporting them to Jackson. In doing so, Gilmor and his men rode for days behind enemy lines without sleep to make certain that Jackson received accurate and timely information.

In August, Gilmor took his command out of the Shenandoah Valley in time to join General Lee's Army of Northern Virginia as they moved toward Maryland in search of a victory on Northern soil. When the Confederate army marched into Frederick, Maryland, Gilmor took the opportunity to visit a friend's house outside of Baltimore. Unknown to him, a contingent of Union soldiers and Baltimore policemen were at the house when he arrived. Gilmor and a friend who was with him entered the yard only to find themselves surrounded by the enemy. Gilmor was charged as a spy and moved to Fort McHenry for confinement. Gilmor was treated humanely and allowed to have visitors at Fort McHenry. On December 6, Gilmor's father posted bond, and he was released, but in January he was ordered to report to General Dix at Fortress Monroe. Finally in February 1863, just as Gilmor was making plans to escape, he was exchanged.[10]

During the action at Kelly's Ford in the spring of 1863, Gilmor distinguished himself to the point that he was noticed by both Lee and Stuart. Lee thanked Gilmor "for marked bravery and cool courage," and Stuart reported that he was indebted to Gilmor for having accompanied him during the action as a volunteer staff officer.[11]

In the midst of the major battles of 1863, Gilmor requested permission to raise his own cavalry battalion. In his proposal, he requested the freedom to recruit only fellow Marylanders to fill his ranks and to be allowed to operate independently in the field. On May 7, the Confederate War Department approved his request and elevated him to the rank of major. When he was unable to fill his ranks completely with men he wanted, Gilmor was forced to accept deserters, former criminals, and men who had been discharged for less than honorable service.[12]

On June 3, Lee left Fredericksburg, Virginia, and marched toward the Shenandoah Valley in the hope of obtaining a victory on federal soil. Gilmor was ordered to scout around Winchester before General Ewell arrived with his corps. In the process, Gilmor encountered an old acquaintance, Belle Boyd, the Confederate spy. She requested permission to accompany him on the trip to Winchester. Gilmor, who did not want to take a woman on such an important mission, informed Boyd that she would have to receive permission from Brigadier General Micah Jenkins, commander of the Valley district. When the two met with Jenkins, Gilmor placed himself behind Boyd and gestured to the commander his displeasure with her request. Jenkins followed Gilmor's lead and denied the request.[13]

At Middletown, the Yankees tried to break through Confederate lines. At the time Gilmor was ill and bedridden, but he quickly dressed and joined his men in the field. Moving to the front of the column, Gilmor rallied his men. He remained in the midst of the melee until he was sure that the Federals could advance no farther. When the bloody battle was over, the casualty count showed that the Marylanders had lost nearly half their men on that day of combat.[14]

On one occasion Gilmor was confronted by a Jessie Scout. The Jessie Scouts were a group of federal spies and rangers formed by General John C. Fremont and were named after his wife, Jessie. Their function was to root out Confederate guerrillas and partisans. They often wore Confederate uniforms but were able to identify each other by a white scarf they wore around their neck. Gilmor discovered the secret of the white scarf, and his use of it led to tragedy for one Union soldier. Wearing a Confederate uniform, but with the white scarf added, Gilmor was on a scouting mission when he was confronted by another soldier dressed the same as he. The rider, a real Jessie Scout, drew his pistol and began to question him. Gilmor's answers put the Yankee at ease, convincing him that he was one of them. Once he had gained the man's confidence, Gilmor threw him off guard by asking to see a piece of his equipment. As the man bent to retrieve it, Gilmor drew his saber and stabbed him just below the heart. Shocked and in severe pain, the Jessie Scout fell from his mount. Gilmor dismounted and tried to assist the wounded man, but he was unable to do so. "My blade had gone too near the heart," he said. "You sold me well, but I don't blame you," gasped the dying man. Gilmor took the man's horse and continued on.[15]

Another of Gilmor's tricks was to send several of his troopers into a federal column with a generous supply of whiskey. They would offer to fill the Union soldiers' canteens. When the unsuspecting soldiers dropped out of the column to do this, they were surprised to find themselves surrounded by Gilmor's men.[16]

In June 1863, Gilmor's battalion was attached to Brigadier General George Steuart's brigade. Steuart's command remained near McConnellsburg, Pennsylvania, for several days while Gilmor's troops searched through the surrounding farmland to requisition horses, cattle, and other supplies. Gilmor was ordered "to leave a pair of plow horses and milk cows on each farm, and to respect all other property." Although the Confederate army was badly in need of supplies, they still wished to preserve their honor in the eyes of the North and the rest of the world. Lee encouraged his men to show restraint when they were on enemy soil and not to take out their anger on the citizens for any wrongs the Southerners had suffered.[17]

In July, Gilmor led his Maryland cavalry to Gettysburg. Only on the last day did he see limited action. On July 4, General Lee ordered his army to retreat. As the Confederate army slipped away, Gilmor rallied his men in anticipation of a federal attack. As Lee's embattled army retreated into Virginia, Gilmor gathered a group of 180 sick and wounded men into a fighting force. Along with the 62nd Virginia, they attempted to disrupt a federal assault on a Confederate supply train. In the process, Gilmor experienced an attack of vertigo and suddenly lost consciousness. When he woke up, he had been taken prisoner. During the night he was forced to sleep under a blanket between his

A bridge of the Richmond and Fredericksburg Railroad destroyed by Confederate raiders.
(Library of Congress)

two guards. When the guards fell asleep, he slipped from under the blanket and escaped, taking with him his weapons and their two horses.[18]

By the end of 1863, after Lee's defeat at Gettysburg and the fall of Vicksburg, the chance for Confederate victory in the war was dwindling. As 1864 approached, the methods of war would change. What had been labeled a "gentleman's war" was rapidly becoming a more destructive "total war." Harry Gilmor approached 1864 with an even stronger determination to fight for the Southern cause.[19]

Throughout January and into February, Gilmor's men made raids and scouted in western Virginia. In February, now serving under J.E.B. Stuart, Gilmor was ordered to destroy the tracks of the Baltimore and Ohio Railroad and to prevent the movement of troops along that line. With just twenty-eight men, Gilmor set up a barricade across the tracks near Martinsburg in western Virginia. His men took up positions in the woods nearby to await the train. An express out of Baltimore carrying wounded furloughed soldiers home and other civilian passengers was stopped. Gilmor entered the mail car in search of the safe as the rest of his men boarded the passenger cars. While Gilmor attempted to open the safe, his men were robbing the passengers. After rounding up those on board, Gilmor ordered the train destroyed.[20]

News of the train robbery reached the Northern papers. The New York press called Gilmor's men a "guerrilla band." Testimony from passengers reported that valuables such as "watches, diamonds, rings, and breastpins" were taken by the raiders. The *Baltimore American* reported that the robbery was undertaken "with all the grace and sang froid of experienced highwaymen.... Even their pocket knives and toothpicks did not escape the plunders." A few days later, some of Gilmor's men robbed a wagon train owned by Jewish merchants who were selling merchandise from Maryland in Richmond. The robbery consisted of $6,000 in gold pieces, several watches, and a Hebrew prayer book. Although Gilmor himself was not present when this occurred, it was later reported that he bragged about planning the robbery.[21]

In March Gilmor was arrested and General John Imboden ordered to investigate the robberies. General Lee was disgusted by the actions of Gilmor's raiders. Such crimes were too similar, he said, to the exploits of the lawless guerrillas that preyed upon helpless citizens. Lee declared that "such conduct is unauthorized and discreditable. Should any of the battalions be captured, the enemy might claim to treat them as highway robbers."[22]

The behavior of Gilmor's men could not have come at a more inopportune time. Confederate authorities were becoming disenchanted with the tactics of these bands operating on their own. Even generals like J.E.B. Stuart and Robert E. Lee began speaking out against partisan companies. Lee told Confederate Secretary of War James Seddon that he "recommended that the law authorizing partisan corps be abolished." On February 17, 1864, the Confederate congress passed legislation that prohibited the creation of partisan commands, but gave Seddon the right to make certain exceptions. The law also directed that all partisan commands organized earlier, Gilmor's command being one of them, be combined with other organizations into battalions or regiments.[23]

On March 21, General Imboden ordered that Gilmor be released and returned to his command until his court-martial. In his memoirs, Gilmor insisted that the robbery was against his orders. In April, Gilmor was tried, acquitted, and returned to his old command, but the whole affair had left a bad taste in everyone's mouth.[24]

On May 5, Gilmor's battalion was mustered into service as cavalry and ordered to report to Major General Arnold Elzey. Gilmor's command became officially known as the 2nd Maryland Cavalry Battalion. Despite being assigned to regular command, Gilmor would continue his partisan activities.[25]

During the spring of 1864, Union troops under the command of Major General Franz Sigel invaded the Shenandoah Valley. While engaged in a battle near Staunton, Gilmor was shot in the lower back. Fortunately for him, the ball first struck his saddle, slowing down the projectile and probably saving his life. Although the wound was painful, it was not serious, and in a short time he was back in the saddle.[26]

In early summer, Union Major General David Hunter posed a new threat for the Valley; his mission: to destroy its railroads, cut Lee's supply lines, and flank him out of his trenches in eastern Virginia. Hunter was opposed by a small Confederate force under Brigadier General William "Grumble" Jones. Gilmor was assigned the task of harassing Hunter's army from the rear. Despite Gilmor's assaults and continued raids, General Hunter continued to push up the Valley.[27]

At Piedmont, General Hunter defeated Grumble Jones, who was mortally wounded in the action. With his path unobstructed, Hunter entered the prosperous town of Staunton. There he ordered the destruction of supplies and the Virginia Central Railroad. A mixed mob of federal soldiers and camp followers plundered local stores.[28] At Staunton, Hunter's command was reinforced, and on June 10, he moved toward Lexington. After driving the Confederates from the area, he torched the Virginia Military Institute and Virginia Governor John Letcher's home. Hunter then marched off toward Lynchburg, hoping to complete the remaining objectives of his mission.[29]

Robert E. Lee realized that something had to be done to meet Hunter's threat. Accordingly, he sent the 2nd Corps of the Army of Northern Virginia under the command of Lieutenant General Jubal Early to the Valley. Gilmor was ordered to go through Hunter's line and make a circuit of his rear. In the meantime, General Early arrived at Lynchburg hoping to make Hunter pay for his "path of destruction." Hunter began to withdraw his army from Lynchburg, and Gilmor was ordered to strike at Hunter as he retreated. Rather than retrace his steps back down the Valley, Hunter retreated into western Virginia. This left an opening for Early to move his men northward toward Washington.[30]

With General Lee's permission, Early took the war to the North, hoping to menace the federal capital and draw Union troops and resources away from Richmond and Petersburg. Early sent Major General John Breckinridge to attack Union forces at Martinsburg, Virginia, with Gilmor's 2nd Maryland placed at the vanguard of his infantry. After destroying the railroads around Martinsburg, Breckinridge crossed the Potomac. News of the movement of Confederate troops into Maryland was filled with wild rumors and exaggerations about the activities and strength of the raiding party.[31]

On July 9, Major General Lew Wallace engaged Early's Confederate army at Monocacy Junction. His command was all that stood between Early's raiding party and Washington. Gilmor was detached from the main army with orders to destroy telegraph and railroad lines behind the Union army. Early easily defeated Wallace and moved to the town of Frederick, threatening to torch the town unless they paid a ransom of $200,000. The town was saved when the ransom was paid.[32]

As Confederate raiders continued to rain havoc on the residents of Maryland, fears and tensions were heightened. Gilmor, not wanting a repeat of the earlier incident on the Baltimore and Ohio Railroad, warned his men not to plunder; they found another way of getting what they wanted, however. The *Baltimore Sun* reported that Gilmor's men resorted to a kind of exchange thievery. While raiding a train outside of Baltimore, they forced the passengers to trade personal items for those belonging to them. One of the passengers was asked to trade his new boots for a pair of cowhide ones without soles. Other Gilmor troopers exchanged articles of clothing with the passengers.[33]

While General Early was moving against Washington, Union General Hunter returned to the Valley, where he continued to burn private dwellings. As a result of Hunter's actions, Early made a grim decision: "I came to the conclusion it was time to open the eyes of the people of the North to this enormity, by an example in the way of retaliation." Chambersburg, Pennsylvania, was selected to bear the brunt of his vengeance. Brigadier Generals John

McCausland and Bradley Johnson's brigades were selected to carry out the raid. Gilmor, with both the 1st and 2nd Maryland Cavalry battalions, was selected to lead the vanguard of the Confederate invading force.[34]

Gilmor's horsemen entered Chambersburg early on July 30 and blocked the routes out of the town. Then they seized several of the town's most affluent citizens and explained to them "that by order of General Early, $100,000 in gold or $500,000 in currency was required to ransom the town." Failing to pay the ransom would result in the burning of the town as retaliation for Hunter's destruction in the Valley. When the money could not be raised, the town was plundered and torched.[35]

Amid the terror and anguish in Chambersburg, Gilmor and two of his men went to one of the houses to be torched. When they told the unfortunate woman her house was to be burned, she broke into tears but did not request that her house be spared. She did, however, ask for time to remove her valuables before the house was sat ablaze. In the meantime Gilmor noticed a breakfast sitting on the table. The woman asked her unwelcomed guest to help himself if he so desired. Gilmor availed himself of her hospitality and sat down to eat. In the conversation that followed, Gilmor asked the woman the name of her husband. She replied, "Colonel Boyd of the 1st New York Cavalry." Gilmor said that her house would be spared, explaining that her husband had a reputation for being kind and gentlemanly to the people of the Valley. He would exchange kindness for kindness.[36]

Early's raid demonstrated that as long as the South controlled the Shenandoah Valley, Washington was in danger. With Chambersburg still smoldering, General Grant replaced General Hunter with Major General Philip Sheridan. His objective was to clear the Valley of Early's troops. On August 10, Sheridan moved his Army of the Shenandoah southward up the Valley. Gilmor, now serving under Major General Stephen Ramseur, was actively involved in the battles.

During the late summer of 1864, Gilmor was shot through the shoulder and collarbone and was taken to a hospital in Charlottesville, where his wound was treated. Later he was moved to Winchester to convalesce at a friend's house. While there, he was promoted to the rank of colonel. His stay, however, was interrupted by the defeat of Confederate forces outside of Winchester. As the Confederate troops retreated through the town, Gilmor realized that he would probably be captured if he stayed in bed. Quickly he put on his trousers and hurried into the street, wearing only his pants and nightshirt. He was recognized by one of his rangers, who gave up his horse to Gilmor. "I must have cut a sorry figure," he later recalled, "tearing through the streets of Winchester without hat, coat, or shoes." Gilmor was able to escape and resume his command in western Virgina.[37]

After returning to duty, Gilmor's physical condition and his feelings of despair were at an all-time low. Still suffering from his wounds, he had to be helped off his horse and, on occasion, fainted in the saddle. By November, Gilmor's health had improved enough that he was to take on another assignment. Early sent him on a mission to determine Sheridan's troop strength. Taking six men with him and dressed in Union blue, Gilmor crossed the enemy lines. When they captured four Yankee soldiers who were on their way to vote in the presidential election, Gilmor took their voting tickets and went to the camp to cast his vote. He could have helped the Confederate cause by voting for McClellan, but apparently it seemed a better joke to vote for Lincoln.[38]

Sheridan was able to clear the Valley of Early's troops except for groups of partisan raiders, who continued to harass his troops. Gilmor's raiders were among these partisan bands. It was the responsibility of Major Henry Young's Jessie Scouts to find Gilmor and bring his raiders under control. In early February 1865, he learned that Colonel Gilmor was a guest in the home of a friend in western Virginia. It was the opportunity for which he had been waiting.[39]

A force of twenty Jessie Scouts was quickly assembled, along with a back-up contingent of 300 cavalrymen. Under early morning darkness, the Jessie Scouts entered the town of Moorefield. It took only a short time to locate where Gilmor was staying. Caught by surprise, Gilmor had no opportunity to fight; he surrendered quietly. Young and his men were deep behind Confederate lines but held off several Confederate attacks, and on February 6, Gilmor was delivered to General Sheridan in Winchester. Gilmor was taken to Fort Warren in Boston Harbor, where he spent the rest of the war.[40]

On July 24, 1865, Gilmor was paroled and released from prison. Sensing that the climate around Baltimore was too hostile for his return, he traveled to Europe and then to Louisiana. During this time, Gilmor fell in love and married twenty-two-year-old Mentoria Strong.[41] Gilmor and his wife returned to Baltimore, where he again became prominent in the social and political activities of the town. In 1873, Gilmor was appointed major of the 1st Battalion

Cavalry of the Maryland National Guard. Later he was appointed police commissioner of Baltimore.[42]

In December 1879, Mentoria gave birth to twin boys. Following their birth, Mentoria died; she was only thirty-four years old. The twins died shortly after.[43] By 1881, Gilmor's health began to fail. He had never fully recovered from wounds he had suffered in his shoulder and jaw. Now the pain became severe, and medical attention was little help. Gradually his health deteriorated until he was paralyzed and almost totally blind. Finally on March 4, 1883, death mercifully came. Gilmor was buried next to his wife in Loudon Park in Baltimore.[44]

An epitaph entitled "Our Gallant Harry" is engraved on his monument in Loudon Park Cemetery. The first three lines, "Dauntless in Battle; Splendid in Success; Constant in Defeat," appropriately describe Harry Gilmor's role in the Civil War.

11

Kill-Cavalry

HUGH JUDSON KILPATRICK

H UGH Judson Kilpatrick, often putting his men in harms way without regard for their welfare, earned his nickname "Kill-Cavalry" because of his usually high casualty rate. His flamboyance and recklessness caused fellow cavalry officers like J.E.B. Stuart, John Hunt Morgan, and George Custer to seem dull. Some say he was the most notorious scoundrel in the Union army. When leading raids into Confederate territory, he often inflated the reports of his success. His fabrications led to his rapid promotions and eventually to the command of a division. Kilpatrick was a passionate man, having both admirers and enemies. To them he was either a hero or, as one Union officer put it, "a frothy braggart without brains."[1]

His character and moral fortitude were just as questionable. Although he did not smoke or gamble, activities common among Civil War soldiers, he lacked integrity and was guilty of more damning vices, such as thievery, adultery, and lying. In 1862, he was imprisoned for three months for profiteering.[2]

Opinions varied on Kilpatrick's ability as a military leader. At times he demonstrated the bravery of a warrior, but on other occasions he would withdraw without a fight. When his raid on Richmond failed in 1864, Major General George Meade relieved him of duty. Later, General William Sherman made effective use of Kilpatrick's abilities during his march to the sea. Sherman later remarked: "I know Kilpatrick is one hell of a damned fool, but I want just that sort of man to command my cavalry." Kilpatrick's performance at the end of the war earned him a promotion to the rank of major general.[3]

Hugh Judson Kilpatrick's physical appearance was anything but romantic. He was plain and small in stature, with pale eyes and frizzy red sidewhiskers. When he was a plebe at West Point, the older cadets made him the object of their amusement. Kilpatrick reacted to their taunts with good-natured repartee and sometimes with his fists. Later, he dressed with flair. He wore a carefully tailored uniform, high black boots, and a black felt hat, always tilted at a rakish angle. A staff officer once said that it was difficult to look at him without chuckling.[4]

Hugh Judson Kilpatrick was born on January 14, 1836, near Deckertown, New Jersey, the second son of Simon and Julia Wickham Kilpatrick. His parents considered him special, typical for children born later in their parents' lives. They made sure that he received a good education. As soon as he could read, young Kilpatrick concentrated on military men, showing no interest in his father's occupation, farming. As he grew older, his dreams expanded to include politics. He dreamed that after gaining fame on the battlefield, he would be elected governor of New Jersey and then president of the United States. Before he was twenty, Kilpatrick was stumping rural New Jersey for a local congressman, George Vail, who was seeking renomination.[5]

Opposite:
Hugh Judson Kilpatrick's looks were unremarkable, but he had quite a colorful personality.
(U.S. Army Military History Institute)

The congressman won and rewarded Kilpatrick with an appointment to the United States Military Academy. At West Point, Kilpatrick dropped his first name, preferring to use Judson. He made good grades, graduating seventeenth in a class of forty-five. During his second year at the Academy, he joined the Dialectic Society, playing major roles in different dramas and developing his ability as a public speaker. As a result, he was chosen to give the valedictory address for his graduating class.[6]

When talk of secession swept the country, Kilpatrick irritated cadets from the South with his pro-Union sentiments. As a result, he found himself involved in several fist fights, but despite his small size, he won more than he lost. He was a strong Unionist and so anxious to defend that position that he got up a petition with classmates' signatures, requesting permission for the Class of 1861 to graduate earlier than usual, so its members could serve the nation as quickly as possible. The petition was sent to the War Department, and the request was granted.[7]

On the same April day that Kilpatrick graduated, he married Alice Nailer of New York. All but ten of his classmates attended the ceremony. After a honeymoon of one night, he left his newlywed for Washington and the war. With him he carried a silken banner bearing his wife's name.

Kilpatrick's first assignment was as a lieutenant in the 1st U.S. Artillery, but he had no desire to fight in the regular army. Rather, he preferred the volunteer service, believing he would have a greater opportunity for promotion there. He asked his mathematics instructor at West Point, Gouverneur Warren, to recommend him for a post with a New York regiment. Soon he was commissioned captain of the 5th New York Infantry in Duryee's Zouaves. Working hard, he quickly molded his company into an effective fighting unit, gaining his men's confidence and respect.[8]

Kilpatrick's first assignment in the field involved scouting and foraging expeditions. At the Battle of Big Bethel on June 10, 1861, he saw his first action against the enemy and became the first regular army officer to be wounded during the war. Although the Confederates were victorious, he received praise in the Northern newspapers. Kilpatrick's first experience in battle was promising. He displayed a knack for organization and the ability to lead and gain the confidence of his troops. His report of the engagement, however, greatly exaggerated his part in the battle. He then compounded his deception by sending a copy of the report to the *New York Times*, which published the entire report.

His desire for recognition and his embellishment of his accomplishments soon created a problem. By putting his personal goals above those of his men and the army, he drew the dislike of his fellow officers.[9]

As a result of his performance at Big Bethel, Kilpatrick was promoted to the rank of lieutenant colonel of the 2nd New York Cavalry. While his command lived and trained in a camp outside of Washington, Kilpatrick moved into Willard's Hotel in the city. Here he associated with politicians who might help his career. To help pay for the expensive room, Kilpatrick had dealings with Union sutlers to steer army contracts their way.[10]

Late in the spring of 1862, General McClellan's Army of the Potomac moved into Virginia. Kilpatrick was ordered to join Brigadier General Irvin McDowell, with the responsibility of repulsing any Confederate attack on Washington. As Kilpatrick moved into Confederate territory, he found ways to enhance his income. He confiscated horses from farmers for the Union army, keeping the best ones for himself and selling them in the North. He stole tobacco from plantations and sold it to the sutlers.[11]

While McClellan was active in Virginia, Kilpatrick conducted raids throughout northern Virginia. During one of these raids near Falmouth Heights, he demonstrated a talent for deception and audacity. Although having only one regiment in his command when he found himself confronted by a superior Confederate force, he shouted orders to nonexistent reinforcements, giving the impression that he had a brigade of cavalry with him. Hearing this, the rebels were fooled into retreating across the Rappahannock River.[12]

During the summer of 1862, Kilpatrick's regiment joined Brigadier General George Bayard's cavalry brigade, a part of Major General John Pope's army. The aggressive Pope gave the cavalry a fighting role, encouraging Kilpatrick's raids behind enemy lines. On July 19, Kilpatrick's raiders left Falmouth Heights for Beaver Dam Station on the Virginia Central Railroad. There they burned the depot and captured one prisoner, a yet-unknown Confederate named John S. Mosby.[13]

Kilpatrick continued his successful raids, even making contact with the Confederate Major General J.E.B. Stuart. He proved to be an undaunted raider, able to slip easily behind enemy lines to disrupt Confederate supply and communication lines. When facing the rebels, he had no second thoughts about ordering his men into battle, which often resulted in large casualties; but he did not lead them. Instead he remained in the background. The label "Kill-Cavalry" was well earned.[14] During July and August 1862, Kilpatrick's raiders conducted a successful raid on Stonewall Jackson's communication lines in the Shenandoah Valley, burning depots and destroying railroad tracks and telegraph lines.[15]

In the fall of 1862, however, a formal complaint was filed with the provost marshal alleging that Kilpatrick had stolen a team of mules from a farmer. The investigation that followed revealed Kilpatrick's dealings with sutlers and his sale of confiscated horses and tobacco, and the taking of bribes. As a result, Kilpatrick was arrested and taken to the Old Capitol Prison in Washington. Sworn statements attesting to his criminal acts were taken from one of Kilpatrick's aides, Lieutenant George Burnham, and two of the regimental sutlers. "The affidavits . . . taken in the case of Colonel Kilpatrick leave little question of his guilt," Secretary of War Edwin Stanton concluded.[16]

Fortunately for Kilpatrick, daring cavalry leaders were in great demand. The solicitor in the case, William Whiting, found that the evidence against Kilpatrick was made "orally and not under oath ... yet they render it proper to give the accused the benefit of the doubt." Whiting recommended that the charge against him be dropped. After spending three months in prison, Kilpatrick was released on January 21, 1863.[17]

Kilpatrick returned to a new cavalry organization. Major General Joseph Hooker, now commander of the Army of the Potomac, had combined the cavalry into a single corps of 9,000 horsemen, led by Brigadier General George Stoneman. Kilpatrick was given command of the 1st Brigade in Brigadier General David McMurtrie Gregg's 3rd Division.[18] During the Chancellorsville Campaign in April 1863, Kilpatrick's brigade participated in General Stoneman's raid on the outskirts of Richmond. Although the operation on the whole was not successful, Kilpatrick's brigade acquitted itself well. With a detached force, they captured towns and destroyed lines of communication. By riding sixty miles a day, he penetrated within two miles of Richmond, putting the Confederate capital into a panic. Finally, Kilpatrick had to retreat down the Peninsula to avoid being captured.[19]

In June, now operating under Brigadier General Alfred Pleasonton, Kilpatrick's men engaged Stuart's horsemen near Brandy Station in saber-to-saber fighting. Kilpatrick's brigade charged in three waves, but the first two were repulsed by Confederate artillery fire. His third regiment, however, was able to smash into Confederate forces and scatter them. Stuart rallied his troops and finally forced Kilpatrick to retreat. After a series of charges and counter-charges, Pleasonton's division retired from the field. Although Kilpatrick's name was absent from the list of officers Pleasonton cited for gallantry, shortly after, on June 14, Kilpatrick was promoted to brigadier general.[20]

On June 17, Kilpatrick spotted rebel troops around Aldie, Virginia. Without bothering to determine the enemy's strength or deployment, he sent the 1st Massachusetts forward to attack. "Kilpatrick's standing order was 'Charge God damn 'em,' whether they were five or five thousand," a newspaper reporter wrote. The Confederates retreated out of town, drawing Kilpatrick's men into an ambush. "My poor men were just slaughtered," Captain Charles Francis Adams of the 1st Massachusetts later recalled. Next Kilpatrick sent the 2nd New York into the ambush; more than a hundred of his men were killed in the crossfire. Kilpatrick was devastated by the carnage, but he was determined to make one last effort to dislodge the enemy. This time he sent the 1st Maine, personally leading the charge. The attack was so ferocious that the Confederates withdrew.[21]

On June 28, 1863, the Army of the Potomac was once again reorganized. When Major General George Meade assumed command, Kilpatrick was assigned the 3rd Division. The unit contained two brigades under the newly appointed Brigadier Generals George Custer and Elon Farnsworth. At noon on July 3, Kilpatrick's division arrived at Gettysburg. After Pickett's charge failed, Kilpatrick seized the opportunity to engage the enemy. He ordered Farnsworth to assault the flank of the retreating Confederates. The ground ahead was heavily wooded and covered with large rocks and boulders; a charge over this ground appeared to be suicidal. When Farnsworth questioned the order, Kilpatrick accused him of being afraid to lead the attack. "I'll lead it," Farnsworth replied, "but you must take the responsibility." Farnsworth led the charge, only to be greeted with a heavy enemy barrage; the result was the shattering of his brigade and Farnsworth's early death.[22] The charge had been a fiasco. Kilpatrick's effort provided one small victory for the Confederates at Gettysburg and lost the confidence of his men and his superiors.

In his official report of the battle, Kilpatrick tried to cover up his error by blaming the infantry's failure to exploit the confusion Farnsworth had caused on the Confederate right. In the same report, however, he praised Farnsworth for his valor: "he baptized his star in blood, and ... for the honor of his young brigade and the glory of his corps, he yielded his noble life."[23]

Immediately after the battle, Kilpatrick tried to make amends for his failure by vigorously pursuing Lee into Maryland. He captured some of Lee's wagons and achieved some degree of success against his weakened forces. In reporting these engagements, Kilpatrick exaggerated the number of prisoners taken and the enemy's casualties. He stated in his report that he had "captured a brigade of infantry, two pieces of artillery, two caissons, and a large number of small arms." Kilpatrick also claimed that he had achieved this success without help. He sent a copy of his report to the *New York Times*, where it was published.[24]

Union Brigadier General John Buford's report of Kilpatrick's encounter was entirely different. "I saw two squadrons from General Kilpatrick's division gallop up the hill," Buford wrote, but "their two squadrons were instantly scattered and destroyed by the fire of the rebel brigade. . . . Not a single enemy was found when the ground was examined a few hours afterward. . . . Having alarmed the enemy, he got across the ford before we could get round to his rear." Confronted with the discrepancy, Meade asked Kilpatrick for an explanation, but he had gone to visit his wife and newly born son.[25]

Up until then, few knew how Kilpatrick had stretched the truth in his reports because there were few witnesses to challenge his exaggerated claims. At Gettysburg, however, Kilpatrick's fellow officers discovered that he was not the heroic figure he claimed to be. They saw that he had stayed in the rear when his troops carried out the suicidal attack against Lee's flank. Now they were appalled at his dishonesty in his battle reports. It seemed as though the less he accomplished, the more he stretched the truth, even shifting his blunders to others.[26]

In October, Kilpatrick encountered J.E.B. Stuart again near Buckland, Virginia. Stuart set a trap for the overeager Kilpatrick. Attacked from both flanks by Stuart and Major General Fitzhugh Lee, the trapped Union troops scattered. Kilpatrick was humiliated and his career seemed to be ruined. At this low point, he was to receive more distressing news. In November his wife died of influenza; two months later his son joined her.[27]

Kilpatrick was anxious to redeem himself; he quickly devised a plan to do so. In early 1864, he expressed the opinion that a raid on Richmond was possible and that he would be willing to lead it. Major General John Sedgwick ordered Kilpatrick to Washington to discuss his plan with Lincoln. Kilpatrick's proposal for the raid on Richmond would involve 4,000 mounted horsemen. En route, he would destroy railroad bridges and distribute Lincoln's amnesty proclamation. Once in Richmond, the raiders would capture Jefferson Davis and free

Union prisoners. He believed the prospects for success were good because the Confederates had few cavalry to defend the capital.[28] Impressed by Kilpatrick's confidence of success, President Lincoln gave his approval.

For Kilpatrick's plan to be successful, he would need to surprise the Confederates. On the morning of February 28, Kilpatrick left Stevensburg, Virginia, with 4,000 troops. Under his personal command were 3,500 troops who were to strike Richmond from the north. A detachment of 500, led by twenty-one-year-old Colonel Ulric Dahlgren, was to attack Richmond from the south. The raid began smoothly enough. Both Kilpatrick and Dahlgren met with little opposition, and they were able to destroy railroad lines and distribute hundreds of copies of the president's proclamation. On March 1, Kilpatrick's raiders reached the outskirts of Richmond. "We were so close that we could ... count the spires of the churches," one of his men recalled. Kilpatrick waited for the sound of rifle fire that would signal Dahlgren's attack from the south. But Dahlgren's progress had been stymied by the high waters of the James River, forcing him to find another route. Dahlgren would eventually attack from the west, much later than planned. Kilpatrick waited outside of Richmond for two hours, but when Dahlgren still had not attacked, he retired east toward the Chickahominy River. At 5:00 P.M., with snow falling, Kilpatrick crossed the river and set up camp near Mechanicsville.[29]

Despite the cold and icy conditions, Kilpatrick decided to make another attempt at completing his mission. His plan was to send two small detachments into the Confederate capital, one to free prisoners and the other to kidnap President Jefferson Davis. But before his men could set off, they were attacked by a small force of 300 Confederates led by Major General Wade Hampton. Not realizing the size of Hampton's force, Kilpatrick withdrew to the safety of the Union camp at New Kent Court House.[30]

In the meantime, Colonel Dahlgren attempted to enter Richmond, but his efforts were thwarted. In an ambush fight, Dahlgren's detachment was cut to pieces, and he was killed.[31] Papers were found on Dahlgren's body describing plans to burn Richmond and kill President Davis and his Cabinet. When the papers were taken to Davis, he found them amusing. "This means you, Mr. Benjamin," he said to his secretary of state. But others in Richmond were not as amused. General Braxton Bragg, Davis's military advisor, wanted the men who had accompanied Dahlgren on the raid to be executed and the papers published. Robert E. Lee, however, was opposed to killing the captives: "Acts in

*After Uric Dahlgren died, plans to assassi-
nate Jefferson Davis were found in his coat.
Though Kilpatrick denied any knowledge of
the "Dahlgren Papers," many believed he had
written them.*

(National Archives and Records Administration)

addition to intentions," he said, "are necessary to constitute crime." The captives were not killed, but the papers were published.[32]

Union leaders believed that the rebels had made up the stories about the
plans to kill Davis to arouse Confederate emotions. General George Meade, on
the other hand, suspected that Kilpatrick was the author of the "Dahlgren
Papers," but when questioned, he denied having given any instructions to
Dahlgren. As a courtesy to Lee, General Meade sent a statement to him indicating that "neither the United States Government, myself, nor General Kilpatrick authorized, sanctioned, or approved . . . any act not . . . in accordance
with the usages of war."[33]

Meade took the botched raid as an opportunity to demote Kilpatrick to
brigade command. As a result, Kilpatrick requested to be transferred to the
western theater; on April 15, 1864, his request was granted and he was ordered
to report to Major General William T. Sherman. Sherman welcomed him.[34]

As a result of his defeat and censure in the east, Kilpatrick was no longer as cocky and self-assured as he had been earlier. Nevertheless, he made an effort to fit into Sherman's command. Soon after joining his new division, he spearheaded the federal drive through Tennessee and into Georgia. In a battle outside of Resaca in May, Kilpatrick was badly wounded in the thigh, but by August 18, he had recuperated sufficiently enough to be able to lead a raid against rebel communications south of Atlanta, destroying miles of track. When his raiders were challenged by Confederate cavalry who threatened to surround them, Kilpatrick mustered up his spirit and led a charge through the Confederate cavalry to safety.[35]

During Sherman's march to the sea, Kilpatrick made a name for himself, becoming infamous to Georgians. His men pillaged one plantation after another. "When the main body of Kilpatrick's army came up," Catherine Whithead, a young lady whose plantation had been ravaged, wrote in her diary, "they commenced the destruction and committed every kind of depredation." Kilpatrick's treatment of the slaves was no better, Whithead wrote: "They took everything from the Negroes, at which I was much surprised as they professed to love them so much. They stole all their clothes and money and whatever would be at all useful to themselves." The plundering began at the top. "Even Kilpatrick asked for silver," she continued, "and when the General condescends to anything of that kind you cannot expect anything more from the men."[36]

At another farm, Kilpatrick confiscated horses to replace his own worn-out mounts. His men collected about 500 more horses than they needed, so Kilpatrick ordered the surplus killed. A farmer watched in horror as the horses were killed, the corpses lying on the ground in his yard. "My God," he said, realizing that he could not bury so many animals. "I'll have to move."[37] Although Kilpatrick's actions during the Union's march through Georgia violated the rules for the treatment of civilians, they were a part of General Sherman's overall policy of total war.

During Sherman's march, Kilpatrick was involved in a running war with Confederate Major General Joseph Wheeler and his cavalry. Because Wheeler was able to slow Sherman's advance, Kilpatrick was called upon to rid the area of the troublesome general. In November, Kilpatrick moved his raiders north toward Augusta. Wheeler took the bait, thinking Kilpatrick's horsemen were the vanguard for Sherman's advance. In the meantime, Sherman was moving unmolested in another direction toward Savannah. When Sherman reached

Kilpatrick and his cavalry destroyed much of Georgia during Sherman's march to the sea.
(James E. Taylor, Western Reserve Historical Society, Cleveland, Ohio)

Savannah just before Christmas 1864, he wrote to Kilpatrick praising his efforts: "The fact that to you, in great measure, we owe the march of four strong infantry columns . . . over 300 miles through the enemy's country . . . , is honor enough for any cavalry commander."[38]

Marching through the Carolinas, Sherman increased his efforts to make the South suffer. At the beginning of the campaign, Kilpatrick issued large quantities of matches to his troops, leaving no doubt about his intentions. "In after years when travelers passing through South Carolina shall see chimney stacks without houses, and the country desolate," he said, "and shall ask 'who did this?' some Yankee will answer, 'Kilpatrick's cavalry.'" To his foot soldiers he said, "There'll be damned little for you infantrymen to destroy after I've passed through that hellhole of secession."[39] On April 26, General Joseph Johnston surrendered his army to General Sherman near Durham Station, North Carolina. Just before the war's end, Kilpatrick was promoted to major general of volunteers and brevet major general in the regular army.

Kilpatrick soon left his post to go home and campaign for one of the Republican hopefuls in the 1865 New Jersey gubernatorial race. When his candidate failed to get the nomination, he went to work for his opponent, Marcus Ward. Of all his talents, Kilpatrick's ability as a speaker was his best. He proved this during the election. As a reward for his efforts for the Republican Party, he was named ambassador to Chile. In South America, he met, courted, and married Louisa Valdivieso, cousin of a future president of Chile and niece of an archbishop of the Catholic Church. In 1869, Kilpatrick was recalled from his post and made an unsuccessful run to be governor of New Jersey. Still entertaining the hope of being president, Kilpatrick ran for a seat in the U.S. House of Representatives, but lost. In 1881, President James Garfield appointed him to his old post in Chile.[40]

On July 20, 1881, while in Santiago, Kilpatrick was struck by Bright's disease, a deterioration of the kidneys. In December, just as it looked like he would recover, Kilpatrick suffered a relapse and died. He was forty-five years old. Kilpatrick was buried in the Valdivieso vaults in the Church of Sagrario in Santiago. A year later, his body was returned to the United States and reinterred in the cemetery at West Point. Classmates and men who served under Kilpatrick contributed money to pay for a monument to mark his grave.[41]

12   *Thunderbolt of the Confederacy*

JOHN HUNT MORGAN

TO MANY in the South, John Hunt Morgan was a symbol of the Southern code of honor, a system of ethics rooted in the past. A Southern gentleman was evaluated based on this code of honor. But Morgan was more than just a symbol of Southern honor; he was a hero. Like Robin Hood, he was a bold outlaw who broke the restraints of traditional warfare. The Confederacy had many heroes — Robert E. Lee, Thomas "Stonewall" Jackson, J.E.B. Stuart, and Albert S. Johnston — but more than others, Morgan was the ideal of a chivalrous knight.[1]

John Hunt Morgan was a fine specimen of a man. His movements were graceful; his physical features, handsome. His boyish smile was one that was hard to forget. "It comes over his face like a laugh over a child's countenance — having in it an innocence of humor which is very beautiful to me," one of his lady friends recalled. All ages and classes of people admired him, but none as much as the young Southern belles. Wherever he went, women flocked to see him, touch him, and get his autograph or a button from his jacket. His horse, Black Bess, had to be guarded to keep his admirers from cutting souvenirs from her mane and tail. His good looks, along with a bit of roguishness, made him a man with a strong sexual attraction. Young ladies who had the opportunity to be with him, even for just a short time, immediately fell in love with him.[2]

Morgan was said to have had "no annoying habits or negative characteristics" to detract from his mythical image. From afar his persona was one that few could emulate; yet when people met him in person, the attraction grew even stronger. Emma Holmes, a Charleston belle, wrote in her diary about an evening a friend had spent with him: "She said he was extremely different from what she imagined. [He was] so mild and gentle in his manner that she would not have taken him for a soldier but for his boots and spurs, so unwarrior-like did he seem."[3]

In the North, Morgan was a source of grief to the military and of fear to the civilians. Federal troops and civilians both referred to him as "King of the Horse Thieves," a label deeply resented by his own men and those who knew him best. In the South he was called the "Thunderbolt of the Confederacy." In Kentucky, especially, one was either for him or against him; there was no middle ground.[4]

Morgan's family ties were all with the South. His father, Calvin Morgan, left his home in Huntsville, Alabama, to go to Lexington, Kentucky, to marry Henrietta Hunt, one of the city's most beautiful women. On June 1, 1825, John Hunt Morgan was born, the first of Calvin and Henrietta's eight children. Calvin

---

Opposite:
John Hunt Morgan's fine physical features and flirtatious manner attracted ladies everywhere he went. (Library of Congress)

Morgan worked as the overseer for his father-in-law's plantation. Morgan was not only inculcated with the South's system of honor valued by his father's family, but he was expected to meet his grandfather's standards of conduct.[5]

Young Morgan was easygoing, softspoken, and very courteous. In the eyes of many he was a typical Southern gentleman who openly expressed his feelings. Those who knew him best said he was either high when he enjoyed success or, if things did not go well, sunk to depths of gloom and despair.[6]

At the age of sixteen, Morgan entered Transylvania College in Lexington. He was described as a restless, undisciplined youth by his instructors and one who was not destined to be an outstanding student. His parents and grandfather were disappointed in his performance. Feeling that it was impossible to live up to their expectations, John compensated by engaging in boyish pranks and engaging other young men in duels. Although dueling was illegal in Kentucky, Southern society recognized it as a test of manliness and the way a young man could demonstrate his status as a gentleman and earn the right to lead. Morgan was unable to gain recognition for his academic achievement, but when he challenged a fellow university student to a duel, he gained the recognition he sought. Because he had violated the university's rule prohibiting dueling, Morgan was suspended for the remainder of the term. He left the university and never returned.[7]

In 1846, when the United States went to war with Mexico, twenty-one-year-old Morgan joined the 1st Kentucky Cavalry and was commissioned lieutenant. He reached Mexico in time to participate in the Battle of Buena Vista. The Kentucky Volunteers gave an excellent account of themselves, and on July 8, 1847, Morgan was mustered out. He now turned his attention to earning a living in the business world, acquiring a hemp factory and a woolen mill. Both enterprises prospered, to the surprise of those who had known him as an immature youth at Transylvania. Morgan branched out to buying and selling slaves and taking a major part in community activities.[8]

During this time Morgan also took on another responsibility, marrying eighteen-year-old Rebecca Grantz Bruce. In addition to being attractive, Rebecca was mild mannered and said to have all the Christian virtues of "gentleness, meekness, forbearance, and long suffering." After their wedding, the two moved in with Rebecca's parents. Five years later, Rebecca gave birth to a stillborn son. Shortly after, she developed pain and soreness in one of her legs and was diagnosed with septic thrombophlebitis, the infection of a blood clot in a vein in her leg. There was no known cure for the condition and as time progressed, she became an invalid. Morgan was frustrated with the situation; there seemed little he could do to help her or make her comfortable.[9]

By the 1850s, his invalid wife was totally dependent on him, and, with the death of both his father and father-in-law, Morgan became the man of both households and father figure for his younger brothers. When frontier conditions and the secession crisis in the South led to the organization of militia companies in Kentucky, Governor Charles Morehead encouraged this movement by offering weapons from the state arsenal, and Morgan raised a company of infantry, becoming its captain. They were known as the Lexington Rifles, and they soon became the pride of Lexington.[10]

After Fort Sumter was fired upon by Confederate guns and the Southern states began to secede, Kentucky hoped to remain neutral. Kentuckians had no desire to see force applied against the rebel states, nor did they desire to secede from the Union themselves. Although many parts of Kentucky had strong Southern sentiments, the state would remain pro-Union. However, in April 1861, when President Lincoln issued a call for volunteers, Kentucky Governor Beriah Magoffin replied with an emphatic no. "Kentucky will furnish no troops for the wicked purpose of subduing her sister Southern states," he said. John J. Crittenden, one of Kentucky's representatives in Congress, spoke in favor of neutrality: "Let us not be forced into civil strife for the North, nor dragged into it for the South — take no part with either." For John Hunt Morgan, there was no dilemma; he would cast his lot with the South.[11]

In July 1861, Rebecca died. With his wife gone, nothing remained to prevent him from joining the Confederacy. Although despondent about the loss of his wife, he moved out on his own, taking his Lexington Rifles with him. Despite the hopes of many Kentuckians for their state to remain neutral, peaceful coexistence was not to be. On September 3, Confederate troops, under Major General Leonidas Polk, moved into Kentucky to fortify the western end of their defense line. Two days later, federal troops under Brigadier General Ulysses S. Grant occupied two strategic points in Kentucky.[12]

In October, Morgan, with a contingent of eighty-four men, was sworn into the Confederate army. Morgan was named captain and his brother-in-law, Basil Duke, became first lieutenant. In November, General Albert S. Johnston ordered Morgan and his Lexington Rifles, now having grown in size, to Bowling Green. Morgan's cavalry had just settled down when the vanguards of federal Brigadier

General Don Carlos Buell's army threatened the area. Morgan was ordered to disrupt the federal supply line by burning the Louisville and Nashville Railroad bridge across Bacon's Creek, south of Louisville. Leaving only burning embers behind, Morgan ordered his men back south. Although the burning of the Bacon's Creek bridge was a minor incident, it marked the first of many such raids against the L & N Railroad by Morgan and his men.[13]

By February 1862, Morgan and his command were camped at La Vergne, Tennessee, southeast of Nashville. General Johnston, fearing he would be trapped behind enemy lines after the fall of Fort Donelson, ordered his army to march to Nashville. Six days later, Morgan served as a rear guard as the army abandoned Nashville. Just behind them was the vanguard of General Buell's Army of the Ohio. While Johnston reorganized his army, Morgan headed for Nashville with a raiding party of fifteen. Under the darkness of the night, Morgan found his target, the steamboat *Minnetonka*, tied up at the wharf on the Cumberland River. After setting the boat on fire, they were discovered by federal cavalry and were forced to flee. Morgan's Raiders suffered their first casualty, one of many that would follow as the war continued.[14]

On March 15, Morgan's Raiders were involved in their first railroad raid. At Gallatin, Tennessee, they stopped a train, putting the locomotive out of operation and setting fire to the freight cars. In addition, they destroyed all of the equipment around the Gallatin depot. Attacks of this type would become the trademark for Morgan's future raids.[15]

In between raids, Morgan had time to socialize. There were frequent trips to the genial Colonel Charles Ready's home for dinner and visitation with his attractive twenty-one-year-old daughter, Martha (Mattie). In a short time a romance blossomed, and he moved his base of operation from La Vergne to Murfreesboro to be closer to her. Mattie had other suitors, and even a proposal of marriage from Illinois Representative Samuel Scott Marshall, but she wanted to marry for love and not for position or convenience. Like other young women of the period, Mattie was caught up in the spirit of romance that was so much a part of upper-class Southern society. It is not difficult to understand why Mattie and the gallant John Hunt Morgan were attracted to each other.[16]

On one occasion Morgan came directly to her house after a raid. When it was discovered that he was there, a large crowd gathered outside just to have a chance to see him. At another time Morgan halted his command before the Ready house, and informed Mattie that he was on his way to Nashville to capture a Union general to exchange for General Simon Bolivar Buckner, who had been captured at Fort Donelson. Promising to return with the prisoner, he mounted his horse and rode away. Dressed with Union overcoats over their uniforms, Morgan's party stopped an unsuspecting wagon train, which assumed that Morgan and his men were Union soldiers checking their passes. When the raiders drew their revolvers, they realized they had been captured and surrendered without a fight. Soon Morgan had eighty prisoners, but no general to trade for Buckner. Morgan continued his masquerade, capturing other officers, but again, no general. When Morgan returned from his mission, he went to the Ready house. Halting the column, he presented the prisoners to Mattie and her sister.[17]

On another occasion, again disguised as Union officers, Morgan and his aide rode into Gallatin and went to the telegraph office. Morgan asked the operator what news he had. "Nothing sir, except it is reported that damned rebel, Captain John Morgan, is this side of the Cumberland with some of his cavalry." The operator then drew his revolver and said, "I wish I could get sight of the damned rascal. I'd make a hole through him larger than he would find pleasant." When Morgan identified himself, the operator dropped his gun in fear and kept quiet while Morgan gathered up his code books and secret dispatches and made good his escape. By now Morgan's pretending to be a Union officer had become a ritual, and he would continue to look for opportunities to employ this practice to throw the enemy off guard.[18]

For the time being, Morgan had to put his romance on hold. Just four days after his visit to Gallatin, he and his raiders were ordered to join General Johnston's army at Corinth in northern Mississippi. On April 4, Morgan received word that he had been promoted to full colonel. Within two days he would be engaged in one of the major battles of the war near a little church called Shiloh.[19]

By the time Morgan's Raiders were engaged, the battle had raged for several hours. It was an eye-opening experience for them; the noise and carnage were unlike anything they had experienced before. In the ensuing battle, the Raiders quickly learned that cavalry units could not fight effectively in a wooded area. Dismounting, they fought like infantry, a tactic they later repeated on other occasions. The casualties were high; Basil Duke, Morgan's second in command, was wounded, but he would live to fight another day. When victory seemed to be in sight for the Confederates, a stray bullet struck General Johnston in the leg. At first the wound was thought to be superficial, but the bullet had severed an artery. That afternoon, when General Johnston died, the Confederates lost one of their best generals.[20] General P.G.T. Beauregard replaced Johnston. When Grant moved 30,000 fresh troops into the battle, the Confederates were forced to give ground in the direction of Corinth; as they did, Morgan's Rangers served as a rear guard.

By the end of April, Morgan was ready to march eastward into Tennessee. On May 4, the Raiders arrived at the outskirts of Lebanon, Tennessee, where they were welcomed with open arms. Many of the residents offered to share their food and shelter. Their stay in Lebanon was interrupted soon after dawn when federal troops rushed into town. One of the guards was able to spread the alarm, alerting Morgan and his men in time for them to mount their horses and gallop out of town. The chase that followed was later described as the "Lebanon Races." In his haste to escape across the Cumberland River on a ferry boat, Morgan had to leave his horse, Black Bess, behind. It was the last time he ever saw his faithful steed. Worse than that was the high number of casualties his command had suffered.[21]

Disheartened at first, Morgan's spirit rose when some of the men he had feared lost found their way back to camp. With replacements added to his command, Morgan was ready to make a raid into Kentucky. On the morning of May 12, Morgan's party rode into the village of Cave City and found a freight train standing in the station. After setting fire to the cars, they blew up the engine. Shortly after, another train approached the station, and it was quickly captured. To their surprise most of the passenger cars were filled with Union soldiers and some of their wives. One of the officers, Major W. A. Coffey, was an old acquaintance of Morgan. When Coffey's wife pleaded with him not to kill her husband, Morgan, always gracious in the presence of women, explained to her that he was not planning to kill anyone. He decided not to burn the train because he did not want the women passengers to be uncomfortable while they waited to be rescued. In searching the train, Morgan's men found $8,000 in federal currency. Taking the money, Morgan invited Major Coffey and the women passengers to join him and his men for lunch at the hotel in town. After lunch, Morgan placed Major Coffey and the women back on the train and told the engineer to take everyone back to Louisville.[22]

Leaving his men at Chattanooga, Morgan traveled to Corinth, Mississippi, hoping to obtain permission to organize a regiment. Whatever loss of reputation Morgan might have suffered as a result of the debacle at Lebanon, it was more than eliminated at Cave City. All along the way to Corinth he was greeted by crowds of admirers who treated him as a hero. An editor in Atlanta wrote: "Hurrah for Morgan! ... Our people would rather get a sight of him than Queen Victoria. Again we say, Hurrah for Morgan!" Southern journalists played up Morgan's successes but paid little attention to his rout at Lebanon. The $8,000 take at Cave City was exaggerated until it became $350,000 by the time the news reached Richmond. What received the most attention, however, was the way Morgan had treated the women on the captured train; it confirmed their belief that Southern men were chivalrous. Morgan's reputation as a "Christian, Southern gentleman, and a humane warrior" was now well established.[23]

Morgan's trip to Corinth proved to be a success. He was authorized to organize the 2nd Kentucky Cavalry regiment with a complement of 400 men, including two companies of Texas Rangers. In a short time the regiment grew to 900 men, not quite brigade size, but Morgan declared it a brigade nevertheless and took the unoffical title of acting brigadier general. In December 1862, Morgan could use the title officially when he was promoted to brigadier general.[24]

On July 4, 1862, Morgan and his men headed for Kentucky. The Raiders' first brush with federal troops was at Tompkinsville. After a short encounter, Morgan's men routed the Federals, taking 300 prisoners, a number of good horses, and a generous supply of food. A detail was assigned to take prisoners back to Tennessee while Morgan moved on.[25]

Startled by the unexpected Confederate raid on Kentucky, Union reactions were to bolster key towns and cities there with additional federal troops. In Glasgow, Morgan issued a proclamation urging local citizens to join him: "Kentuckians! I have come to liberate you from the hands of your oppressors." Although the message was highly publicized, few responded.[26]

At Horse Cave, Kentucky, Morgan sent George Ellsworth, a telegrapher, on a night mission to tap telegraph lines and intercept Union messages. Ellsworth was able to cut into the lines, engage the enemy in conversation to obtain information, and then send bogus dispatches designed to mislead and confuse them. As a thunderstorm struck, Ellsworth cut into the telegraph line connecting Louisville and Nashville. Despite the storm that at one point caused sparks to fly from his telegraph keys, Ellsworth was able to gather information to allow Morgan to select a route for his march that would elude enemy troops. For his effort at Horse Cave, "Lightning" Ellsworth, as he became known, was given a position on Morgan's staff.[27]

With the information he needed, Morgan headed for Lebanon. Before the day was over, the Raiders had captured the town without a single casualty, taking over 200 prisoners and destroying supplies valued at $100,000. Again Morgan issued a proclamation calling for "the willing hands of fifty thousand of Kentucky's brave" to join him in destroying the Union invaders. Once more the response was less than encouraging.[28]

As Morgan's troopers moved further into Kentucky, destroying railroad bridges and lines of communication, Union commanders throughout the state panicked. Brigadier General Jeremiah Boyle, commander of the troops in Louisville, was in such a state of frenzy that he fired off telegrams to Washington which grossly overestimated Morgan's strength, pleading for help.[29]

From Lebanon, the Raiders moved through the Kentucky towns of Springfield, Herrodsburg, and Versailles. When Morgan learned that there were several thousand troops at Lexington, he wisely changed his plans and headed for Georgetown. Morgan then sent a few of his men into Lexington with recruiting posters, which they placed throughout the town. As a result, sufficient recruits showed up the next day to form a new company.[30]

With the Federals close on their heels, it was clear to Morgan that he had to leave Kentucky as soon as possible or run the risk of being captured, or worse. Weary, but pleased, the Raiders crossed the Cumberland River. A few days later they were safe in Tennessee. In what is referred to by historians as Morgan's First Kentucky Raid, Morgan started with 900 men, returned with over 1,200, traveled over 1,000 miles, captured 1,200 troops, destroyed bridges and military supplies, and disrupted communication lines. His casualties during the twenty-four days totaled only ninety killed, wounded, or missing. Morgan's success on his Kentucky raid helped to raise Southern morale and demonstrated that the North was vulnerable to attack by raiding parties.[31]

Although Morgan was popular with his men, he often had difficulty with his superiors. General Braxton Bragg was critical of Morgan's disciplinary procedures. His form of discipline was consistent with his own behavior. He permitted his men to keep their independence in personal matters as long as it didn't interfere with their official duties. If a man disappeared from base camp for a few days between raids, Morgan would not question this as long as he was available for the next raid. "I prefer fifty men who gladly obey me, to a division I have to watch and punish," he said. Fighting behind enemy lines required men who often had to operate on their own; this, Morgan believed, required self-motivation, unity of purpose, and loyalty. Morgan knew his men and showed interest in their welfare. He was courteous and gracious, and he acknowledged his subordinates' achievements. He disregarded seniority for promotion, basing it entirely on merit. "Seniority means deeds," he said. In battle, Morgan led by example. His men admired his disregard for danger, energy, and dedication to the cause.[32]

In July 1862, General Bragg received recommendations from Generals Forrest and Morgan that convinced him to attack Union General Don Carlos Buell in Kentucky. Morgan believed that there were 30,000 Kentuckians anxious to join the Confederate army; Forrest believed that only arms and support were preventing them from doing so. The plan of attack would come from two fronts. Bragg would move northwest across Tennessee and cut Buell's supply line. Brigadier General Edmund Kirby Smith would move north from Knoxville and cross into Kentucky. Bragg believed that the people of Kentucky had been forced to remain in the Union and, if given the opportunity, would rebel and force the Yankees from their state. Then the liberated Kentuckians would be free to join his Army of Eastern Tennessee. On August 10, Morgan received orders to raid the L & N Railroad at Gallatin and cut off all of Buell's supply lines from Louisville. This, they hoped, would be a successful raid, drawing Buell's army northward.[33]

On August 12, Morgan's men captured the federal troops at Gallatin, burned a train and a nearby bridge, blocked a tunnel, and destroyed large stretches of tracks. The wrecking of the railroad tunnel and the cutting off of supplies from Louisville got Buell's attention just as Bragg had hoped it would. With 30,000 men, General Bragg marched out of Chattanooga toward Murfreesboro. A few days later, General Buell's army of 35,000 moved northward to take up a position at Murfreesboro. At Richmond, Kentucky, General Smith captured 4,000 federal troops and then moved northward to threaten Cincinnati, Ohio. With the Confederates at their gateway, a citizen's army of 50,000 was formed to protect the city from Smith's invasion.[34]

In the meantime, Morgan found a printing press. Gathering together members of his command who had newspaper experience, he published the first issue of a short-lived newspaper. He named it the *Vidette*, after a mounted sentry in advance of an army. In one of the first issues, Morgan published his policy of retaliation. It also contained information about the Raiders' activities, military operations, and letters from friends in Kentucky. The paper did not survive beyond November, but it was unique, particularly because the paper was produced by a cavalry unit while in enemy territory.[35]

On August 28, Morgan received orders from General Smith to join him in Lexington. Morgan and his 2nd Kentucky arrived at Lexington on September 4. Wearing his best full-dress uniform and followed by his entire command of 900 men, Morgan rode into town; it was a moment of triumph for him. Friends and Confederate sympathizers crowded the streets, cheering and waving as Morgan made his way to his family home. Friends and admirers presented him with gifts, including a thoroughbred gelding name Glencoe; it was, indeed, his finest hour.[36]

With Bragg between General Buell's army and Louisville, Buell had nothing left to do but fight, and fight he did. On September 20, Buell attacked Bragg at Munfordville. Quickly Buell pushed past Bragg and made his way to Louisville, where he had a chance to rest and receive reinforcements. Bragg's plan to liberate Kentucky had failed. The 30,000 Kentuckians did not revolt, and Bragg and Smith were forced to return to Tennessee. Despite the overall failure of the mission, Morgan was acclaimed for his part in the venture. News of his victories and the presence of 1,400 prisoners, following Confederate reverses and a period of low morale, were particularly welcomed. War clerk J. B. Jones wrote in his diary: "Glorious Colonel Morgan has dashed into Kentucky, whipped everything before him, and got off unharmed. He has but a little over a thousand men, and captured that number of prisoners."[37]

Near the end of November, Bragg's army returned to Murfreesboro and began to prepare their winter camp. At the same time, Morgan was planning for a raid on Hartsville, Tennessee, forty miles north of Murfreesboro, where one of his scouts had discovered a federal storehouse loaded with supplies. Despite the fact that 2,500 Union troops stood guard, Morgan was confident he could capture the garrison. On December 7, 1862, Morgan and 1,250 men rode toward Hartsville. Despite freezing cold, the men arrived at their destination, catching the Union troops off guard. Although the Federals put up a determined fight, Morgan's Raiders quickly scored another victory. In addition to wagonloads of much needed supplies, Morgan took 2,000 prisoners. General Bragg congratulated Morgan, writing, "The intelligence, zeal, and gallantry displayed by [Morgan] will serve as example and an incentive to still more honorable deeds." Soon after, Morgan was promoted to brigadier general, and Basil Duke to colonel.[38]

After returning from Hartsville, Morgan took time out to marry Mattie Ready in the parlor of the Ready residence. General Leonidas Polk, wearing his Episcopal bishop's robe, performed the ceremony. Four other generals — Bragg, Hardee, Cheatham, and Breckinridge — were in attendance. Morgan did not have long to spend with his new bride. Soon after the wedding, he met with staff members to plan another raid. General Bragg received information that Union Major General William Rosecrans was stockpiling supplies at Nashville in preparation for a spring offensive. Morgan proposed a raid north into Kentucky to cut the supply lines behind Rosecrans. He assured General Bragg that it would be an easy matter to slip into Kentucky. The difficult part would be in getting his men back safely after destroying the bridges and rail lines.[39]

On December 21, Morgan assembled his men. His command had now grown to seven regiments. The plan was simple; General Forrest would operate in west Tennessee to harass Grant's supply line while Morgan swept north around Rosecrans's garrison at Nashville.[40] The next morning Morgan left Murfreesboro with 4,000 horsemen. By nightfall on the twenty-third, the Raiders had crossed into Kentucky. On Christmas Eve, they entered Glasgow and overpowered a small contingent of federal troops stationed there. On Christmas day, Morgan's Raiders were met with stiff resistance, but soon they were able to sweep past it. In short time, the first break was made in the Union supply line. "Lightning" Ellsworth cut into the telegraph line and sent fictitious messages up and down the line. The raid continued with little opposition, allowing Morgan's men to move at their leisure and to destroy selected targets.[41]

Morgan's activities did not go unnoticed. The size of Morgan's command made it difficult to move without being seen or reported. Pursued by federal cavalry and harassed along the way by local militia, Morgan found it much easier to get into Kentucky than to leave. On December 30, a big snowstorm struck southern Kentucky, making Morgan's trip back to Tennessee even more difficult. On January 25, 1863, Morgan's Christmas raid came to an end; the regiment rode into Smithville, Tennessee with 2,000 prisoners and a large quantity of supplies. Morgan's losses were unbelievable — only two killed and twenty-four wounded. In addition, Morgan had accomplished his objective of disrupting Rosecrans's supply lines.[42]

While Morgan was busy in Kentucky, Rosecrans had marched from Nashville toward Murfreesboro to challenge Bragg's army. When the battle was over, both armies withdrew from the field badly bloodied; Bragg fell back to Tullahoma. Although Morgan's Kentucky Christmas raid had been a success, his efforts had come too late to hinder Rosecrans.[43]

During the winter of 1862–63, Morgan set up his headquarters at McMinnville, forty miles east of Murfreesboro. As a result, Morgan was united with his wife again. The Raiders kept active during this time, but Morgan was not with them on most of their raids, preferring to spend more time with his wife and less with his military duties. When his absence became noticed, one of Morgan's uncles wrote to Mattie: "I feel you are sticking too close to your husband." In Morgan's absence, his command had become careless and had failed to detect a group of Federals who were able to slip through their lines. His second in command, Colonel Basil Duke, was injured in a raid. Confederate morale was dipping. Morgan sensed that it was time for another raid, something spectacular to lift Confederate morale. The opportunity would soon present itself.[44]

During the summer of 1863, General Bragg's army was in danger of attacks from both General Rosecrans at Murfreesboro and Major General Ambrose Burnside near the Ohio River. As a result, Bragg decided to fall back to Chattanooga to a safer position. To cover his withdrawal, Bragg dispatched Morgan's Raiders to harass and delay any federal forces moving south in Kentucky. But he also gave very specific orders to Morgan to stay south of the Ohio River so he could be recalled quickly if needed.[45] Morgan did not tell his men; only to Basil Duke did he confide that General Bragg's orders restricted him to operate only in Kentucky.[46]

Morgan, confident because of his earlier successes, decided on a bold move. Despite Bragg's orders, he would cross the Ohio River into Indiana, hoping to draw Union forces away from Bragg. Then he would march into Ohio and return to Confederate territory by way of western Virginia. On July 2, Morgan's Raiders, now 2,500 strong, crossed the Cumberland River. Scouts were sent ahead to the Ohio River to find a safe place to cross. On July 4, he encountered Union troops at Tebb's Bend. After a three-hour battle, the Raiders moved on, but the effort had been costly; Morgan had seventy-one dead or wounded and the Federals had been alerted. Newspapers spread the word, greatly exaggerating the size of his force, with figures ranging from 4,000 to 11,000 men.[47]

On July 8, Morgan reached the Ohio River at Brandenburg, using steamships

Morgan and his men set out for a raid in this romanticized illustration. (Library of Congress)

that had been captured earlier by the advanced force to cross. Federal gunboats and the home guards fired on them, but by midnight they had safely made the crossing. Morgan had the boats burned behind him so that none of his men would think of returning to Kentucky. At Corydon, Indiana, the Raiders encountered a group of 500 armed civilians, but they were easily brushed aside. From then on Morgan would be constantly attacked and harassed by small groups of civilians and militia, all of which would take their toll on his command.[48]

Despite the constant harassment, the Raiders found Indiana to be a land of milk and honey. Here the farms had not been touched by the war. With the approach of the Raiders, many families fled, leaving food and supplies for the taking. At Indianapolis, the governor declared a state of emergency. Notices asking all male citizens to arm themselves and form militia companies were posted throughout the city. More than 60,000 men throughout the state answered the call. Terror spread as Morgan made his way to the Ohio border. On July 13, Morgan crossed over the Whitewater River into Ohio, passing just to the north of Cincinnati. As the Raiders passed through the Ohio towns, the pillaging and looting increased. Morgan's men stole horses, broke into stores, and helped themselves to whatever they wanted.[49]

Morgan soon realized that he had made a mistake by going as far as he had. Local militia and armed citizens contested his advance at nearly every town. "It was a terrible, trying march," Duke wrote. "Strong men fell out of their saddles for want of sleep." By now it became apparent to the federal troops who were pursuing Morgan that he was heading for Buffington Ford at Portland, a small steamboat landing, where he could cross the Ohio into western Virginia. Here a strong Union column under Brigadier General Edward Hobson intercepted Morgan. Tired by over two weeks of constant riding, often as much as twenty-one hours a day, and outnumbered, a portion of Morgan's command under Colonel Duke surrendered. Duke was able to hold the enemy at bay until Morgan could escape with a contingent of 1,200 of his men.[50]

Morgan's band wandered through Ohio with Union troops in close pursuit. When Morgan reach Senecaville, he knocked at the door of a house to get directions. A woman, whose husband was serving in the war, opened the door and invited him in. They talked for a few minutes and she gave him directions. As he was leaving, she confessed that she had almost shot him through the window as he approached but had decided against it. Morgan replied that she had not pulled the trigger because "at that moment my wife is on her knees praying for my safety."[51]

The sweltering temperature now began to take its toll on Morgan and his Raiders; each day more men were lost. Finally on July 26, Morgan and the remainder of his command surrendered to Captain James Burdick. When Brigadier General James Shackleford arrived, he refused to accept Morgan's formal military surrender. Morgan asked to be returned to the field, preferring to die in battle rather than be taken as a criminal, but his request was denied.[52]

Early the next day, under heavy guard, Morgan was taken to Cincinnati. Vengeance was swift. Ohio's Governor David Tod insisted that he and his men should be treated as civil prisoners. Morgan, in his typical optimistic manner, believed that he would be exchanged or paroled. But because of his marauding actions, Morgan would not be treated as a soldier, but rather as a horse thief.

On July 28, General-in-Chief Henry Halleck directed that Morgan and the officers captured with his command be sent to the Ohio State Penitentiary at Columbus.[53]

Morgan and his men were insulted and degraded; authorities at the prison shaved their heads and beards as if they were civilian criminals. Prison rules were strictly enforced. The Raiders were held in separate three-and-a-half-by-seven-foot cells, and they were not permitted to speak to each other except during mealtime. Violation of any of the prison rules meant confinement in the "dungeon." Morgan found imprisonment intolerable. Gradually the restrictions were lifted, and the men were allowed to talk with each other.[54]

Morgan soon began to think about escaping. It was suggested that they could dig a tunnel. The fact that the floor of the prison was concrete made the idea seem out of the question at first. After some thought and discussion, however, a plan was devised. Two table knives were smuggled from the dining room and used to chip away the floor. Eventually they worked their way through the floor to the air duct below and then began to dig the tunnel. Just after midnight on November 27, Morgan and six of his men made their way through the tunnel to the prison yard and over the wall. From there they went to a friend's house, where they were provided with horses. A reward of $5,000 was offered for Morgan's capture, but at Christmas, the general was united with his wife.[55]

In January 1864, Morgan and his wife were honored in Richmond. The adulation came from the people, but not from the Confederate high command. Morgan believed that the cool reception he had received from President Davis was the fault of General Bragg, who was now serving as his military advisor. Bragg, Morgan rationalized, was still angry with him for disobeying his orders on his recent raid. For Bragg it was more than that. During the Battle of Stone's River, when he needed Morgan's cavalry, they were unavailable.[56]

For nearly three months Morgan campaigned for authorization to organize a new command so that he could continue his raids on Kentucky. When authorization didn't come, he blamed Bragg. Finally he issued a proclamation in an effort to recruit his own command. Morgan's personal magnetism still worked; men came from all parts of the South to serve under him. By the middle of May, his brigade had grown to 2,000 men. Near the end of the month, Morgan sent a message to the Confederate War Department, not requesting permission, but informing them that he was going to make another raid into

Kentucky. By the time the message reached Richmond, the raid into Kentucky was already under way.[57]

After ravaging and robbing the bank at Mount Sterling, Morgan headed for Lexington. An intelligence report indicated that the Union army had 5,000 horses quartered there. On June 10, Morgan's Raiders rode into Lexington. Within minutes, warehouses and other buildings along the railroad were torched. As the fires raged, Morgan ordered his men to take the horses and head toward Paris. In the meantime Morgan took the opportunity to visit Hopemount, to see his mother. On the way he was spotted by a federal patrol, who gave chase. Soon Morgan was nowhere to be seen. Although the patrol searched the area, they found nothing. Morgan had escaped detection by riding his horse through Hopemount's big front door. After visiting with his mother and making certain that the federal patrol was gone, he led his horse out the back door and galloped off to join his command. It was the last time he would see Hopemount.[58]

As the Raiders made their way through Kentucky, they gathered 1,000 horses and nearly 1,000 prisoners. Before returning to Virginia, Morgan decided to spend the night at Cynthiana, north of Lexington. He allowed his men to sleep late and have a leisurely breakfast. Without warning, federal troops under General Stephen Burbridge swept down on Morgan and his men. Although outnumbered and surprised, Morgan and half of his command were able to escape. It was several weeks before his scattered troops found their way back to Virginia. The raid had been a failure. In their haste to escape, they were not able to bring a single prisoner or horse back with them.[59]

In August, Mattie came to see her husband, hoping to raise his spirits. His last raid had been a failure. Because of the pillage and looting by his Raiders in Mount Sterling, he had lost much of the support of his friends in Kentucky.[60] To add to his misery, three of his brigade commanders had become embittered by his actions in the last raid. Now they were demanding an investigation of the bank robbery at Mount Sterling and other unlawful acts by members of his command. Questions were also being raised in Richmond by Secretary Seddon about his ill-fated raid into Kentucky without orders.[61]

As a result of the investigation, the Confederate War Department charged Morgan with allowing "excesses and irregularities" associated with the armed robbery of the bank in Mount Sterling. The $59,000 taken from the bank belonged to private citizens. Under the rules of war, stealing private funds was illegal. Not only had the men taken private funds, but they had failed to transfer them to the Confederate treasury. They had kept the loot for themselves. There is no evidence that Morgan approved of the robbery at Mount Sterling or the pillage of private property, but he failed to take action against those who were responsible. As commanding general, he would have to answer for the actions of his command.[62]

Morgan responded to the charges in a letter to Seddon. He admitted that members from his command had robbed the bank at Mount Sterling, but the critical nature of the situation had prevented him from making an investigation on the scene. On August 30, Seddon announced the appointment of a court of inquiry to investigate the matter. It was scheduled for September 10, but Morgan would be dead before it had a chance to convene.

On September 3, Morgan arrived in Greeneville, Tennessee. He deployed his cavalry division on the outskirts of town. Union Brigadier General Alvan Gillem, commanding forces at nearby Bulls Gap, received information that Morgan was in Greeneville. He made plans to march his troops all night and attack Morgan's headquarters in the morning. At 5:00 A.M., federal cavalry slipped through a gap in Morgan's line. Charging into Greeneville, they surprised the few Confederate troops in town.[63]

Morgan was awakened by rifle shots in the streets below his bedroom. A staff officer rushed into the room to warn him of the immediate danger. Morgan quickly slipped on his pants and boots and ran down the steps, a colt revolver in each hand. He attempted to reach the stable and his horse, but he was spotted and had to turn back, taking shelter in the bushes near the house. A spectator pointed out his hiding place to the Union soldiers searching for him. Unarmed and defenseless, Morgan came out from his hiding place with his hands raised. "Don't shoot. I surrender," he said. "Surrender and be God damned — I know you," one of the Union soldiers replied as he raised his carbine and fired at point-blank range. Morgan groaned and fell to the ground. "I've killed the damned horse thief!" the soldier told his comrades.[64]

The jubilant troopers threw Morgan's body across a horse and paraded their trophy around town before stripping him down to a pair of underpants and throwing his body into a muddy roadside ditch. Two of Morgan's staff were allowed to retrieve his body and place it in the house where he had been sleeping. After the enemy withdrew from Greeneville, his body was claimed and taken to Abingdon, Virginia. His wife, now pregnant with their daughter, had his body moved to a vault in Richmond. After the war, he was returned to Kentucky, the land he loved, for interment in a cemetery in Lexington.[65]

John Hunt Morgan's raids behind enemy lines made him famous, and he terrorized citizens in three states. To Northern citizens, he was a rogue and a common horse thief. To his own army he was a maverick. For most Southerners, he was a chivalrous knight, the gallant cavalier of romantic literature.

Part 3 Fighting Under the Black Flag

GUERRILLA WARFARE

THE CLASH of Union and Confederate armies during the Civil War was one of the tragic periods in American history; sometimes brother was fighting brother. Even more frequent and tragic was the struggle on the home front between families and neighbors. A desire to settle the slavery issue often erupted into acts of violence and the growth of bands of marauders known as guerrillas.[1]

The term *guerrilla* originated in the early 1800s and referred to those who were engaged in the Spanish resistance against Napoleon. Historically, guerrilla wars have been brutal, savage affairs fought by small groups of men behind enemy lines. Because the fighting was so ferocious and outside the conventional rules for war, it is often said that the guerrillas were fighting under the black flag. To the guerrillas this meant that they would give no quarter; one savage act was repaid in kind with another. Using the elements of surprise and mobility, guerrilla bands were able to conduct raids on both military and civilian targets and then quickly disappear. This hit-and-run tactic proved very successful.

The guerrilla war between North and South began in the region known as Trans-Mississippi before any Southern states had seceded from the Union. Pro-slavery and antislavery factions had been fighting with each other for six years before the war began. After 1861, the fighting continued under the Confederate and Union banners. The early conflict on the border shaped the pattern of warfare that would follow.[2]

Before and throughout the war, pro-slavery guerrillas were prominent in Missouri, Kansas, Kentucky, and Virginia. They were able to keep their cause alive even after rebel forces had been driven from the area. In Missouri, for example, the Union gained control of St. Louis and all the surrounding area; however, many of the inhabitants were pro-South and considered the state part of the Confederacy. Confederate attempts to gain control of Missouri were unsuccessful, and thousands of young pro-Southern men lived under Union domination. Some slipped South and joined the Confederate army, but others thought they could serve the cause by working behind enemy lines. Southerners believed that one Confederate could beat a dozen Yankees, so the fact that they were outnumbered did not bother them. Guerrilla warfare, they believed, was a way of evening the odds. Not all guerrillas, however, supported the Southern cause. One fact was true for these irregular fighters on both sides — no quarter was given, none was asked, and those that survived the war carried the scars for life.

Guerrillas on either side seldom wore uniforms. Their usual attire consisted of a slouch hat, high boots, and a fancy shirt (with ruffles, and often called a "guerrilla shirt"). Around the waist, they wore a belt housing several revolvers. A number of pistols were often carried in their saddle bags. In battle, the guerrillas proved themselves equal to many of the military units they opposed. They were generally excellent horsemen and could ride into action with the horse's reins between their teeth, using their knees to direct the animal's movements, enabling them to fire two pistols at once.[3]

Born of a turbulent frontier and a tragic political situation, Confederate irregular bands roamed the borders from Missouri to Texas during the Civil War. They were led by dangerous men such as William Quantrill, Bill Anderson, Champ Ferguson, and others. Many guerrillas were only boys, but they fought like men; it was a war that turned a stable society into a conflict felt by all who encountered it. This was not a war between great armies, but a bloody local insurrection. It was a war between men and women who had once been friends and neighbors but now were bitter enemies. It was a Civil War in the exact definition of the phrase. This war was held hundreds of miles behind the battlefronts. It was a war fought without rules; in addition to killing each other, the guerrillas attacked civilians and destroyed personal property. Ambush, arson, executions, and murders were commonplace. In this area, civil law and the legal rights of the people were either suspended or ignored.[4]

The conditions that gave birth to guerrilla warfare began several years before the Civil War. On May 30, 1854, the delicate balance between the supporters and opponents of slavery had been shaken when President Franklin Pierce signed the Kansas-Nebraska Act. The act provided for "popular sovereignty" — the idea that the people living in the new territories should decide for themselves whether to allow the extension of slavery. The boundary lines for the territories set by the act were from the western border of Missouri to the Con-

"Bloody Bill" Anderson earned his nickname by ruthlessly murdering over fifty people.

tinental Divide and a part of the Rocky Mountains, an area 200 miles long by 700 miles wide.

The issue of slavery had pervaded the country for decades, particularly in the South, and had been the subject of many debates. Under the Missouri Compromise of 1820, states were admitted into the Union on the basis of maintaining a balance between the free and slave states. Slavery was outlawed from all United States Territories north of the 36° 30' parallel, Missouri's southern boundary. In 1850, California was admitted to the Union as a free state, which meant the next state to be admitted, Kansas, should enter as a slave state. But since the Kansas-Nebraska Act provided for an election to determine the status for the state's entry into the Union, this was not certain.

The idea of popular sovereignty seemed fair and democratic on the surface, but many people, including Abraham Lincoln, believed it to be dangerous. Opening up new areas of the country to slavery, they reasoned, would create violent competition between the opposite forces. Just as Lincoln and the others feared, the competition over the future of Kansas and the surrounding areas erupted into a bloody war zone.[5] Pro-slavery and abolitionist supporters invaded the Kansas Territory to press their point of view. In November 1854, several thousand pro-slavers from Missouri crossed into Kansas to vote for a delegate to Congress. They felt they had as much right to vote as the Northerners who had emigrated there, as they believed, for the sole purpose of voting. Their actions were not necessary, since the census records showed that a majority of the voters living in Kansas were from slave-holding states.[6]

In the spring of 1855 a flood of free-staters poured into Kansas. Rumors were spread that the election had already been bought by abolitionists for $100 a vote, and, worst of all, these Northerners were criminals and other undesirables. In Missouri, the newspapers urged pro-slavers to enter Kansas again. As a result, some Kansasans began to prepare for war. Rifles and ammunition were shipped into the territory, often in boxes marked "books." In Lawrence, Kansas, a cannon arrived in a crate labeled "machinery."[7]

One of the prominent abolitionists to come to Kansas was a former congressman from Indiana, James H. Lane. He hoped to organize a Democratic Party, but when that failed, he changed sides and became a "Free State" Republican. His Free State Army challenged the pro-slave group from Missouri known as the Border Ruffians. The term "Border Ruffian" was initiated by Northern newspapers to degrade pro-slavers and was used to describe lower-class whites. Soon rival bands on both sides were exchanging raids across the border, unleashing a series of murders, lootings, and pillaging. On May 21, 1856, the Border Ruffians attacked the town of Lawrence, Kansas. The fanatic John Brown, who had come to Kansas from Ohio, swore to avenge it. Three days later, aided by his four sons, he attacked the houses of five men, dragging them out and murdering them in front of their families. The community was outraged over the murders, and Brown was forced to flee the state. As a reprisal for the Brown raid, the Missouri Border Ruffians murdered five free-state men; and so it went on and on and on.

In the years preceding the Civil War, a succession of raids and counter-raids developed into fierce hatred, paving the way for the violent struggle that would take place on the border when the war began. Even before Fort Sumter, the abolitionists from Kansas were known as "jayhawkers," and the Missourians who supported slavery were called "bushwhackers."[8] Both labels originally were meant as insulting terms, but soon they came to be worn as badges of pride. "We jay-hawked. I don't suppose you know the meaning of the word," one jayhawker wrote in a letter to his sister. He explained: "we come to the home of some leading secesh [secessionist]. Then we take his horses and property, burn his house, etc. or as we say, clean them out."[9] Bushwhacker continues to be used today as a verb describing an act of ambush on an enemy.

By 1861, the seeds of hatred and distrust had been planted. Now the Kansas raiders of the 1850s believed they had the authority of the United States government to move freely into Missouri as an occupation force, considering all Missourians as disloyal to the government. In return, the Missouri guerrillas were to take revenge against the citizens of Kansas. All along the border, men were waiting for the opportunity to avenge the wrongs inflicted upon them during the years preceding the war. Although there were only a few secessionist elements in Missouri, their influence went far beyond their numbers.[10]

One of the first to enter the war was James H. Lane. On January 29, 1861, he was elected to the U.S. Senate representing the free state of Kansas. Lane's feelings about slavery and his hatred of Missourians were well known. He had been involved with Kansas and its border war from the very beginning. Within months after Lincoln took office as president, he appointed Lane a brigadier general in the Union army. Lane gathered together the jayhawkers who had previously been involved with him in their battles with the Missourians. With these men he formed the 3rd, 4th, and 5th Kansas regiments, which became known as the "Redlegs" because of the red leggings they wore.[11]

During the spring of 1861, McClellan's forces occupied western Virginia and gained control of the strategically important Baltimore and Ohio Railroad. The majority of the inhabitants of this region were loyal to the Union and accepted the federal takeover, but a group of Confederate sympathizers in the area did not. A reporter from the *Cincinnati Times* wrote: "the war in western Virginia is far from being at an end. . . . They [secessionists] are committing murders daily, lying in ambush for that purpose. Not only the Union volunteers, but their own neighbors, who peaceably and quietly sustain the cause of the Union, are the victims of their malice and blood-thirsty hate. They steal from our pickets and murder them. They shoot down their neighbors ... and burn their property to ashes. . . . no neighborhood is safe from their depredation, unless protected by Federal bayonets."[12]

To combat the guerrillas, the Unionists organized a band of anti-guerrillas

known as the "Snake-Hunters." Although the Snake-Hunters were able to capture a number of bushwhackers, there continued to be ready replacements. The
struggle between the two groups continued throughout the war, with neither
side gaining advantage.

After Confederate troops under General Sterling Price defeated federal forces
in the battle at Wilson's Creek in August 1861, Price led his troops north
through Missouri, where they were welcomed and cheered in nearly every town
they encountered. Infuriated by this, Lane crossed into Missouri with 1,500 of
his Redlegs and destroyed the farms and settlements of all those that he suspected of being Southern sympathizers. The jayhawkers did more than meet
Lane's order that "everything disloyal, from Shanghai rooster to a Durham cow,
must be cleaned out." On September 22, Lane reached the town of Osceola in
western Missouri. Discovering military supplies in a warehouse, Lane used this
as an excuse to torch and plunder the town. His men burned buildings, robbed
banks, stores, and private homes, and shot civilians believed to be disloyal to
the Union. When he left the town, many of his men were so drunk that they
had to be carried in wagons they had stolen. With them they also took numerous horses, mules, and 200 newly freed slaves. Lane took for himself a carriage,
piano, and a number of silk dresses for his female friends. The sacking of Osceola would be remembered for a long time by the people of Missouri and would
later become a battle cry of Confederate guerrillas. Two years later, shouting
"Osceola!" a band of Missouri bushwhackers massacred the inhabitants of a town
in Kansas.[13]

Another outsider who moved to the Kansas-Missouri border was Charles R.
Jennison. Born in New York, he moved to Wisconsin, where he studied medicine before moving to Kansas in 1858 and settling in Mound City. Jennison
was small in stature but habitually wore a tall, Cossack-type fur cap to give the
illusion of being taller. He had strong abolitionist feelings and came to Kansas
because of his convictions. He rode for a time with a group of jayhawkers but
later became part of a vigilante committee that became notorious for dispens-
ing justice at the end of a noose. In the fall of 1860, Jennison and his jayhawkers raided the village of Trading Post and rounded up all those believed
to favor slavery. Among those was a man named Russell Hinds, a bounty hunter
who captured and returned runaway slaves. Hinds was tried on the spot by the
jayhawkers, found guilty, and hanged.[14]

During the early stages of the war, Jennison's guerrillas became part of a

Kansas militia company, calling themselves the Mound City Sharp's Rifle Guards. On occasion, Jennison's men joined Jim Lane's jayhawkers in a series of hit-and-run raids. By the end of the summer, Jennison was named colonel, and his men were mustered into the 7th Kansas Volunteer Cavalry. Jennison knew nothing of military operations and, as a regimental commander, was a failure. His attempt to train and drill the men in his command turned into utter confusion. Assigned to routine duty with the army, he and his men became bored. They soon turned their attentions to more interesting activities. For the next few months, Jennison's jayhawkers laid waste to the Missouri countryside. When Jennison's men reached Harrisonville, Missouri, they found that another marauding gang had arrived before them and had removed everything of value except for some Bibles belonging to the American Bible Society. The jayhawkers took the Bibles.[15]

Union Major General Henry Halleck commanded the Department of the West. When he learned of the undisciplined jayhawker raids, he was disturbed, saying that they were "no better than a band of robbers." Because of their actions, some Missourians who had been Unionists now were switching their allegiance to the Confederacy. "The conduct of these forces," Halleck said, "had done more for the enemy in this state than could have been accomplished by 20,000 of his own army. These men disgrace the name and uniform of American soldiers and are driving good Union men into the ranks of the secession army." In March 1862, Halleck ordered the 7th Kansas to New Mexico for duty in Indian country. Jennison's days of marauding and plundering were over.[16]

In Missouri, men were banding together in response to the jayhawker raids. Motivated by hate, revenge, and in some cases simply adventure, they spread a wave of terror across Kansas. The most infamous leader of these bushwhackers was William Clarke Quantrill. Leading his men in a sudden charge, he would attack the enemy. Each of his guerrillas was armed with several Colt revolvers, providing them with more firepower than their adversaries. Against such weaponry, even the Union cavalry was often outmatched. In raid after raid, Quantrill and his guerrillas terrorized the Kansas-Missouri border. They are best known for sacking Lawrence, Kansas, an act so horrendous that it brought national attention and condemnation.[17]

By the late stages of the war, guerrillas — Confederate, Union, and just plain bandits — were in operation in all the border states. Tennessee's most infamous Confederate guerrilla was Champ Ferguson, who waged ferocious war in the Cumberland Mountains. Not just satisfied to shoot his victims, Ferguson often stabbed them as well. On one occasion, he went to a hospital, pushed aside a physician who tried to stop him, and with a rifle, blew out the brains of a soldier who was lying helplessly in bed. Just after the war, he was apprehended as an outlaw and hanged.[18]

At the end of the Civil War, some in the South talked of continuing the war by engaging in large-scale guerrilla operations against the Union occupation forces. General Robert E. Lee advised against this, telling his army at Appomattox to return home and be peaceful, law-abiding citizens. By 1865, the people of the South were tired of war. When a civilian questioned one of Lee's veterans, asking why he had not taken to the mountains and fought guerrilla warfare, the soldier replied, "Look! I've been in thirty-five battles since this war started, and I'm plumb satisfied!" Any effort to continue the war would have only prolonged the South's misery and increased the vindictiveness in the North.[19]

When the spring of 1865 began, citizens along the western border were braced for another round of bloody guerrilla warfare, but in April, Lee surrendered. In Kansas, the celebration was spontaneous and unforgettable; church bells and cannon proclaimed the victory. In Missouri, however, there was only silence. After years of marching armies, raiding jayhawkers, and uncontrolled outlaw action, the western Missouri countryside had become a blackened wasteland that some called the "Burnt District." Returning home from exile, the Reverend George Miller was stunned by what he saw: "My wife and I came through Johnson, Cass, and Jackson Counties, and, for miles and miles, we saw nothing but lone chimneys to mark the spots where happy homes stood. It seemed like a vast cemetery — not a living thing to break the silence. . . . man no longer existed there."[20]

During the four years of war, the most destructive guerrilla war in American history had been carried out. Both sides had experienced death, destruction, and barbarity at the hands of the guerrillas. When the war was over, the spirit of hate and mistrust persisted. The Missouri guerrillas, however, remained relatively quiet in the days after hostilities ceased. Their ablest leaders were dead or disheartened by defeat, like those who had fought in the regular army.[21]

After Appomattox, the bushwhackers laid down their arms, hoping to live out the remainder of their lives in peace, but for some there was no peace. Jim Cummins, a returning bushwhacker, stated: "I . . . fought for things I thought

Jesse James, America's most celebrated outlaw.

(Dictionary of American Portraits, Courtesy Mercaldo Archives)

was right. When the war was over and I wanted to settle down they would not let me, but pursued me with a malignant hatred." A number of Missouri guerrillas were hunted down and shot; others fled the state. Some quietly yielded to the punishment inflicted by the victors. There were a few, however, who refused to give in. Many of these men, young in age, had known nothing but war. For them, the war was not over.[22]

13

Fanatical Abolitionist

JOHN BROWN

I T WAS Sunday, October 16, 1859. The sun had just slipped behind the
Allegheny Mountains to the west, and an evening chill and light rain were
beginning to settle over the area. On the Kennedy Farm in Maryland, John
Brown gave the command: "Men, get your arms; we will proceed to the
Ferry."[1] In a short time eighteen men, well armed with rifles and pistols, were
ready to move out. All went on foot except their leader, Brown, who drove an
old wagon. Their destination was Harpers Ferry, a little more than five miles
to the south; their objective: its capture.

Harpers Ferry is a narrow neck of land at the point where the Potomac and Shenandoah Rivers meet. Baltimore is eighty miles due east of Harpers Ferry, and Washington less than sixty miles southeast. On the eve of Brown's raid, there were several small towns and villages nearby, but the mountain setting gave Harpers Ferry "an air of remoteness." The population of slightly more than 2,500 included 1,250 free blacks and eighty-eight slaves. Because of the cold climate and mountainous terrain, there were no large plantations in the region. Harpers Ferry contained a combination of homes, saloons, hotels, and shops extending along the two rivers and dotting the Bolivar Heights. Along Potomac Street was a fire-engine house, the federal armory, and an arsenal, where arms and weapons were stored. Nearby, on an island in the Shenandoah, stood Hall's Rifle Works, where firearms for the U.S. Army were manufactured. Several hundred persons were employed there, producing 10,000 stands of arms each year.[2]

Brown selected Harpers Ferry as the site for his raid for several reasons. The arsenal would provide him with weapons needed for arming slaves in the insurrection he planned. Harpers Ferry was close to the large slave population in Virginia that, he believed, would come to his aid in the revolt. Finally, it was located at the junction of two important rivers; these would provide him with the means to go down the Shenandoah Valley as he spread his revolt to plantations throughout the South.

Leading his small army were Brown's four captains: John Kagi, A. D. Stevens, John E. Cook, and Charles P. Tidd. Brown had only the vaguest plan for the operation he hoped to carry out at Harpers Ferry. Kagi and Stevens were to capture the bridge watchman while Cook and Tidd cut the telegraph wires on both the Maryland and Virginia sides of the Potomac River. He assigned the other men to take positions in town and to hold the two bridges that entered Harpers Ferry.[3]

For John Brown the attack on Harpers Ferry was the culmination of years of efforts to eliminate slavery. His feelings about slavery had begun early in his life. His father had inculcated in him a devout Calvinist faith and an extreme hatred of slavery. Brown was born on May 9, 1800, at the turn of the century

---

Previous page:
As children, John Brown's sons feared him and his unforgiving wrath, but as adults, they were his allies in the violent fight against slavery. (Library of Congress)

Harpers Ferry, a remote town nestled at the junction between the Potomac and Shenandoah Rivers. With only 88 slaves and no large plantations, Harpers Ferry was unprepared for abolitionist John Brown's raid. (Library of Congress)

and at the aftermath of a "great religious awaking" that swept the village of West Torrington, Connecticut. His parents, Ruth and Owen Brown, were devout Calvinists who believed all people were sinners in the hands of an angry God. The third of six children, Brown was a thin, serious child. His parents insisted that he and their other children develop sound religious habits.[4]

Brown's fanatic zeal was a natural outgrowth of his childhood experiences. Owen Brown, a tanner and shoemaker, was an ambitious man whose business ventures often took him away from home. The family was transient, staying only a short time in one place. As a child, Brown had to endure strict discipline; his father believed to spare the rod would spoil the child. When Brown was eight years old, his mother died. He was stricken with grief. His father remarried, this time to a much younger woman, setting a pattern that Brown would follow later.[5]

Brown followed his father in terms of his treatment of his family and his religious beliefs. He believed in the divine authenticity of the Bible and that it was an infallible guide to life. "The Bible," his daughter Ruth said, "was his favorite volume, and he had a perfect knowledge of it." Many parts of it he learned completely by heart.[6]

From his stern, Calvinist father, Brown first learned about the evils of slavery. Later, when he was twelve years old and the family moved to Ohio, he experienced these evils firsthand. While helping to move some cattle, Brown saw a slave being whipped. He remembered that horrible scene the rest of his life. He later wrote: "This brought me to reflect on the wretched, hopeless condition of fatherless and motherless slave children. For such children have neither fathers nor mothers to protect and provide for them. I sometimes would raise the question, 'Is God their father?'" Brown longed to be God's instrument for the freeing of slaves and the smiting of their owners. Later, as his fanaticism grew, he began to believe himself to be an avenging angel of the Lord.[7]

Brown had little opportunity to attend school, but he was able to read and write. He dreamed of attending a seminary and becoming a minister, but it never came to fruition. Rather, he stayed at home to work in his father's tannery. At the age of nineteen, he built his own tannery and went into business for himself.[8] By the time he was twenty, Brown was already a man of strong, uncompromising opinions. His opposition to slavery continued to grow, thanks to his father and his antislavery friends. One of Brown's employees remembered, "Brown was always of one mind" about slavery. He believed that slavery was a sin against God and that it was his duty to help eradicate it by assisting slaves in escaping to freedom. Brown was serious about what he said, having already helped one fugitive slave escape and offering to shelter any other runaways who came to his house.[9]

In 1820, John Brown married Dianthe Lusk. Dianthe bore seven children: four sons and one daughter survived. During the early years of their marriage, Dianthe was able to temper Brown's radical views. Now with a family, Brown set about to make himself a model Christian businessman and a leading figure in the community. His zeal for religion, however, did not stay in check for long; he began to teach Sunday school, telling his students to be honest and always fear God. He made church attendance mandatory for his employees and required them to attend worship services in his cabin every morning. If any of his employees defied him or did anything wrong, he punished them with an

Old Testament vengeance. One form of punishment Brown used frequently was to order his employees to shun the one who was being disciplined, not allowing them to talk to him under any circumstance.[10]

John Brown ruled his family in the same way; it was said that he had a rod in one hand and the Bible in the other. Insisting that his children learn "good order and religious habits," Brown would not allow his children to play or to have visitors on the Sabbath. His uncompromising attitude toward the family had a telling effect on Dianthe. Early in their marriage she had shown signs of serious emotional problems. Now these symptoms returned and unfortunately to a greater degree. Brown showed great concern for his wife, staying up nights to care for her and praying constantly for her to recover. The gentleness that Brown displayed at this time would be remembered by his children all their lives. Despite his efforts and prayers, his wife's health grew worse.[11]

Hoping to help Dianthe recover, Brown sold his business and moved eastward, to Randolph Township in the Pennsylvania wilderness. There he opened another tannery business, built a log house, and cleared twenty-five acres of land for farming. He quickly established himself in the new community and served as postmaster of New Richmond, a section of the township, from 1828 to 1835. He was responsible for the first school in the township, building the schoolhouse himself and employing a woman to teach there. Although Brown was generous in helping his neighbors, he was still unyielding in matters of religion and politics. When a newcomer moved into the area, Brown made a point of inquiring about his views on religion and slavery. If they agreed with his, it was fine; if they did not, he looked upon the person with suspicion. Brown had a zealous obsession with moral behavior, and he waged a campaign against sin (as he saw it) in any form. On one occasion, when a man was arrested for stealing a cow and released because he was needed to support his family, Brown was outraged. He intimidated the constable into re-arresting the man. While the man was in jail, Brown provided for the family himself.[12]

Brown continued his strict discipline with his children, using the whip frequently. He required his boys to keep an account book of punishment they were due. When the total reached a predetermined level, Brown would inflict the punishment. On one occasion when John Jr. was being whipped, Brown stopped before completing the number of lashes his son was due. Then to his son's surprise, Brown took off his shirt and fell on his knees. Giving his son the whip, he ordered him to "lay it on." "I dared not refuse to obey, but at first

I did not strike hard," John Jr. said. But when Brown insisted that he strike harder, John Jr. did until "drops of blood showed on his back." At first John Jr. didn't understand what his father intended to prove by this unusual behavior. Later he came to realize that it was his attempt to illustrate the doctrine of atonement. "I was too obtuse to perceive how justice could be satisfied by inflicting penalty upon the back of the innocent instead of the guilty," John Jr. said.[13]

In 1831 Brown's business fortunes began to deteriorate, and he became ill. For more than a year he suffered from a malarial-type fever, which severely weakened him. It was also the year that his four-year-old son Frederick died and Dianthe developed heart trouble. Then in 1832, his wife became pregnant again. This time, in her weakened condition, she died shortly after her newly born son died. Brown was left with four young children to care for.[14]

Less than a year after Dianthe's death, Brown married again. This time it was his housekeeper's sixteen-year-old sister, Mary Ann Day. She was the perfect wife for him. Brown moved from place to place for much of his life; Mary was able to endure the hardships of this lifestyle. In addition, she had the right temperament. She had been trained that a wife's role was to bear children, maintain a household, and obey her husband. Her most endearing virtue was that she never complained. She would bear him an additional thirteen children, of which only six survived childhood. When she became a widow in 1859, only four of her children were still alive.[15]

During the following years, Brown's tannery business continued to lose money. Despite this, he hoped to establish a school for former slaves. Unfortunately, by the end of 1834, his financial troubles reached the point that he did not have enough money to operate his tannery, let alone establish a school. It was time to move again.[16]

Brown continued to move from place to place, just as his father had. It was difficult for him to earn a living, so it was necessary for him to go where he thought the prospects would improve his situation. In Ohio, where he owned a tannery, Brown had little success. He worked as a farmer, postmaster, and shepherd. In Springfield, Massachusetts, Brown entered the wool business.[17] Although Brown found it difficult to support his family, he never gave up on his main interest in life — the abolition of slavery.

As part of the Compromise of 1850, Congress passed a fugitive slave law which provided that runaway slaves, and even free African Americans, could be seized and returned to slavery in the South. At Springfield, Brown organized a group of men whom he named the "League of Gileadites." Their function was to aid former slaves, runaways, and free African Americans living in the North in joining together to prevent their being forcefully returned to the South. Should one of them be in danger of being returned, Brown told his followers, they should unite together to prevent it from happening. Brown did not join any antislavery organizations or participate in the Underground Railroad. He would assist fugitive slaves in his own way; unfortunately, he became obsessed with solving the slavery problem by the use of violence.[18]

The issue of slavery continued to be debated in Congress. The Missouri Compromise of 1820 had set the pattern for admitting new states to the Union. In 1854 the Kansas-Nebraska Act was passed, providing for "popular sovereignty" and repealing the Missouri Compromise. There seemed to be little doubt that the Nebraska Territory would enter as a free state; the status of Kansas, however, was in question. By allowing the settlers of Kansas and Nebraska to determine whether or not their territory would allow slavery, the door was opened for violence, and Kansas became a battleground for the two sides.[19]

Pro-slavery elements from Missouri, known as Border Ruffians, entered Kansas to harass free-staters and vote illegally in the elections. While the Border Ruffians moved to seize control of the Kansas Territory, the free-staters were busy, too. Efforts were made to promote emigration to Kansas, and residents organized into militia units to defend their homes and communities.

During the summer of 1855, John Brown's sons went to Kansas to join the free-staters in their opposition to the imposition of slavery on the territory. They settled at Osawatomie near the home of their uncle, the Reverend Samuel Lyle Adair. Brown did not plan to go until his son, John Jr., wrote to him, telling him of the conditions in Kansas: "We need guns more than we need bread; every slave state from Texas to Virginia is trying to fasten slavery upon this glorious land." He appealed to his father to come to Kansas to fight with them; in 1856, Brown arrived, stating, "I have only a short time to live. Only one death to die. And I will die fighting for this cause. There will be no more peace in this land until slavery is done for."[20]

Only a few days after the Browns has arrived in Kansas, they were visited by a band of Border Ruffians who inquired where their loyalties lay. From the moment they responded that they were free-staters, the Browns were marked for trouble. Now that John Brown had arrived, the family was ready to meet violence with violence. In May 1856, the Border Ruffians struck in force at

Lawrence, Kansas, sacking the town and killing two abolitionists. When the news of the atrocities reached Brown, he and an armed force headed for Lawrence, but the Border Ruffians were already gone.[21]

Brown, hearing that five abolitionists had been killed at Lawrence, planned to retaliate by killing five pro-slavers. On May 23, he and six others, including four of his sons, approached the pro-slavery settlement along the Pottawatomie Creek. Calling themselves the Army of the North, they first went to the cabin of James Doyle. He and his two sons had been involved in pro-slavery activities and were well known in the area. Taking the three men outside, Brown's men murdered them, hacking their bodies to pieces with broadswords. The murders were committed in front of the rest of the family. Mrs. Doyle later testified that her youngest son was spared because she had pleaded with them not to kill him.[22]

Just after midnight, Brown's band reached the home of their fourth victim, Allen Wilkinson, a well-known pro-slave leader. Mrs. Wilkinson later testified that four of Brown's men entered their cabin and told her husband to put on his clothes. "I begged them to let Mr. Wilkinson stay with me, saying I was sick and helpless," she said. Brown refused. Mr. Wilkinson wanted at least to get someone to stay with her, promising to remain in the cabin until the morning. Again, Brown refused. He would not even allow Wilkinson to put on his boots before taking him outside and slashing him to death. Then his body was dragged into brush nearby.[23]

After four brutal murders, Brown's desire for retribution had not yet been satisfied. He had vowed to kill five pro-slavers, and five it would be. His last victim was William Sherman. Like the others, he was taken from the house and cut down outside. Then his mutilated body was thrown into the creek. Finally, the killings were over; as John Brown had promised, five men had died.

The Pottawatomie Massacre was the beginning of the violence that would be referred to as "Bleeding Kansas." The fighting in Kansas took the form of guerrilla warfare, with each side claiming an eye for an eye. To some, John Brown was a hero of the abolitionist movement; to others, he was a brutal murderer. Brown was now a wanted man; he went into hiding and eventually returned to Ohio. Now notorious for his actions in Kansas, Brown attempted to raise money to purchase weapons. He hoped to arm slaves so that they could participate in the revolt to overthrow slavery. If successful, Brown hoped to create a revolutionary state for African Americans. He even drew up a constitution for the new government.[24]

During the three years between the Pottawatomie Massacre and the raid on Harpers Ferry, Brown was involved in guerrilla warfare and raising funds. He spent six months in 1857 traveling to the northeastern part of the United States, pleading his cause, and enlisting a dedicated core of followers.

Brown's favorite biblical passage was Hebrews 9:22: "Under the law almost everything is purified with blood, and without the shedding of blood, there is no forgiveness of sins." Brown was willing to shed his blood for the cause. This willingness won him the ardent support of a small group of Northern abolitionists. Among them was Frederick Douglass, a former slave. By 1858, Brown had decided to strike his major blow at slavery at Harpers Ferry. Douglass declined Brown's offer when he was invited to join the raid, believing it to be a suicidal effort. "His zeal in the cause of freedom was infinitely superior to mine," Douglass later wrote of Brown. "Mine was as the taper light; his was as the burning sun. I could live for the slave; John Brown could die for him."[25]

During the summer of 1859, Brown moved to Maryland and rented a house near Harpers Ferry. Brown used the name of Isaac Smith and grew a flowing white beard to conceal his identity. In order not to arouse suspicion, he pretended to be a cattle buyer and kept his men under cover as much as possible. All summer long, Brown studied local maps and statistics and waited for recruits to arrive, but the large volunteer force he had anticipated never materialized. Brown had twenty-one followers, most of whom were young. Included in the group were four of his sons — Watson, Oliver, Owen, and John Jr. Among the group was Dangerfield Nubie, an African American who had to leave Virginia because it was illegal for free blacks to live there. He had joined Brown in hopes of liberating his family, who had to remain in Virginia as slaves. Finally, on October 16, the long wait came to an end; Brown and his small army headed for Harpers Ferry.[26]

Brown and his army crossed the river over the old railroad bridge. When they approached the railroad station, they were confronted by Hayward Shepherd, a baggage master. Brown's men ordered him to halt; when he didn't, they shot him. Ironically, the first man killed at Harpers Ferry was an African American who was neither a slave owner nor a defender of slavery, but a free black.[27]

The raiders took over fifty hostages, though some were able to escape. One of the hostages was Colonel Lewis Washington, the great-grandnephew of George Washington. The raiders surrounded the armory and arsenal, where only a night watchman was on duty. Brown quickly seized his first objective; it had been carried out with dispatch and little effort. But now his trouble was just beginning. Brown had not expected much opposition from the townspeople, but once they realized what was happening, the alarm went out that slaves and abolitionists were raiding and looting the town. In a short time they came, in force and armed. Brown was forced to retreat into the fire-engine house. As he did so, Dangerfield Nubie was shot. The angry mob hauled off his body, mutilated it, and fed it to the hogs.[28]

With the townspeople organizing, Brown was at a loss for what to do; his avenues of escape had been blocked. He tried desperately to negotiate his group's safe passage in return for the hostages, but the offer was refused. When Brown sent two couriers out under a flag of truce, they were shot. One of Brown's sons, Watson, fell mortally wounded but was able to drag himself back to the engine house. Brown had counted on slaves in the area to come to his aid and join in the revolt, but this help did not materialize.[29]

When the news of the attack on Harpers Ferry reached Washington, President James Buchanan called in U.S. troops. Lieutenant Colonel Robert E. Lee was ordered to take command of the military forces at Harpers Ferry; Lieutenant J.E.B. Stuart of the 1st Cavalry was assigned as Lee's aide. Lee's first inclination was to attack at once, but he decided not to for fear of harming the hostages.[30]

During the night, Brown surveyed his situation. Two of his sons, Watson and Oliver, lay dying on the floor. It was cold, and they had not eaten for over twenty-four hours. Oliver was in pain and begged his father to kill him to end his misery, but Brown refused. "If you must die, die like a man," Brown replied. A little later he called to Oliver and got no reply. "I guess he is dead," Brown said.[31]

In the morning Brown realized that he was now surrounded by marine troops and no longer by farmers and townspeople. Stuart was sent to deliver Lee's terms for surrender, but Brown refused to accept them. With that, Stuart gave the signal for the marines to attack.[32] The marines battered the door down, charged inside, and attacked the raiders. The encounter took only three minutes. The hostages were freed unharmed, and all of Brown's troops in the engine house were captured or mortally wounded. Brown was wounded and bleeding profusely around the head and neck. Of Brown's army, nine were dead, and a tenth, his son Watson, died later in the day. The final count for Brown's efforts: seventeen dead — ten as the result of the action at Harpers Ferry, seven on the gallows. John Brown was incarcerated in nearby Charlestown, Virginia, to await trial.[33]

News of John Brown's raid electrified the nation. Southern whites were both angry and frightened. They accused the North and Republicans of a plot to subdue the South with a slave rebellion. Republicans tried to disassociate themselves from Brown; some even hoped that he would be tried and hanged as quickly as possible to spare them more embarrassment.[34] Hearing of Brown's plight, Boston abolitionist John La Barnes engaged attorney George H. Holt to represent him. Brown's trial began on October 25, exactly one week after his capture. The trial was highly publicized, with people crowding the courtroom, hoping to get a look at the fanatical abolitionist. Brown was charged with three counts: treason to the commonwealth of Virginia, murder, and conspiring with slaves to commit treason. Because his wounds had not healed, Brown spent most of the trial lying on a stretcher. When Brown's attorneys attempted to show that insanity was hereditary in his family, he angrily rose from his stretcher and proclaimed: "I am perfectly unconscious of insanity, and I reject, so far as I am capable, any attempt to interfere in my behalf on that score."[35]

During the trial, Brown took the opportunity to express his position. He put not just slavery on trial, but blamed the country for allowing slavery to exist. Brown defended his actions, saying: "I believe that to interfere, as I have done, in the behalf of God's despised poor is not wrong but right. Now if it is deemed necessary that I should mingle my blood further, . . . I say let it be done." He talked of the evils of slavery and predicted that it was doomed to be ended only by violence.[36]

Three weeks after Brown's failed raid on Harpers Ferry, the trial was over, and he was found guilty. Judge Richard Parker sentenced him to be hanged one month later, on December 2.

Immediately after the trial, some came to Brown's defense. A reformer, Wendell Philips, spoke out on his behalf: "History will date Virginia emancipation from Harpers Ferry. John Brown has loosened the roots of the slave system. It only breathes; it does not live hereafter." Ralph Waldo Emerson, the leading New England poet, said that Brown was "a new saint awaiting his martyrdom." Jefferson Davis, however, the future president of the Confederacy, said that

Brown deserved to suffer "a felon's death." Even the New England abolitionists were appalled by the bloodshed at Harpers Ferry for which John Brown was responsible.[37]

During the last month of his life, Brown remained composed and unrepentant. In doing so he inspired his followers who faced the same fate. He spent the time visiting with the people who thronged to see him and writing letters to his family and friends. In his letter to John Jr. he said, "A calm peace ... seems to fill my mind by night and day." To his wife Mary he wrote, "Give thanks to our Father in Heaven, for 'He doeth all things well.' Kiss our children and grandchildren for me. Both of us have been called upon to make a sacrifice in our beloved cause, the cause of God and humanity. It is not too much, I would have sacrificed more!"[38]

As the day of his execution drew near, Mary Brown came by train to be with her husband. At the same time, Colonel Lee arrived with 250 soldiers and instructions to protect the town against a possible Northern invasion. On the day of Brown's execution, Charlestown was quiet. As he left the jail to go to the gallows, John Brown handed a sheet of paper to one of the guards. On it were these words: "I, John Brown, am now quite certain that the crimes of the guilty land will never be purged away, but with blood. I had as I now think vainly flattered myself that without very much bloodshed it might be done." He was right; much blood would be shed before slavery came to an end.[39]

Brown was driven from the jail steps to the gallows in the back of a wagon that also carried his coffin. His arms were bound, and he sat on the coffin. The streets along the way were filled with soldiers and militia because of the rumors that there would be an attempt made to rescue him. After the hanging, John Brown's body was taken to his home in North Elba, New York, where he was buried in a simple grave near other members of his family.

Martyr or insane fanatic, John Brown became an American legend. Within two years of his death, Union soldiers marched to a battle tune that went, "John Brown's body lies a mouldering in the grave; his soul goes marching on."[40]

L. H. LIGHTFOOT,
Leaf Tobacco Dealer,
RICHMOND,
VA.

14 Guerrilla with a Vendetta

CHAMP FERGUSON

CHAMP Ferguson was dressed in a new black cloth frock coat, vest and pants of the same material, and a neat white shirt, provided by the "ladies of the South." His hands were tied behind his back at the elbows and wrists. "He appeared," said a witness, "like a man who was about to make a speech on some leading topic, and had simply paused to refresh his memory." Ferguson appeared to be in excellent health, a fine picture of a man, but he seemed impatient, looking about, as if he considered the whole twenty-minute procedure unnecessary. As Colonel Shafter, the post commandant, read the charges against him, Ferguson acknowledged their truth by bowing or shaking his head as a way of denying them. After reading the sentence, Shafter said, "In accordance with the sentence I have read you, Champ Ferguson, I am going to have you executed." Showing no emotion, Champ replied, "I am ready to die."[1]

When the Reverend Bunting invoked the blessing of God upon him, Ferguson was deeply affected by the words, showing his emotions for the first time. Tears glistened on his cheeks, and he asked Colonel Shafter to wipe his face. As he did so, Shafter expressed the hope that Ferguson would have no hard feelings toward him or his men for performing their duty. Champ said that he wouldn't and thanked him for his kindness. Asked if he had any final remarks, Champ replied that he had plenty, but he didn't know how to say them. His only request was that his body be turned over to his wife. "I do not want to be buried in such soil as this," he said. A white cap was placed over his head. "Lord, have mercy on my soul!" were his last words. The trap door fell.[2] Thus ended the life of Champ Ferguson, one of the most infamous guerrillas to serve the Confederacy, a man accused of personally killing fifty-three people, including children and a wounded soldier in his hospital bed.

Champ Ferguson, the eldest of ten children, was born on November 29, 1821, near Albany, Clinton County, Kentucky. Little is known about his family or his childhood except that he had little formal education. Later he would say, "I never had much schooling, but I recollect of going to school about three months, during which time I learned to read, write, and cipher right smart." In 1843, Champ married Anna Eliza Smith, who bore him one child, a boy; Eliza and their son died from illness three years after their marriage. He married Martha Owens two years later. They had one child, a daughter. Ferguson's one redeeming trait in his character, some thought, was the deep love he had for his wife and daughter.[3]

Before the beginning of the Civil War, Champ Ferguson was well known along the Kentucky-Tennessee border. He lived the usual life of men in the area, farming in the mountains and hunting to provide for a large part of his family's food needs. His knowledge of the Cumberland Mountains would serve him well as a guide and scout during the war and help him escape from his enemies when he needed to.[4]

In 1861, Champ was in the prime of life. He was adept in the use of a gun and knife and was an excellent horseman. Ferguson was robust, fond of liquor and fine horses, and he easily caught the eye of women in the community. Later, a reporter for the *Daily Press and Times* described Ferguson: "For twenty years he had borne a loose character. He had been known as a gambling, row-dyish, drinking, fighting, quarrelsome man. He seemed to always be in hot water."[5] At the age of forty, Champ Ferguson seemed quite ready to assume the role of guerrilla.

Before the war began, Ferguson had killed his first man, Constant Jim Read, in what might have been considered self-defense, but Champ's case never came to trial. When the Civil War began, he was induced to join the army on the promise that all prosecution in the case would be dropped.

Most of Ferguson's neighbors in Clinton County, including his own family, supported the Union. Even his brother Jim joined the Union ranks. All of these people resented his taking up the Southern cause. The code of the mountains was elemental; when a man took sides, all the other side became enemies. This was the situation with Champ Ferguson and his family.[6] According to Confederate sources, a band of eleven neighbors, seeking vengeance for what they considered Ferguson's betrayal, went to his house. In Ferguson's absence, they humiliated his wife and daughter by forcing them to remove all their clothes. The act infuriated him to such an extent that he would seek vengeance against the "marked eleven" and all other Unionists. If the story is true, it scarcely explains, and does not excuse, his savage acts of retribution against all those he faced during the war.[7]

During Ferguson's trial at the end of the war, he explained his actions as simply self-defense, that he only killed those who would have killed him if they had the chance. The feud in the mountains of Tennessee and Kentucky between Unionists and rebels was deadly; it was a case of kill or be killed.[8] The Kentucky-Tennessee line divided the North and South politically, but many families within those boundaries were divided in their allegiance. In Kentucky, the Confederates were in the minority; in Tennessee, the Federals were outnumbered. In both cases these minorities were strong. Early in 1861, residents of Tennessee had voted to remain in the Union, but when Lincoln called for troops, the sentiment changed; by June the vote was for secession. Kentucky remained neutral but was occupied by federal troops early in the war, and an all-out effort was made to recruit men there for the Union army. Guerrilla warfare began in earnest along the border; the price of survival was constant vigilance. Danger was always present and little mercy was shown by either side. "No quarter given" was the general rule.[9]

On November 1, 1861, Champ Ferguson killed William Frogg, a member of the home guard. Ferguson contended that Frogg had tried to kill him and that he had acted in self-defense, but Frogg's wife denied this. She testified that her husband and Ferguson had always been on friendly terms, and that he had never made any threat against him or in any way wanted to kill him.[10]

One month later, Ferguson shot and killed Reuben Wood, the second of fifty-three persons with whose murders he would later be charged. Ferguson went to his home and accused him of being a Lincolnite and being a member of the federal home guard. "Why, Champ, I nursed you when you were a baby. Has there been a misunderstanding between us?" Wood inquired. "No," said Ferguson. "Reuben, you have always treated me like a gentleman." Ferguson nevertheless stated his intention to kill Wood. Wood's daughter begged Ferguson not to shoot her father, but to no avail. Again, Ferguson's excuse for killing a man was the same. "If I had not killed Reuben Wood first, he would have killed me," Ferguson said later. The war had not yet begun in Kentucky and Tennessee, and yet Ferguson had already killed two Union sympathizers in cold blood.[11] Shortly after, Ferguson moved his family across the mountains into Tennessee for their protection.

By the spring of 1862, the Confederates had suffered serious reverses in their operations in Kentucky and Tennessee. The capture of Fort Donelson and Fort Henry in February by General Grant had forced the Confederates to retreat all the way to northern Mississippi and allowed the Federals to enter Nashville, Tennessee. Colonel John Hunt Morgan, the Confederate raider, however, was operating in the area. Ferguson rode with Morgan as a scout and guide. One evening while on scouting patrol, Ferguson encountered a sixteen-year-old boy. When Ferguson asked him his name, he replied, "Fount Zachery." When Ferguson heard the word "Zachery," he pulled out his gun and shot the youth; then, getting off his horse, he stabbed him. Fount Zachery was the first of four members of the Zachery family whom Ferguson would kill. The brutal way that these men were killed suggests that they may have been members of the eleven that he had marked for death.[12]

The war in the Cumberlands, especially at the beginning, was fierce and deadly. Bands of common thieves, under the guise of home guards, were robbing friends and foes alike. It was difficult to trust anyone. It is easy to see why Champ Ferguson considered it a good policy for self-preservation to shoot first and ask questions later, to kill those suspected of being his enemies before they killed him.[13]

Sometime during the spring, Champ Ferguson was authorized by the Confederate government to form a company of cavalry. Ferguson was elected captain and Henry Sublett first lieutenant. On June 1, 1862, Ferguson and his men went to Elijah Kogier's house and killed him. After the shooting, the group searched his house. Kogier's wife asked Ferguson if he planned to kill all her friends. He said there were a few more he intended to kill, but he did not identify them. Later, when Ferguson was asked why he had killed Kogier, he said, "He was a treacherous dog and richly merited his fate." On that same day Ferguson killed James Zachery, grandfather of young Fount Zachery.[14]

In July 1862, Morgan, with a brigade of nearly 900 men, made his first raid into Kentucky. To be successful, raids of this size depended on good information. Accurate reports of enemy strength enabled Morgan to know when he had overpowering numbers. Champ Ferguson and his men were helpful in both scouting and providing him this information. At the same time, Ferguson saw this as an opportunity to settle a personal vendetta against Tinker Dave Beatty and his men, who he believed were responsible for the earlier humiliating experience of his wife and daughter. He vowed to kill every one of Beatty's men; riding with Morgan provided him with the opportunity to search for them. Ferguson found Beatty and killed him, but he was never charged with his death. Ferguson's brutality was not condoned by Morgan. Basil Duke, Morgan's second in command, warned Ferguson not to kill any of the prisoners of war. Ferguson only partially agreed to the order, replying, "I know it ain't looked on as right to treat regular soldiers taken in battle in that way. Besides I don't want to do it. I haven't got no feeling against these Yankee soldiers, except they are wrong, and oughtn't to come down here and fight our people. I won't touch them; but when I catch any of them hounds, I've got good cause to kill, I'm going to kill em."[15]

The month of October was a bloody one for Champ Ferguson. One of the deaths for which he was responsible was an old man by the name of Boswell Tabor. Ferguson encountered Tabor, one of the men he believed involved in the abuse of his wife and daughter, while delivering some prisoners through his farm. When Tabor saw him, he pleaded for his life. Taking his pistol from his belt, Ferguson shot him through the heart. Then he put his pistol next to Tabor's head and fired again. Hearing the first shot, Tabor's wife and daughter came running from their house, screaming and crying, but it was too late to save him. Later, at Ferguson's trial, when questioned about Tabor's death, he implied that it was a "good deed well done." "I killed Boswell Tabor," he said; "he had killed three of my men a few days previous. He was in front of his house when I shot him. He ought to have been killed sooner."[16]

During the same month, Ferguson was responsible for the brutal murder of John Williams, David Delk, and John Crabtree. In his statement to the court at his trial, Ferguson intimated that the men who had been killed had made two mistakes. The first mistake was in hunting for him; the second was in finding him.[17]

Champ Ferguson and his men took part in Morgan's famous Christmas Raid in 1862–63. Near the end of the raid, on New Year's night, Ferguson split off from the main force to settle a personal score with Elam Huddleston.[18] Huddleston had first joined the Union army, but after a while had withdrawn and formed his own guerrilla band, operating in the Cumberlands. Of the Union guerrilla leaders in this section during the war, Huddleston was one of the most feared. The war between Huddleston and Ferguson was fierce and brutal.

Approaching Elam Huddleton's house, Ferguson and his three companions opened fire. Then, breaking down the door, Ferguson grabbed the startled Huddleston and stabbed him to death. Next the guerrillas went to the home of Peter and Allen Zachery. According to Champ, the struggle with the two brothers had been "desperate," but the result was the same. Both were killed. These deaths brought the total of men he had killed who had made the flagrant error of insulting Ferguson's family to ten. Ferguson's private vendetta was almost complete; there was one more murder yet to come, but it would be near the end of the war before Ferguson would settle the score with him.[19]

By the spring of 1863, Champ Ferguson and his guerrillas were ranging farther afield and in greater numbers than earlier. He still continued to work closely with Morgan's men, but not actually under his command. Champ and his men, however, were aiding the Confederate cause in the Cumberlands, proving more than just an annoyance to the Federals in the region. Ferguson and his men proved to be so much of a problem for Union troops that in December 1863, in a report to headquarters on the capture of some of Ferguson's men, Union Brigadier General E. H. Hobson wrote, "What shall I do with the

Union Colonel William Stokes raised the black flag, an act that led eventually to Champ Ferguson's death.
(Library of Congress)

prisoners? They are the meanest of Ferguson's guerrillas. Would it not be well to have them shot?"[20]

By 1864, the Federals had driven Confederate armies out of Tennessee, but guerrilla activities were still a big problem. As long as there were irregular bands operating in any force, there would be no security in the homes of the loyal Unionists. This is not to say that Southern sympathizers in the area went unscathed. Upon returning home, Confederate soldiers who lived in this section often found that Union troops and guerrillas had burned their houses. Many of these veterans joined Ferguson and other guerrilla bands as a way of retaliating against federal troops in the area.

Union Colonel William Stokes raised the black flag against all known guerrillas in the area and sent word that he would take no prisoners. Ferguson was ready to return in kind. When he received information of Stokes's movements in February, he planned an ambush. With a force of forty men (Stokes reported 300) he waited for the Union troops on their return to Sparta. As the Federals filed into the valley, they were startled by a shot and saw two men riding rapidly down the road. Quickly the Union troops pursued them, falling into

Even Confederate Major General John Breckinridge could not condone Ferguson's murder of 41 Union soldiers at Saltville.
(Library of Congress)

Ferguson's trap. When Ferguson attacked, the Yankees were completely surprised and fled in all directions, losing half their men in the process. The next day, when Stokes sent out a party to recover the dead and wounded, they found forty-one bodies lying side by side. Thirty-eight of them had been shot to death; the heads of the other three had been crushed by rocks.[21]

During the Battle of Saltville, Virginia, in October 1864, Ferguson's actions would lead to a controversy. At his trial ten months later, Union Captain Orange Sells of the 12th Ohio Cavalry testified that he had witnessed Ferguson kill a number of prisoners and wounded soldiers. Even Confederate Major General John Breckinridge considered it a reprehensible crime.[22] But of all the murders and atrocities committed by Champ Ferguson, the one that ranks the highest in the minds of federal authorities was the killing of Lieutenant Smith of the 13th Kentucky Cavalry. While Smith was a prisoner lying wounded in a Confederate hospital, Ferguson entered the ward and shot him in the head.[23]

According to the folklore in the Cumberlands, Smith was the eleventh and last man on Ferguson's hit list of those that abused his family. At his trial, Ferguson admitted killing Lieutenant Smith in the Emory and Henry Hospital, but not for the reason speculated. "I had a motive in committing the act," he said. "He captured a number of my men at different times, and always killed the last one of them. I was instigated to kill him. . . . He is the only man I killed at or near Saltville, and I am not sorry for killing him."[24]

Ferguson's killing of Lieutenant Smith was reported to General Breckinridge. By his command, Ferguson was arrested by Confederate authorities and held in jail at Wytheville, Virginia, pending trial. He was incarcerated for two months but released on April 5, 1865, on an order from Brigadier General John Echols, and told to join his command.[25]

On April 9, General Robert E. Lee surrendered his Army of Northern Virginia to General Ulysses S. Grant at Appomattox Court House. The terms of their agreement provided that "each officer and man be allowed to returned to their homes, not to be disturbed by the United States authority so long as they observe their parole and laws in force where they reside."[26]

The terms of the agreement were clear in purpose and should not have been difficult to carry out. An exception to this agreement, however, was the case of Champ Ferguson. Before the war ended, federal authorities had determined that Ferguson would not be allowed to surrender. Champ Ferguson was unaware of this decision or he would not have allowed himself to be captured. Knowing the Cumberlands as well as he did, he could have easily hidden out in the mountains and made it impossible for them to find him. In an interview in the *Nashville Dispatch*, Ferguson stated: "When I surrendered I never dreamed of being arrested. I did suppose, however, that they would make me take all the oaths in existence, but that, I was willing to do, and live up to them. Why, I could have kept out of their hands for ten years and never left White County."[27]

On July 11, 1865, Champ Ferguson was indicted on two charges: practicing guerrilla warfare, and murder. There were twenty-three specifications of murder, charging that he had killed fifty-three persons. Since it would be more difficult to prove a charge of murder against a soldier, who would be acting under the orders of his superiors, it was to the prosecutor's advantage to have the accused treated as a guerrilla. The trial would last almost two months. Ferguson was defended by one of the ablest lawyers in Tennessee, Judge Jo Conn Guild. It was probably due to his excellent defense that the trial dragged on so long. The counsel for the defense tried as hard as he could to delay the trial, hoping that the hatred from the war would cool; the longer the delay, the less likelihood of retribution, he reasoned.

Judge Guild's efforts to save Ferguson included three pleas: first, to post-pone the trial; second, to claim that Ferguson was exempt from prosecution under the terms of Lee's surrender to Grant; and third, to question whether a military court had jurisdiction to try a private citizen now that the war was over. The court ruled against all three pleas. With all legal efforts exhausted, the trial began. Ferguson pleaded "Not guilty" to all charges and specifications.[28]

On September 26, 1865, the military commission reached a decision and transmitted it to the general commander of the District of Middle Tennessee. Two weeks later the findings of the commission were approved; Champ Ferguson was to be hanged: "The Court do therefore find the said Champ Ferguson guilty and sentence him to hang by the neck until he is dead at the time and place as the General Commander may order, two-thirds of the members of the Commission concurring in the sentence."[29]

On October 20, 1865, the order of the court was carried out, and Ferguson was executed. Ferguson's last request as he stood on the scaffold was to have his body returned to his home in White County, where he could be buried in good rebel soil. Ferguson's wife complied with his last request. She stayed by her husband's side during life and was faithful to him in death. There were not many that were.[30]

15 Deadly Duo

WILLIAM QUANTRILL AND "BLOODY" BILL ANDERSON

WILLIAM Clarke Quantrill did not look like a killer. He always appeared younger than he was and had soft, wavy blond hair to complement his slender body. Some people remember him as a handsome, clean-shaven young man with a deceptive smile. It was hard to believe he possibly could have killed two men before he was twenty-one years old.

Much the same can be said of Bill Anderson. The handsome, well-dressed guerrilla was easily identified by his dark, full beard and mustache and long hair which fell to his shoulders in ringlets. From head to toe he dressed entirely in black; he was lean and muscular and appeared taller when in the saddle than five ten, his actual height. His easygoing, entertaining, and affable personality belied the real person. Below his exterior was a dangerous, sadistic, brutal man. He was said to have tied a knot in a cord every time he killed a man. The final tally would exceed fifty. His cold stare gave the impression of a "cross between an eagle and a snake." A maniac in battle, he showed no fear or regard for his own life and his men's welfare. Quantrill was known to occasionally spare a life, but Anderson never did. He was aptly named "Bloody Bill."[1]

William Quantrill was the product of chaotic times. The oldest of twelve children, he was born at Canal Dover, Ohio, on July 31, 1837, to Thomas Henry and Caroline Clarke Quantrill. His father was an author and a tinsmith, but just prior to his death in 1854, he served as a principal of the school at Canal Dover. At sixteen, Quantrill himself was a teacher. On other occasions he was a cook for a freight outfit that crossed the plains, a dishonest gambler in a Rocky Mountain gold camp, and a chief suspect of at least two murders — all of this before he was twenty-one years old.[2]

As a child, Quantrill was cruel and showed no mercy toward animals. He was without pity or remorse, delighting in the torture of animals and their cries of pain as they died. When his father spanked him, he never cried. Young Quantrill enjoyed what he called practical jokes. He frequently kept small snakes in his pocket to throw at girls to scare them. On one occasion he locked a teenage girl in the belfry of a church. She spent a terrifying twenty-four hours in the belfry without food or water until she was found. Quantrill enjoyed her horror, thinking it was a good joke.[3]

Young Quantrill had few friends, preferring solitude to social interaction. He never got along with his father but was the favorite of his mother. To his

---

Previous page:

(Right) A photographer shot this picture of Anderson before his body was put on display in a Missouri courthouse for everyone to see. (Used by permission, The State Historical Society of Missouri, Columbia, all rights reserved)

(Left) William Clarke Quantrill looked more like a statesman than a murderer, but he was cruel and merciless, paving the way for the James boys.

(Dictionary of American Portraits, Courtesy Smithsonian Institution)

mother, little Bill could do no wrong. To her he could be charming; to all others he was stubborn, cruel, and deceitful.[4]

Quantrill was a superior student and acquired a good education. At the age of sixteen, he became a teacher. The townspeople said he was the "best teacher they ever had." In his spare time he studied bookkeeping, hoping to take up that occupation later on. During the summer of 1856, Quantrill took courses in chemistry, physiology, Latin, and trigonometry.[5]

When Quantrill was twenty he moved westward, going as far as Utah before returning to Lawrence, Kansas, to take up residence. Before long, he was running with the local thugs and jayhawking across the border into Missouri. By 1860, Quantrill had become a confirmed bandit, thief, and murderer, yet as a criminal he might have remained unknown, ending at a lynching party, had there not been the Civil War. His name in Kansas was "Charley Hart," and in the free-soil town of Lawrence he called himself an abolitionist. He joined the Northerners who vowed to abolish slavery and were part of the Underground Railroad, through which slaves moved to freedom in the North. The Southerners, of course, wanted to get their runaway slaves back and were willing to pay handsomely for their return. Charley Hart seized the opportunity, going into business and revealing how ruthless he could be.

One day he and a friend, Frank Baldwin, encountered a young runaway slave; the slave was exhausted, frightened, and obviously a fugitive. When the fugitive asked for directions to Jim Lane's house, Quantrill offered to take him there. The runaway followed the two, thanking them for their help. When the opportunity presented itself, Quantrill and his companion arrested the fugitive and took him to Westport, Missouri, where the owner paid them a $500 reward for his slave's return.[6]

In December 1860, Quantrill accompanied five young Quaker jayhawkers on a mission to free some slaves of a Missouri slaveholder named Morgan Walker. When they neared the farm, Quantrill rode ahead on a pretext of taking a look at Walker's farmhouse. Arriving at the house, Quantrill revealed the imminent raid. Walker rounded up some of his neighbors and lay in wait. The next day, when the jayhawkers arrived to demand the freedom of the slaves, they rode right into an ambush. Three of the abolitionists were killed and the slaves remained with their master.[7]

Quantrill's betrayal was exposed, but he was quick to find an excuse for his behavior. He explained that the Quakers had been members of a jayhawker gang that had been responsible for the murder of his older brother. His betrayal, he said, had been a way of avenging his brother's death. His new status as an "avenging angel" left him on the side of the pro-slavery Missourians. Quantrill still continued to operate across the border, but now as a bushwhacker.

Early in the war, Quantrill served briefly with the Confederate cavalry at the Battle of Wilson's Creek, but when Southern forces retreated into Arkansas, he left the army. At this time, Quantrill was living in Blue Springs, Missouri. Shortly after his return from the army, a band of Kansas jayhawkers started raiding farmhouses north of Blue Springs. Quantrill joined a posse under the leadership of Andrew Walker to pursue the Kansas raiders. They traced the jayhawkers to a farmhouse. It had been looted and set afire, and the woman of the house had been beaten. In the 1860s, striking a woman, it was believed, was an unpardonable sin; there was no way to justify such outrageous behavior. Walker and his men were determined to make the raiders pay. They caught up with the jayhawkers as they were leaving another burning farmhouse. The posse attacked, yelling and firing. One of the raiders was killed instantly. Two others were mortally wounded and died soon after; the others got away.[8]

By December 1861, after participating in raids with other marauders, Quantrill had found a place for himself in the war. When Walker stepped down as the leader of the marauders, Quantrill quickly took his place, organizing his own band of bushwhackers. Consisting mostly of country men familiar with guns and horses, his band was a mixed group of idealists, opportunists, and vagabonds. Before the war, some of these men had been criminals; others were driven by their hatred for jayhawkers they believed had wronged them. However, not all of the men who rode with Quantrill were savage killers. Many joined Quantrill because a relative or neighbor had done so.[9]

While Quantrill and most of his lieutenants were in their early to mid-twenties when the war began, many of his subordinates were still in their teens. Frank James was sixteen in 1860. His brother Jesse and Cole Younger's brother Jim were just twelve. The men and boys who rode with Quantrill came from the same geographic area; many were related to each other. It is believed that at least half of Quantrill's men either had a brother or cousin riding with them. The fact that there was such a clanlike structure for the group greatly increased the chances of a family member being killed by the enemy, further increasing the command's desire for revenge.[10]

Many of Quantrill's men had ties to the South, but they were not slaveholders or even large landowners. Most of his recruits lived and worked on small family farms or were laborers on somebody else's farm. Although their service with Quantrill branded them as outlaws to federal authorities, the guerrillas did not see themselves as such.[11]

Quantrill had little difficulty in recruiting men after they realized that there was no other organized group to deal specifically with the border situation. Quantrill had a questionable background and no real military experience, but he was able to gather a dedicated group of men who were anxious to defend their homes against the jayhawkers. The band grew quickly in size.

Acting as a Confederate officer, Quantrill trained his men to be expert shots and first-class riders. They also learned how to evade capture and live off the land. Quantrill was exceptionally intelligent, quick-thinking, brash, and confident. He was totally convinced of his invincibility and enjoyed outwitting his enemies.[12]

With his strong personality and power of command, he welded the band into a hard-hitting force called Quantrill's Raiders. Quantrill's men were tough, hardy farm boys, expert horsemen, and among the best shots of any outfit, North or South. They were young, carefree, and willing to take chances. Although armed with carbines, Sharps rifles, and shotguns, their basic weapon was the six-shot Colt .44. Most of Quantrill's men carried two Colts in their be. .d two more in a saddle holster; some carried as many as eight weapons. V. ngaged in battle, they could call on more firepower than their opponent, never having to stop to reload; when one gun was empty, they simply pulled out another. Union troops who carried single-shot carbines that had to be reloaded after every shot were no match for the guerrillas.[13]

Quantrill's men did not follow traditional methods of fighting, preferring to ambush some unsuspecting Yankee patrol. After an attack, the guerrillas would strip the victims' bodies, take their horses and weapons, and disappear into the woods. Another tactic used by Quantrill's men was to dress in Union uniforms, allowing them to approach federal troops closely before opening fire on them. Quantrill's bushwhackers were a menace to all Union forces in the region.[14]

Quantrill was now twenty-four years old, of average height and slight build, with a pale complexion and a mustache that gave him the appearance of a riverboat gambler. His appearance was deceiving; it was hard to believe that he was the leader of a group of killers. Only his cold stare gave any indication of the natural killer instinct that lay below the surface.[15] Despite his appearance, Quantrill was able to secure his leadership by providing his men with immediate action through continued raids on Union sympathizers.

In raid after raid, Quantrill's bushwhackers established themselves as the terror of the Missouri-Kansas border. On March 22, 1862, one hundred members of his gang burned a bridge and murdered the tollkeeper in the presence of his little boy. Then they killed a Union guard. This, Quantrill said, was the answer to an order issued by General Henry Halleck that any bushwhacker who was captured would be hung as a robber and murderer.[16]

On April 21, 1862, Quantrill and his men officially were declared outlaws in Special Order No. 47, issued by Brigadier General James Totten, the commanding Union officer in Missouri. It read, in part, "All those found in arms and open opposition to the laws and legitimate authorities ... will be shot where they are found perpetrating the foul acts."[17] Quantrill's reply to General Totten's order was to "raise the black flag," which meant that he, too, would give no quarter — no prisoners would be taken. Surprisingly, the outlawing of his band not only made his men more desperate, but it actually increased their ability to recruit new members.

Like so many of the bushwhackers, "Bloody Bill" Anderson was a country boy, born in 1840 at Salt Springs Township in Randolph County, Missouri. Anderson's father, Bill Anderson Sr., moved from place to place, trying to make a living. He even traveled to California looking for gold; like most, he didn't find it. Then in 1855, when Kansas opened up to settlers, he moved his family there. The Andersons were of rough stock, and, according to Judge L. D. Bailey, "their reputation as to horse flesh was somewhat unsavory." As teenagers, young Bill Anderson and his brother Jim helped to support the family by stealing horses. In 1860, Anderson's mother died when a lightning bolt struck her. She was thirty-six and left behind six children, Bill being the oldest.

On May 12, 1862, Anderson's father was killed by a man named Arthur Baker. The Anderson boys made no immediate attempt to avenge their father's death, biding their time until the opportunity presented itself. Two months later, Anderson, with his brother Jim and a friend, confronted Baker and his brother-in-law in Baker's store. Baker drew his gun and fired, striking Jim in the leg. Bill returned fire, hitting Baker. Then, locking Baker and his companion in the cellar of the store, Anderson set fire to the building. After making sure that Baker was dead, they torched his house and barn.[18]

Later, Bill Anderson would change the story of his father's death, saying he had been tortured and killed by Yankees. After a while, he actually seemed to believe the story himself. In a letter to the editors of a Lexington, Missouri, newspaper on July 7, 1864, Anderson wrote, "I have chosen guerrilla warfare to revenge myself for the wrongs that I could not honorably revenge otherwise. I lived in Kansas when the war commenced. Because I could not fight the people of Missouri, my native state, the Yankees sought my life, but failed to get me. Revenged themselves by murdering my father, destroying all my property, and since that time murdered one of my sisters and kept two in jail twelve months."[19]

In Missouri, Bill and his brother began their full-time bushwhacking, first operating in Jackson County to the south and east of Kansas City. Early in the fall of 1862, William Quantrill received complaints that the Andersons were robbing pro-Southerners as well as Unionist civilians. Quantrill had the pair apprehended and warned them to be more careful in those they mistreaded or they would be killed. Anderson moved his operations to another part of Missouri, but he never forgave Quantrill for the humiliation.[20]

In Missouri, Bill and Jim joined a guerrilla gang composed mainly of men from Kansas who claimed to be Southern sympathizers. By the summer of 1863, Anderson had formed his own bushwhacker gang and was making regular raids in Missouri and Kansas. During this time "Bloody Bill" joined up with Quantrill. Together they terrorized the citizens of Kansas and gained nationwide publicity for their atrocities.

All through 1862, Quantrill's band robbed, ambushed, burned, and attacked Union troops. They killed soldiers and civilians. On one occasion in September 1862, they attacked Olathe, Kansas, burning the newspaper office and killing three civilians. Quantrill swaggered about the town, informing old Kansas acquaintances that he should now be addressed as "Captain." Quantrill's raids were so frequent that a Kansas City paper stated, "Quantrill & Co. do rule in this section of the state."[21]

As 1862 drew to a close, Quantrill's fame continued to grow. In less than a year he had leaped from an unknown Border Ruffian to the captain and leader of a group of partisan rangers, the most formidable guerrilla band in Missouri. Already he was famous in the West; now he wanted the rest of the country to know his name. These thoughts were on his mind as he traveled to Richmond, Virginia, for an interview with Confederate Secretary of War James Seddon.

Quantrill asked Seddon to commission him as a colonel under the Partisan Ranger Act.[22] He also suggested that the whole Confederacy should "raise the black flag" and refuse to take prisoners, killing the captured enemy troops instead. Seddon rejected the idea, stating that in the nineteenth century it was barbaric to fight under the black flag. Although Quantrill's request for commission as a colonel was not granted, he had his picture taken in a colonel's uniform and signed all his dispatches and orders with that rank.[23]

Seddon's action disappointed Quantrill. He had been ignored by the high ranking officials in Richmond. There were no dinners or balls in his honor to recognize the sacrifice he had made for his country. Richmond had many heroes, but he was not one of them. When he returned to his command, he was surprised to see the reduction in its size in his absence. His men had joined Major General Thomas Hindman's troops for several battles in Arkansas and southern Missouri, but they soon tired of the regimentation and discipline required of soldiers in the regular army.[24]

When Quantrill complained about his disappointment to Major General Sterling Price, he assured Quantrill that there would be another chance to gain distinction. Price urged him to quit bushwhacking and form his men into a regular army unit if he wanted recognition from the Confederate officials in Richmond. Quantrill considered Price's advice and presented it to his men. It turned out to be an ill-advised action. As a result, he lost the close allegiance and loyalty that he had enjoyed with his command. Many of his men began to strike out on their own, often under the leadership of George Todd.[25] Illiterate, hotheaded, and always looking for a fight, Todd was highly respected by the younger guerrillas. Eventually he would challenge Quantrill for the leadership of the gang.

By the summer of 1863, Quantrill's control of his command was deteriorating. Then, an act by Union Brigadier General Thomas Ewing revived his flagging leadership. On June 16, 1863, Ewing assumed command of the border district. It was the same day that Quantrill's guerrillas ambushed and killed fourteen Union soldiers. The disaster increased Ewing's determination to escalate the campaign against the bushwhackers. Ewing issued orders to attack guerrillas in ambush whenever possible and to infiltrate their ranks as spies. His methods were somewhat effective, at least for a time, and residents on the border did

notice some change. There were fewer guerrilla raids, and Union patrols returning from a mission often had with them dead guerrillas.[26]

Despite his success and praise from the Kansas newspapers, Ewing was not
satisfied. It was not enough to keep bushwhackers in Missouri; he wanted to
rid the area of them altogether. To accomplish this, Ewing would clear the
region of the guerrillas' families, friends, and anyone who supported them.[27]
Many of the local population were friends or relatives of the guerrillas and
could be counted on for horses, food, clothing, and information about troop
movements. Out of fear, those who were secret Union sympathizers had no
choice but to aid the bushwhackers.[28]

Ewing sought approval of his plan from Major General John Schofield,
commander of the Department of the Missouri. Schofield approved of his plan
but cautioned him that he should move with care; only the greatest offenders
should be removed. He also warned him that Quantrill's men would probably
retaliate.[29]

Ewing immediately issued General Order No. 10: "Arrest, and send to the
district provost-marshal for punishment, all men (and all women not heads of
families) who willingly aid and encourage guerrillas, with a written statement
of the names and residences of such persons and of proof against them.... The
wives and children of known guerrillas, and also women who are heads of families and are willfully engaged in aiding guerrillas, will be notified by such officers to remove out of the district and out of the state of Missouri forthwith.
They will be permitted to take, unmolested, their stock, provisions, and household goods."[30]

Starting in July, Union troops began arresting Missouri women believed to
be aiding partisans. Among those arrested and taken to prison were three of
Bill Anderson's sisters. The women were imprisoned in a three-story brick building until they could be sent south to Confederate territory. The building was
old, poorly constructed, and allowed to deteriorate. On August 14 in the early
afternoon, the building collapsed with the women inside. When they were
pulled from the rubble, the survivors were bloody and hysterical, accusing the
Federals of murder. Bloody Bill's sister Josephine and four other women were
dead. The rumor was circulated that Union authorities had deliberately undermined the building's foundation so that it would collapse and kill all those
inside. The accusation was ridiculous, but the guerrillas believed the act had

been intentional. Many Southern sympathizers believed it, too, including Bill Anderson. "Vengeance is in my heart, death in my hand; blood and revenge are hammering in my head," became the battle cry.[31]

After the treatment of his sisters, Anderson's killing of enemy soldiers became an end in itself, one driven by hatred. Anderson became a homicidal maniac in his desire to kill Union troops.[32] Anderson and Quantrill's gangs now contained several hundred members, making it larger than some Confederate regiments. A special hatred had developed between these Confederate guerrillas and the Kansas free-staters and jayhawkers for whom Lawrence, Kansas, was a haven. The town had become a symbol for all that the bushwhackers hated.[33]

Quantrill met with his captains to outline plans for what he believed would be the greatest raid of the war, an attack on Lawrence. Lawrence, Kansas, epitomized everything the South despised in the North. Its New England reformers and its widely circulated newspaper had excited the nation with abolitionist propaganda for many years. Quantrill also had received word that the hated Jim Lane was home on vacation. This would be a perfect opportunity to destroy some old enemies and build on his reputation as a raider. Quantrill's captains listened sullenly to his proposal, and then, with a yell of approval, the men voted for the raid. "We could stand no more," one guerrilla said.[34]

On August 19, 1863, Quantrill and a band of 300 men set out for Lawrence, the town that would forever be associated with his name. In this column rode Cole Younger and Frank James. Both were to win notoriety later, at the end of the Civil War, as bandits and outlaws.[35] En route, the Missourians picked up 150 more men.

At dawn, on August 21, they reached Lawrence. Some of the men wanted to turn back, fearing the town had been warned of their approach and that they were riding into a trap. "You can do as you please," said Quantrill. "I'm going into Lawrence." He drew his pistol from his belt, spurred his horse, and shouted "Charge!"[36]

Roaring into Lawrence on separate streets, the guerrillas reached the Kansas River and cut the ferry cable. Then the bushwhackers fanned out to complete the raid. Half awake, citizens armed themselves and stepped outside only to be cut down by gunfire from the marauders. So complete was the surprise that the citizens who chose to fight had to do it individually and had no chance.[37]

Down the streets of Lawrence, the marauders galloped, with Quantrill urging his men to "Kill! Kill! Lawrence must be cleansed, and the only way to

Quantrill and his men destroyed Lawrence, Kansas, his former home.
(Used by permission, The State Historical Society of Missouri, Columbia, all rights reserved)

cleanse it is to kill." The first victim to be shot down was a minister named Snyder, who was milking his cow. Yelling their vengeful cry "Osceola," in memory of the Missouri town destroyed in 1861 by the Kansas Brigade, the mounted bushwhackers next encountered a detachment of twenty-two Union army recruits. Surging over the drowsy soldiers, they shot some and trampled the others. In all, seventeen men were killed.[38]

The bushwhackers surrounded a downtown hotel. A guest hung a white sheet from the window and asked Quantrill what he wanted. "Plunder," he answered, and the guests were ordered out and robbed while the gang torched the hotel.[39] Then, while Quantrill ate breakfast in another Lawrence hotel, the band carried out his orders to "kill every man big enough to carry a gun."[40] Quantrill took no part in the actual killing, preferring to observe the massacre from the vantage point of the hotel. Horror-stricken survivors sought sanctuary in his care.[41]

The guerrillas spread out over the town, carrying lists of those to be executed and houses to be burned. One group of guerrillas went to Jim Lane's house to capture him and take him back to Missouri for a public hanging. Awakened by the noise in the street just before they arrived, Lane removed his nameplate from the door and hid in a nearby cornfield. The guerrillas ransacked his house, took his sword and flag, and torched his house to the ground, but they didn't find him.[42]

The massacre at Lawrence, Kansas, was unparalleled in Civil War history. Houses and buildings were looted and then torched; men were pulled from their houses and shot in cold blood before their wives and children. Others were burned alive inside their homes. Two wounded men who had managed to crawl out of the flames were thrown back in.[43] One woman threw her arms around her husband and begged the raiders to spare his life. Resting their pistol on her arm, they shot him dead anyway. The powder from the pistol burned the sleeve of her dress.[44] When the mayor of Lawrence tried to hide from the invaders at the bottom of a well, he was suffocated by the smoke from a burning building nearby. Quantrill's men, many of whom were drunk from whiskey they had appropriated from saloons in town, rode up and down the streets, dragging American flags in the dust behind their horses.[45] Bill Anderson personally killed fourteen men; he made his victims crawl at his feet and beg for mercy before killing them. "I'm here for revenge," he said, "and I have got it."[46]

At nine o'clock, the massacre ended when scouts reported that Union troops were approaching from the north and west. They left behind a devastated town with dozens of fires raging and at least 150 dead, all men and boys. Women, by Quantrill's orders, had been spared. None had been injured or physically violated. The property damaged was estimated at 2 million dollars. Only one of Quantrill's men was killed at Lawrence; Larkin Skaggs was so drunk that he did not hear the call to leave and was left behind. When the survivors discovered him, he was promptly shot, and the angry mob tore his body to pieces. Several other guerrillas were captured in the pursuit and were executed.[47]

The New York Daily Times reported, "Quantrill's massacre at Lawrence is almost enough to curdle the blood with horror. In the history of the war thus far, full as it has been of dreadful scenes, there has been no such diabolical work as this indiscriminate slaughter of peaceful villagers."[48] The Lawrence massacre was unlike the sacking of any other town during the Civil War. It had no real military purpose, nor was it a part of any grand strategy. It was a scene of blood and destruction, inspired, led, and carried out because of the hatred and desire for notoriety of one man — William Clarke Quantrill.[49]

Quantrill may have believed that his leadership in the destruction of Lawrence would be recognized and rewarded by the Confederate government. It was recognized, but not rewarded. The event was not viewed with favor; rather, the South repudiated it. Any chance he had of receiving a commission and being recognized as a legitimate officer of the Confederacy dissipated with the act. Now, more than ever, he was despised by both the blue and gray.[50]

From a military point of view, the Lawrence raid was a resounding success for the guerrillas. Quantrill had penetrated deeply into enemy territory with minimum losses to his command. He had coordinated a variety of factors needed for a successful raid — speed, daring, skill, and total surprise. The long-term effects, however, were disastrous for the people of Missouri.[51] In retribution for Quantrill's raid, General Ewing issued one of the most repressive measures ever inflicted on an American civilian population. Under his General Order No. 11, the inhabitants of three Missouri border counties and half of another were given fifteen days to leave their homes and remove all their belongings. Even those citizens who could demonstrate proof of their loyalty to the Union were required to leave.[52] Federal troops drove thousands of people into the open prairie, while the jayhawkers followed behind, raiding the refugees, stealing even such personal things as wedding rings. "The very air seems charged with blood and death," a newspaper reporter wrote. "Pandemonium itself seems to have broken loose, and robbery, murder ... and death runs riot over the country."[53] Houses were razed, crops burned, and possessions stolen or destroyed.

As a result of General Order No. 11, the population of Cass County was reduced from 10,000 to 600. After the war, when the exiles were allowed to return to their homes, they found the roads and fields overgrown and their homes in ashes. For many years the term "Burnt District" was applied to the counties of Bates, Cass, and Jackson. Although the loss of life was relatively small, when the families were forced to move, they suffered large financial loss.[54] It would be a long time before the folks in those three counties forgot their mistreatment. Their ill feelings would be an asset to the outlaws who roamed that region after the war.

General Ewing had hoped he could put a stop to the guerrilla activity by destroying their cover and food supply, but the evacuation hardly bothered them. They easily avoided both Union troops and roving jayhawkers, living off the land and food supplies left behind by the departing Missourians. Quantrill's guerrillas operated well away from any assistance from Confederate forces and were outnumbered and ruthlessly hunted. Nevertheless, they were still able to continue to be a thorn in the side of the Union and to avoid capture.

In October 1863, near Baxter Springs, Kansas, Quantrill's Raiders confronted a column of Yankee cavalry and a wagon train led by Major General James Blunt. Whooping and hollering and disguised in federal uniforms, the Confederate guerrillas wiped out the column in a few minutes. Never satisfied just to kill the enemy, Quantrill and his men mauled the bodies and burned them, some beyond recognition. Only Blunt's swift horse saved him from the fate of most of his party. Nearly a hundred were killed, and some of the bodies were stripped and mutilated.[55]

Anderson's men were not present at this massacre but arrived in time to ransack the wagons; this, however, did not satisfy Anderson. He craved Yankee blood, not loot, and he tried to convince Quantrill to resume an attack on a fort nearby. Quantrill refused, saying, "We've done enough. Let's not take any more chances." Anderson was disgusted; he wanted another chance to kill more Yankees despite the risk.[56] After the incident at Baxter Springs, Anderson broke with Quantrill, taking a portion of his command with him. Among those who followed him were Frank and Jesse James. Anderson soon began a series of raids on federal supply lines, attacking trains and railroads.[57]

The Confederate government was growing increasingly more disenchanted with the uncontrolled actions of the guerrillas, particularly Quantrill's Raiders. The guerrillas were becoming a terror to the citizens and an injury to the Southern cause. Confederate officials were not only concerned about their immoral and lawless acts, but also about the loss of many young men who were joining the partisan companies to avoid regular service. Generals such as J.E.B. Stuart and Robert E. Lee spoke out against these guerrilla bands. "The evils resulting from their organization more than counterbalance the good they accomplish," Lee told Secretary of War Seddon in January 1864. Lee recommended that the law authorizing these partisan corps be abolished. The Confederate congress followed his advice and on February 15, 1864, repealed the Partisan Ranger Act. At this stage of the war, however, the Confederate government had no means of enforcing the law, and the guerrilla bands continued to operate.[58]

After the Lawrence and Baxter Springs massacres, Quantrill reached the height of his career; he was now the most famous guerrilla commander in the entire Confederacy. Nevertheless, there was still a challenge to his leadership. The rival was George Todd, Quantrill's first lieutenant. Todd lacked Quantrill's tactical sense, and it was said that he "knew only one way to fight — charge straight ahead." His foolhardy courage made him the hero of the younger, more reckless guerrillas. Some declared that Todd, not Quantrill, should receive credit for the events at Lawrence and Baxter Springs. For several months, Todd had been the real leader of Quantrill's band; Quantrill had learned to treat him with caution.[59]

After Baxter Springs, Quantrill and 400 of his men relocated to Texas to escape the cold weather of Missouri and the hot pursuit of the Union troops out to avenge the massacre at Lawrence. In Texas, Brigadier General George McCulloch assigned Quantrill the responsibility of rounding up deserters and Union raiders; of those they pursued, the bushwhackers shot more than they brought back. When not on duty, the guerrillas relaxed in their winter quarters. On Christmas day a gang of Quantrill's men rode into Sherman, shooting their guns and shouting. They shot up the church steeple, rode their horses into a hotel lobby, and ransacked several places of business. On New Year's Day some of the same men were engaged in a brawl in Sherman. In both cases, Quantrill had to be called to restore order, apologize, and pay for the damage. During the next few months the unruliness of Quantrill's men increased until General McCulloch called for the arrest of the entire command.[60]

On March 30, Quantrill was ordered to present himself at McCulloch's headquarters. There, he was immediately arrested, but he easily outfoxed his guards and escaped. With a portion of his command, Quantrill left Texas and returned to Missouri to continue his independent operation.[61]

Quantrill's precipitous fall from power came sooner than expected. Some of his men left the band after charging him with an unequal distribution of loot taken in some of the raids. Others were shocked by the ruthlessness of some of their own comrades and decided to leave. But the main reason was a dispute with George Todd. Shortly after leaving Texas, the long-brewing showdown between the two men came to a head. During a card game, Quantrill accused Todd of cheating, a charge that was true. When Todd threatened him, Quantrill replied that he was not afraid of any man. Todd drew his revolver and shoved it into Quantrill's face. "You're afraid of me, aren't you Bill?" he snapped. Knowing what the consequences would be if he gave the wrong answer, Quantrill swallowed his pride and choked out the words, "Yes, I'm afraid of you." Todd put down the gun, a smile of triumph on his face. He had humiliated Quantrill in front of his men. Without saying a word, Quantrill got up, went outside, and rode away.[62]

In the summer of 1864, Quantrill's former associate Bloody Bill Anderson was in Kansas. On July 15, 1864, Anderson's bushwhackers raided Huntsville, his own home town, robbing merchants and a bank of $45,000 and shooting a passerby who tried to stop him. Anderson did, at least, make his men return money they had taken from some of his former schoolmates. On July 23, Anderson's men destroyed the railroad station at Renick. The next day they ambushed a company of the 17th Illinois Cavalry, and two of the slain Union soldiers were scalped. To one soldier's collar they attached a note: "You come to hunt bushwhackers. Now you are skelpt."[63]

All of central Missouri was terrified by the actions of the guerrillas. They, however, had the support of many Confederate sympathizers across the state who tended to overlook their brutal actions or dismissed the acts as exaggerated rumors spread by the Yankees. Anderson sent letters to the Union troop commanders daring them to leave their forts and fight.[64]

Provoked by editorials in the newspapers urging the readers to fight the guerrillas, Anderson sent a threatening letter to the papers: "Listen to me, fellow citizens. Do not take up arms if you value your lives.... It is not in my power to save your lives if you do. If you proclaim to be in arms against guerrillas, I will kill you. I will hunt you down like wolves and murder you. You can not escape.... Be careful how you act, for my eyes are upon you."[65]

On the morning of September 27, 1864, Anderson carried out one of his most outrageous and barbaric massacres. With a band of eighty men disguised in Union blues, he rode into Centralia, a whistlestop on the North Missouri Railroad. Anderson's mission was frivolous; he wanted to have some fun and see what his men could steal. Entering the town, the bushwhackers met no resistance. They spread terror among the residents and seized everything they wanted. What they didn't want, they destroyed, breaking china and amusing themselves by unrolling long bolts of cloth and dragging it through the streets.

At the depot the raiders found a barrel of whiskey and several cases of new boots. They helped themselves to both. Filling the boots with whiskey, they used them as cups from which to drink. In a short time, many of the men were drunk and in a murderous mood.[66]

At 11:00 o'clock, a stage arrived, and the guerrillas quickly relieved the passengers of their money. At noon, the westbound train from St. Louis came into view. Just before Anderson's gang entered Centralia, the local telegraph operator had sent word up the line that there were guerrillas in the area and that it would be dangerous to come without guards. The conductor, however, ignored the warning, reasoning that he had twenty-five soldiers on board and, although unarmed, the sight would be enough to scare the bushwhackers off. It was a decision he would regret.[67]

When the crew and passengers saw the smoke from the town and the armed men at the station, they realized what was happening and the potential danger. Seeing the problem, the engineer hoped to run the train past the town, but the bushwhackers had thrown railroad ties on the tracks, forcing the train to stop. When it did, the guerrillas swarmed through the cars, firing pistols at the ceiling and robbing the passengers. Anderson went for the baggage car and had no trouble getting the clerk to open the safe.[68]

The bushwhackers forced the civilians off the train, and Anderson asked the soldiers to surrender. "Do as we tell you, and you'll be treated as prisoners of war," he said. All but two complied immediately. The two that held back were shot by Anderson, their bodies falling down between two of the cars. Once off the train, the civilians and soldiers were separated into two groups on the platform. All of the soldiers were on furlough; some were wounded or sick, and one was on crutches. Anderson surveyed the soldiers for a few minutes and then, in an angry voice, shouted, "You Federals have just killed six of my men, scalped them, and left them on the prairie.... I will show you that I can kill men with as much skill and rapidity as anybody. From this time on I ask no quarter and given none. Every Federal soldier on whom I put my fingers shall die like a dog. If I get into your clutches I expect death. You are all to be killed and sent to hell."[69]

Anderson's guerrillas lined up opposite the soldiers, some of whom fell to their knees, begging for mercy; some stood straight and stared at their killers. When Anderson gave the command, his men opened fire. Some soldiers fell immediately from the first shots; the rest tried to escape until another round of gunfire stopped them. The other train passengers watched in horror as the guerrillas slaughtered the soldiers and then scalped and mutilated the bodies. After setting fire to the train, Anderson and his men rode out of Centralia, leaving behind a devastated town and twenty-four dead Union soldiers.[70]

Two hours after Anderson left Centralia, Union Major A.V.E. Johnson, with 150 men of the 39th Infantry searching for bushwhackers, saw smoke rising from the town. When they arrived, the townspeople pleaded with Johnson to wait for reinforcements before he went after Anderson. Most of Johnson's men were new recruits, poorly armed, and mounted on plodding horses and mules. He would be no match for Anderson, but in spite of the warning, Johnson set off after the guerrillas.[71]

When Anderson saw that he was being pursued, he set a trap for Johnson, splitting his troops into three parts, concealing all but a few that he left in the open as bait; then he waited for Johnson. Johnson ordered his men to dismount and form a skirmish line while the others held the horses of the dismounted men. "My God, the Lord have mercy on them!" exclaimed one of Anderson's men. "They are dismounted to fight!" For several minutes, the battlefield was quiet. Finally Anderson gave the orders: "Boys, when we charge, break through the line and keep straight on for their horses. Keep straight on for their horses." He then raised and lowered his hat three times, the signal for the attack. Johnson watched the small party of guerrillas advancing; this is what he hoped for. Then, from out of the woods, from three sides, came the rest of Anderson's men. Johnson had marched himself into a trap from which there was no escape.[72]

Johnson's men had time to fire only one volley, which killed three bushwhackers and wounded three others. Before they could reload, the guerrillas swarmed upon them, killing some of the soldiers where they stood; the others turned and fled in wild panic, many throwing down their weapons. Some threw their hands up to surrender, only to be shot down or trampled by horses. Those left behind to guard the horses mounted them and tried to escape, but they were overtaken and killed. Johnson was killed with one shot to the temple. The battle lasted only three minutes.[73]

Bloody Bill's men robbed, scalped, and mutilated the bodies. A number of the dead were beheaded, and their heads were placed on fence posts. As trophies from his victory, Anderson placed scalps on both sides of his saddle.

Later, seventy-nine unclaimed bodies were buried in a mass grave near Centralia.[74]

Bill Anderson's name would forever be associated with the slaughter at Centralia, and his reputation now challenged that of Quantrill. On October 7, 1864, the *Leavenworth Daily Bulletin* compared Anderson to Quantrill: "As Anderson is taking the place of Quantrill in the management of cutthroats in Missouri, the question is often asked: 'Who is this Anderson, who is more bloodthirsty than Quantrill?' He is more of a fiend, if possible, than Quantrill."[75]

When Confederate General Price learned of the massacre at Centralia, he was aghast. But Price needed the help of Anderson's bushwhackers and made peace with him, accepting a pair of silver revolvers from him. Price ordered Anderson to destroy the North Missouri Railroad. As ordered, Anderson's men destroyed railroad cars, downed telegraph lines, and tore up tracks, leaving a trail of destruction behind them. As they moved eastward, they sacked Danville and burned depots at New Florence, High Hill, and Renick, and left numerous homes and barns in flames.[76]

In the middle of October, General Price ordered Quantrill's rival George Todd and his men to join Brigadier General Jo Shelby's cavalry. On October 21, Shelby's men engaged Union General James Blunt in battle. Still smarting from his defeat at Baxter Springs, Blunt was beaten again. As Todd and his men pursued Blunt, a single shot from a Union sharpshooter dropped him. The bullet entered his neck, shattering his throat, leaving him paralyzed. Todd died two hours later, before he could receive medical treatment.[77]

By the end of October, time was running out for Bill Anderson, too. Wanted for murder, robbery, and reprisal, he was hunted by Major Samuel Cox in northeast Missouri. Cox had assembled a force of cavalry to pursue Anderson. As they approached Richmond, Missouri, a farm woman informed Cox that Anderson was camped near Albany, just a few miles away. At first Cox was suspicious, fearing ambush; however, some of his men knew the woman and vouched for her.[78]

About half a mile from Anderson's camp, Cox had his men dismount and hide on both sides of the road. Then he sent a small cavalry force ahead to attract Anderson's attention. When Anderson saw the Yankee horsemen, he prepared his men to attack. Giving the rebel yell, he led his men in chase of the small federal unit. The concealed Union cavalry waited until he and his men were in range before they fired. Anderson had fallen for the same trap as the one he had set just a few weeks earlier for Major Johnson and his men. Anderson continued to charge forward, running the gauntlet until two bullets struck him in the back of his head. He toppled backward off his horse onto the ground, still clutching his revolvers in both hands.[79] Several soldiers approached Anderson's body. A bullet had blown away a portion of his skull behind the left ear, and another had penetrated his left temple. He had died instantly.[80]

After determining that the body was that of Bill Anderson, Cox had it placed in a wagon and taken back to Richmond, Missouri, where a local photographer was called to take a picture of the corpse. When Anderson's body was placed on display in the county courthouse, hundreds filed by to see it. Before he was buried in a shallow grave on the edge of town, one of the soldiers cut off Anderson's finger to get his ring. That evening two Union militia visited the cemetery to pay their last respects; they urinated on the grave. Bloody Bill Anderson was dead and buried at last.[81]

Following the death of Todd and Anderson, Quantrill went into action. With remnants of his guerrilla force, which he called his Black Flag Brigade, he raided a few small-town stores and worked his way through Arkansas and Tennessee into Kentucky. In Kentucky, the guerrillas became nothing more than outlaws who pretended to be serving the Confederate cause. They stole horses, robbed and looted villages, and murdered soldiers and civilians.[82]

After the collapse of the Confederacy, Quantrill and his men decided to surrender along with Southern forces in Kentucky. In this way, they hoped to avoid execution as enemy guerrillas. Before they could surrender, however, they were ambushed by a company of federal troops under the command of Captain Edwin Terrill. Just one day after Lee's surrender, Terrill caught up with Quantrill. Under a barrage of fire, Quantrill was hit in the back and his spine shattered, paralyzing him from the shoulder down. One of Terrill's men watched Quantrill fall from his horse face down in the mud, and then he fired again. This shot blew off Quantrill's right trigger finger. The soldier took Quantrill's boots, pistol, and money. When questioned, Quantrill claimed to be Captain Clarke of the 4th Missouri Cavalry. Not realizing they had Quantrill, the troops left to continue their search for him.[83]

After the federals left, Quantrill's friends brought a doctor to help him, hoping to hide him until he could recover. The paralyzed Quantrill declined, saying, "Boys, it is impossible for me to get well, the war is over, and I am in reality a dying man, so let me alone. Goodbye." Two days later, after learning who the wounded man was, Terrill returned for Quantrill. Quantrill was loaded into a wagon and taken to a prison in Louisville. Placed in a military prison hospital, he was cared for by a Catholic priest. Before he died, Quantrill made a full confession and converted to Catholicism. He lingered in great pain for nearly a month, dying in the hospital on June 6, 1865.[84]

Quantrill was buried in the Old Portland Cemetery in Louisville. The priest who officiated at the burial refused to have a tombstone erected at the gravesite, fearing someone might steal the body.[85] In 1877, his mother had his bones exhumed under the guise of moving them to the family burial plot in Ohio. When she received the bones, however, they were not reburied; rather, she sold them to curiosity seekers.

Myths evolved about the Missouri bushwhacker. To some, Quantrill was a hero, defending the South against the evil North. In reality, he was a notorious killer, responsible for the death of many innocent people.

Quantrill was the master of guerrilla warfare. He recruited country boys who were already familiar with horses and guns. Then he drilled them relentlessly until they had no equal in riding and shooting. He maintained an elaborate intelligence network, which proved helpful in locating enemy movements and their strength. This method of waging war was effective during war and could be equally effective for outlaws on horseback in peace time — hit the target by surprise, with lightning speed, then scatter into the surrounding countryside to hide in places they had scouted in advance.[86] In just a short time, the James-Younger Gang would put these concepts into practice. Quantrill's legacy would live on.

Epilogue   The Aftermath of Violence

J UST after 2 o'clock on February 13, 1866, a band of twelve men rode into Liberty, Missouri, dressed in blue coats and other bits of Union Army apparel. Some wore six-shooters strapped outside their coats. The first three riders dismounted in the town square, getting into positions where they could watch the surrounding streets. The others rode up to the Clay County Savings Association, where two dismounted and entered the bank. The others remained outside to guard the entrance.

Inside the bank, cashier Greenup Bird and his son William were working at their desks behind the counter when two strangers entered. One of them walked to the teller's window and asked to have a bill changed. William Bird left his desk and went to the counter to change it. As he did, the second stranger drew a revolver and demanded the bank's money.[1]

With businesslike speed, the bandits cleaned the open vault of gold and silver coins, as well as greenbacks and some bonds, all estimated to be worth $60,000. The cashier was forced into the vault with his son, and one of the bandits smiled and said, "Stay in there. Don't you know all Birds should be caged?" Leaving the father and son shut in the vault, the bandits dashed outside and galloped off.[2]

The robbery at Liberty was the first daylight, peacetime bank robbery in American history. Later, a posse was formed to pursue the bandits, but by that time the outlaws were well out of sight and reach. Having the finest mounts available, they easily outran their pursuers. It is doubtful that the posse wanted to tangle with twelve well-armed desperadoes anyway.

The men responsible for the robbery were members of the James-Younger Gang. No serious effort was made to catch the perpetrators, yet some people must have known who they were. None of the outlaws wore masks, yet after the robbery the Birds said they couldn't identify any of the men; no one in town came forward to name them either. It was this type of protection or fear that enabled the James-Younger Gang to remain so long at large.

Rather than earning the disdain of their countrymen for their outrageous actions, the gang skillfully capitalized on lingering frustration from the Civil War and public sentiment against large banks, the railroads, and agents from the Pinkerton Detective Agency, who were sent to capture them. Jesse James and his gang came from the farm state of Missouri, which had suffered greatly during the Civil War. After the war, farmers needed money to restore their farms. Many banks took advantage of the situation by charging exorbitant interest rates. Railroad companies were the object of scorn for holding a monopoly on transporting crops to large eastern markets. Law-abiding citizens applauded when the gang robbed a bank or railroad and were able to elude the Pinkerton men.[3]

The gang would remain at large for almost two decades. Jesse James, their leader, was only eighteen years old when the war ended. He and his brother Frank, along with their cousins the Younger brothers, became America's most famous outlaws. Today, more than a century later, they retain that distinction.

President Theodore Roosevelt called Jesse James "America's Robin Hood." He had become to many the handsome outlaw who rides the western plains on a magnificent horse and steals only from the rich (railroads and banks) to help the poor. Nothing could be farther from the truth. Countless stories about the James-Younger Gang — most unsupported with hard evidence — have been told, stories of their prowess as horsemen, their skill with a Colt revolver, their courage, and their love for their fellow man. These are the stories from which myths and legends are made; while memorable, they are exaggerated and without foundation.

Alexander Franklin James was born on January 10, 1843, the first son of Robert and Zerelda James. When Frank was four years old, Zerelda's third child, Jesse Woodson James, was born. By 1850, Robert James was a prosperous man, owning 275 acres of land that he farmed with the assistance of seven slaves. His estate included more than fifty books on a wide variety of subjects, including Shakespeare. The family foundation of Frank and Jesse was solid.

When gold fever swept the country in 1848 and 1849, Robert James left his established farm to accompany a party of gold rushers to California. Robert almost changed his mind about the trip when little Jesse, crying and clinging to his father's legs, looked up and begged him not to go. But he had given his word to the others in the party, and a man could not go back on his word.[4] He joined the rush to California to find gold; instead he found illness and death.

Zerelda married Benjamin Simms, but they were together only a few months before he picked up and moved out. Zerelda's last husband, Dr. Reuben Samuel, was a good husband and father and was supportive of the boys, even when they were pursued by the law. He and Zerelda had four children together.[5]

Every Sunday the family drove to church. Jesse and Frank regularly attended Sunday school and church, and Jesse remained steadfast in his religious beliefs as long as he lived. He always carried a small copy of the New Testament with him, which he had marked up indicating constant usage. The boys attended the Prairie Grove School during the winter, helping with chores in their spare time. During the summer they tended crops, hunted, and fished. Jesse was well liked, fun loving, sociable, and enjoyed being with people. He made friends easily, but he had one serious problem — he inherited his mother's violent temper. Jesse didn't have much use for "book learning" and had little interest in reading or writing.[6]

Frank was more like his father. He loved to read books, especially the classics. According to one story, Frank had stayed at the home of a well-to-do farmer and had ingratiated himself with the grandmother of the household by

Frank James lived to regret his life of crime, but, after turning himself in, he was able to start anew. (Dictionary of American Portraits, Courtesy Mercaldo Archives)

his behavior. He expressed great interest in her copy of *Pilgrim's Progress.* Frank borrowed the book, and the bookmark indicated that he had almost finished reading it when he returned it to her. When the grandmother learned that Frank was a desperado, she wouldn't believe it — after all, how could someone who had been so courteous and had such reading habits be an outlaw?[7]

The Younger boys were the product of a stable family. Thomas Coleman Younger was the seventh of fourteen children of Bursheba Leighton and Henry Washington Younger. He was born on January 15, 1844, at Lee's Summit. His brother James Hardin Younger was born four years later. Their father was very enterprising; he borrowed money from his father-in-law to create a ferry business, which he quickly parlayed into a small fortune. By 1850, he was wealthy enough to purchase over a hundred acres of prime farmland.

In 1851, John Harrison Younger was born. John killed his first man at the age of fifteen. He was arrested but acquitted on the ground of self-defense.[8] Robert Younger, the baby of the Missouri brothers who followed the outlaw trail with Frank and Jesse James, was born in 1853. Robert and his brother John were too young to fight in the Civil War, but later they were old enough to become members of the James-Younger Gang.

While living in Harrisonville, Cole and Jim attended school; education was

Cole Younger began serving with Quantrill at eighteen years old before joining forces with his brothers and the James boys, his cousins. (Dictionary of American Portraits, Courtesy Mercaldo Archives)

After his parole, Jim Younger could not go on living without the love of his life, Alix J. Muller, whom he could not leave Missouri to marry. (Dictionary of American Portraits, Courtesy Mercaldo Archives)

Bob Younger died in prison before he could be paroled. (Dictionary of American Portraits, Courtesy Mercaldo Archives)

very important to the Younger family. Cole was a handsome young man who exhibited an air of outward confidence, and he developed a quick mind and captivating personality.[9]

Years before the Civil War officially began with the firing on Fort Sumter, warfare had broken out on the Kansas-Missouri border. Missourians had always expected Kansas to enter the Union as a slave state. Northern abolitionists poured men and money into Kansas to swing the vote in favor of its entry as a free state. Each side sent armed raiders to ensure that their political views were represented. This was still frontier territory, and men were accustomed to settling disputes with a gun. Frank, Jesse, and the Younger boys were raised in this atmosphere of turmoil and hatred.

On May 4, 1861, eighteen-year-old Frank James joined a pro-Confederate militia outfit when Major General Sterling Price, commander of Missouri's troops, came through recruiting. His younger brother, Jesse, watched enviously as his brother marched off to war. Home on a furlough, Frank was arrested by federal officers and released on parole. He did not honor the parole, and shortly after, he joined Quantrill's band. One of Quantrill's first recruits, Frank rode with him until the final fatal days.[10] When Jesse tried to join Quantrill, he was rejected because he was too young.

Dr. Samuel, the boys' stepfather, was well known for his outspoken pro-slavery views. During the summer of 1862, Union militia hung him from a tree and left him for dead. He was saved, however, by his wife, who quietly followed behind the troops and rushed to her husband's aid the moment they left. Cutting him down, she found he was still alive and nursed him back to health. Continuing along, the militia found Jesse plowing a field. They beat him and told him if he continued to support the guerrillas, they would return and hang him, too.

Cole Younger was serving with Quantrill when his father was killed. Henry Younger was found dead "with his pockets turned inside out" and about $400 missing. The attack, believed to have been made by pro-Unionists, devastated his family. The following February, the Younger home was burned to the ground, adding fuel to the Youngers' desire for revenge.[11]

When Jesse was almost seventeen, he rode off to join Quantrill's Raiders, serving under the direct command of Bloody Bill Anderson. In his first battle, despite several wounds, Jesse distinguished himself. He also was credited with several personal killings, drawing the attention of his leader. Bloody Bill admired the young boy's courage and said of Jesse, "To have no beard, he is the keenest fighter among us."[12]

Jesse fought with Bloody Bill in Missouri in the spring of 1864, when the end of the war was near and the rebels were getting desperate. They robbed several Union banks and a railroad train as well. Jesse was involved in the Centralia massacre of September 27, 1864, and the slaughter of the Union militia a few days later. He drew attention to himself in this encounter by shooting the militia commander, Major A.V.E. Johnson. Just a month later, a Union troop led by Major Samuel Cox surprised Anderson and his men. Although most of the guerrillas escaped harm, Bloody Bill was killed.[13]

Following Quantrill's death, Frank and the remaining members of the band surrendered to Union forces in Kentucky. After taking the oath of allegiance, they were released. When news of Lee's surrender reached Missouri, most of the guerrillas were ready to put down their weapons and stop fighting if they could be assured of a peaceful life. The federal authorities promised they would not take action against them, but they would allow the civil authorities to prosecute them if they so desired. With this assurance, many of the guerrillas surrendered.

On April 15, 1865, Jesse led the remnant of his band toward Lexington, Missouri, to surrender. Riding in the lead, he carried a white handkerchief tied to a stick as a flag of truce. When Jesse encountered a squad of Union cavalry, the party did not see the flag, or disregarded it, and opened fire at once. Jesse was hit in his right lung, and his horse was killed. The main body of the cavalry went after the five remaining guerrillas, while several troopers pursued Jesse. In spite of his severe wound, Jesse was able to reach cover. Weak from the loss of blood, he managed to fire off shots, killing the lead horseman and wounding a second trooper. That was enough for the others to pull back and leave.[14]

For two days, Jesse lay in the woods delirious and suffering from his wound. A farmer found him, took him to his house, and notified his friends. Four days later, more dead than alive, he was taken to Lexington. The provost marshal, Major J. B. Rogers, was certain the wound was fatal. He gave Jesse a pass and allowed him to return to his mother's home to die.[15] But even a bullet hole through a lung complicated by pneumonia could not stop Jesse. He managed to make it home with the help of friends, and with the medical care of his stepfather, Dr. Samuel, he was able to recover.

At the end of the war, the Youngers were forced to sell their livery and dry goods store to provide the funds needed to put together their shattered lives. Several of their farms, including their residence, had been destroyed, and they needed to sell all their remaining property to recoup some of the money lost since their father's death. The Youngers' house in the center of Harrisonville had been spared destruction, so they returned there to live.[16]

When the war was over, thousands of men and boys stayed on the road, having grown used to lives of fighting and surviving while on the run. Some were permanently displaced from their homes and families; some suffered from alcoholism and other physical and emotional problems. Some went looking for work; others wandered about looking for a stake, a quick fortune, or a new start. Many headed for Missouri, Kansas, Oklahoma, and farther west. The Western frontier of the 1860s offered opportunities for quick fortunes and power, and its lack of strong law enforcement tempted all sorts of personal and social misbehavior. For many, the chaos of the war became habit forming; they had learned to love the violence and excitement.[17]

Some Confederate guerrillas continued to carry on as they had during the war. They robbed banks and railroads, mostly owned by wealthy Northerners. These ex-guerrillas, now outlaws, had no desire to settle down on a farm with a meager existence. Under Quantrill and Anderson, they had ridden and pillaged with relative impunity; now they could continue these activities, using the same tactics they had as guerrillas. This was more appealing than returning home to the less glamorous, dull routines of the farm.[18]

Most of the men returned to their homes in Missouri, but some found it difficult to resume their normal lives. The Missouri Unionists viewed the ex-guerrillas with resentment and subjected them to harassment. Even so, the majority of the guerrillas who wanted to settle down and lead peaceful, law-abiding lives were able to do so. The trouble was that some of them didn't want to or, at least, did not try very hard. This was especially true for those who had criminal tendencies. The war, and their bushwhacking activities, had provided an opportunity for them to develop and expand these tendencies.[19]

What made it even harder was that hatred still flamed in Missouri. People in the Burnt District could not forget or forgive what was done to them. Men who had served or sympathized with the guerrillas were often beaten or killed by masked gangs of men who called themselves "Regulators." Ex-guerrillas were particular targets of hatred. The general amnesty given Confederate soldiers after the war did not include men who had served under Quantrill, who were declared to be outlaws. With such bitter feelings and everything unsettled, conditions were ripe for a new type of outlaw — men with bitter resentment, deadly with weapons, and anxious for action.[20]

It was difficult for Cole Younger to adjust to civilian life. He was still a wanted man, and he felt he would never be free unless he surrendered and stood trial. The chance of having his case go to trial was slim. Several of the guerrillas had been hung by posses before having a trial. Others were driven from Missouri by threats of violence against them or their families. Not wanting to expose his family to continued danger, Cole joined Jesse and Frank James to form an outlaw gang.[21]

Jesse James had little trouble convincing his ex-guerrilla friends that there was more excitement and profit in riding with him than they could find in farming or running cattle. In addition to Frank and the Youngers, Jesse's associates included former guerrillas Ed and Clell Miller, Wood and Clarence Hite, George and Ol Shepherd, Bill Ryan, Charles Pitts, Jim Cummins, Tom Little, Payton Jones, Arch Clements, Dick Burns, and Andy McGuire. They were all tough characters who had seen war at its bloodiest and had been killers and robbers. They all accepted Jesse James as the leader of the gang.[22] Jesse was well suited to his position as leader; he was a criminal at heart and had a good imagination. He invented bank robbery and perfected train robbery.

Jesse selected the Clay County Savings Association Bank in Liberty as the first to rob because of his familiarity with the town and the bank. His technique for bank robbery consisted simply of an adaptation of the old Quantrill guerrilla tactics, tailored to fit a new situation. A band of whooping riders would sweep into town and "hurrah" it (run around yelling and screaming). This terrorized the citizens into getting off the street, allowing them to roam freely and to get out of town unmolested. At Liberty, such a display was sufficient to do just that. The gang repeated this process many times in the years that followed.

At noon on October 30, 1866, the gang struck at Lexington, Missouri. The town was quiet; most of the residents were at lunch. The bank's busy cashier, J. R. Thomas, looked up to see a customer approaching. The customer asked Thomas if he could change a bill. Thomas said he could and opened the cash drawer to get the money. When two more strangers strolled into the bank, Thomas became suspicious. He asked who they were and what they wanted.

"We're bank examiners," was the response as they drew their guns. Following the outlaws' instructions, Thomas put all the money from the cash drawer into a sack, but he refused to open the vault. The robbers threatened to shoot him, but he claimed not to have the key. The bandits left in a hurry with only $2,000, a far cry from the $100,000 rumored to have been in the bank vault. The five men went to their horses in the alley and quietly rode out of town. A posse was formed but was unable to find the bandits. The local paper reported that the robbers were probably "Kansas redlegs," but old-timers all state that the nineteen-year-old Jesse James was the "bank examiner."

On May 22, 1867, with pistols firing and the rebel yell, Jesse James and his gang rode into Richmond, Missouri. Six of the outlaws entered the Hughes and Mason Bank and secured $4,000 in gold. This time the citizens of Richmond fought back. With Mayor John B. Shaw leading the way, men from behind trees, fences, and upper stories of buildings began firing on the outlaws. In the exchange of fire, the mayor and two of the townfolks were killed, but the gang was able to make their escape without suffering a single loss.

As the James-Younger Gang's crime spree continued, many banks hired the Pinkerton National Detective Agency to apprehend the criminals. The Pinkertons had acquired a reputation of dogged pursuit, but the agency soon found that the James-Younger Gang was a very worthy opponent, more slippery and deadly than any they had encountered.

The first case the Pinkertons were called upon to solve was the March 20, 1868, robbery of the Long and Norton Bank at Russellville, Kentucky. Cole Younger and two other men, one believed to be Jesse James, entered the bank and asked for change for their fifty-dollar bill. The cashier, Nimrod Long, told them it was counterfeit. "I reckon it is," said Cole, "but this isn't." Aiming a revolver at Long, he demanded that he open up the vault. Long ran for the door but a fourth man entered the side door, ordering Long to halt. When he didn't, one of the bandits fired a shot, grazing the side of his head. Somehow he was able to escape and give the alarm. Jesse and Cole gathered up $14,000 in gold, silver, and greenbacks and left. As they stepped outside, they were greeted by a hail of bullets. Despite the heavy fire, the bandits were still able to make their escape.[23]

The Pinkerton agents had very little success in apprehending members of the gang. They were received very poorly in rural Missouri, viewed with suspicion because of their past reputation as spies for the Union and the railroads.

Moreover, they had no idea what the James boys or other members of the gang looked like. The hunters would not have recognized the quarry even if they met face to face.

After Russellville, the gang split up and returned home, hoping that their wartime careers would have been forgotten. Jesse claimed that when he was home he was continually harassed, but both Frank and he were able to live at home for a while without a serious incident. By December 1869, however, the bandits were back in action. This time they robbed the Daviess County Savings Bank at Gallatin, Missouri. The cashier was Captain John Sheets, a former Union officer. Jesse studied Sheets very carefully and then fired a bullet into his head, killing him instantly. This murder is believed to be a case of mistaken identification. Jesse thought the man behind the counter was Major Cox, the man responsible for the death of his old guerrilla pal, Bloody Bill Anderson. He believed he had kept his vow to avenge his dead comrade.[24]

As they left the bank, the outlaws were greeted with gunfire, which frightened Jesse's horse. When the horse bucked, Jesse was thrown to the ground. Returning under heavy fire, Frank caught Jesse by the arm, pulled him up onto his own horse, and galloped down the street. Safely outside of town, they appropriated a horse from an unlucky farmer they met on the road and headed back to Clay County.

Jesse's horse was caught and identified as belonging to the James family. As a result, a $3,000 reward was offered for his capture. The murderer of Captain Sheets was to be "shot down in his tracks" stated one local newspaper. With the evidence uncovered from the Gallatin robbery, Deputy Sheriff John Thomason and a posse set out for the Samuel farm to arrest Frank and Jesse. As they approached the farm, they were surprised to see the two burst out of their barn on horseback and gallop away. In the chase that followed, Thomason's horse was shot, and the chase ended. Thomason had to borrow another horse from the Samuel's stable to get back to town.[25]

The James boys continued to be the object of media attention. One of their admirers was John Edwards, editor of the *Kansas City Times*. Edwards, who had been a major in the Confederate army, published a letter from Jesse, who claimed he had not been involved in the Gallatin robbery and played no part in the murder of Sheets. He said he had run from the posse because he thought he would be unable to get a fair trial if captured. After each robbery, there would be another letter.[26]

Early in June 1871, the James-Younger Gang robbed the bank at Corydon, Iowa. On April 29, 1872, they robbed the bank at Columbia, Kentucky. In late September 1872, three horseman, believed to be Frank, Jesse, and Bob Younger, snatched a tin box containing $978 from the hands of one of the sponsors of a fair at the Kansas City fair grounds. After seizing the cash box, they spurred their horses and rode right through the crowd, shooting into the air as they went. The Kansas City caper caused lots of talk and journalistic fervor. A front-page editorial by John Edwards praised the offenders for their daring and nerve: "a deed so high handed, so diabolically daring and so utterly in contempt of fear that we are bound to admire it and revere its perpetrators."[27]

Over a period of years, the reputation of the James-Younger Gang gained national recognition. The gang was a loose association of as many as twenty-eight men. Only five or six members normally took part in a single robbery, after which they would split up into even smaller groups, assuming false names and the roles of ordinary citizens. They usually went into hiding with relatives or friends and rarely had to fight with pursuers. Preceding each robbery would be months of planning and preparation. During this time, the bandits resumed their normal lives as quiet farmers. These methods were very successful, resulting in fifteen or more robberies in the decade from 1866 to 1875.

It was difficult to prove that Frank and Jesse James were involved in all of these robberies. There were often marked discrepancies when witnesses were interviewed. Photographs were usually not available, and there was no simple means of tracing stolen money.

In 1873, the gang extended its practice of robbing small and isolated banks to attacking trains, drawing on their guerrilla experiences from the war. On the night of July 21, 1873, the James-Younger Gang robbed a Chicago Rock Island and Pacific Railroad train near Adair, Iowa. The gang pulled away a loosened rail, sending the train off the tracks and into the ditch. The engineer was crushed against the side of the cab and killed. After finding only $2,000 in the express car, the outlaws passed through the passenger cars, robbing those inside. When the gang was finished, they saddled up and rode away, firing their guns in the air and shouting their farewells.[28]

The Pinkertons redoubled their activities to capture the James-Younger Gang. In spite of the Pinkertons' all-out efforts, the members of the gang remained at large. On January 15, 1874, members of the gang robbed a stagecoach near the town of Malvern, Arkansas. The passengers were asked to get out of the coach so they could be searched for cash and other valuables. As the passengers emptied their pockets, one of the outlaws asked if anyone had served in the Confederate army. George R. Crump replied that he had and named his company and company commander. His watch and money were returned and the outlaws declared that the gang never stole from Southerners, particularly not from ex-Confederate soldiers.[29]

Two weeks later, the gang robbed the Iron Mountain Express as it entered the station at Gad's Hill, Missouri. While robbing the passengers, one of the outlaws ordered them to hold out their hands for inspection. They examined each person's hands carefully. If their hands were rough and work-hardened, no money was taken, but those with smooth hands were assumed to be wealthy and were ordered to turn over their valuables. The robbers explained, "Hard-handed men have to work for their money; the soft-handed ones are capitalists, professors and others who get money easy."[30]

In the spring of 1874, a Pinkerton agent named James W. Whicher dressed in rough working clothes and set off for the Samuel farm at Kearney. Disguised as a drifter, he hoped to be hired as a farmhand. He had been told that his plan was dangerous, but Whicher refused to listen to good advice. His body was later found near Independence with a bullet in his heart and one in his head. Within two weeks, Pinkerton detectives Louis J. Lull and James Wright and Deputy Sheriff Edwin Daniels picked up the trail of the Youngers. Lull and Wright appeared at St. Clair County, posing as stock buyers, looking for cattle and horses. The people living in the Ozark Mountain country were suspicious of all strangers, so when the two Pinkerton men appeared, word of warning went out to the Youngers. The trio stopped at the farm of Theodore Snuffer, a friend of the Youngers, and asked for directions. Snuffer obliged and watched them ride off.[31]

Unknown to the intruders was that John and Jim Younger were inside the Snuffer home. The two Youngers leaped on their horses and set off after them. Pulling their guns, the Youngers ordered the men to halt. The three law enforcers found themselves staring into a double-barreled shotgun and a revolver. Wright fled, spurring his horse in the direction of town. A bullet from Jim Younger's gun took off his hat, but he was able to escape. Lull and Daniels pulled up to the side of the road and dropped their guns as ordered, but Lull had another gun concealed in his clothes. "What are you doing in this part of the country?" John Younger demanded. "Just rambling around," replied Lull. But the outlaws knew different: "Detectives have been hunting for us, and we're going to stop it." Daniels began to plead, but Lull pulled the small concealed pistol he had and fired. He hit John Younger in the neck, but John managed to press the trigger of his shotgun, tearing a gaping hole in Lull's neck before dropping to the ground, dead.[32]

Daniels tried to escape in the excitement, but Jim Younger shot him down. Jim went to help his brother, but it was too late; at the age of twenty-four, John Younger was the first of the notorious gang to die. Despite his wound, Lull managed to escape. After making his affidavit concerning the events, he died six weeks later.

After the death of John Younger, Jesse and Frank left Missouri, returning only long enough to marry their sweethearts. In April, Jesse married his first cousin, Zee Mimms, culminating a nine-year engagement. About the same time, Frank married a young schoolteacher by the name of Annie Ralston, the daughter of Colonel Samuel Ralston, a highly respected citizen of Independence, Missouri.

In January 1875, Pinkerton agents received information that the James brothers were going to visit their mother. On a clear, cold night, the agents surrounded the Samuel farmhouse. Frank and Jesse were not inside, but Dr. and Mrs. Samuel, their two youngest children, and an African American servant woman were. One of the Pinkertons opened a window and tossed a flare into the house to light up the room. Dr. Samuel rushed to put out the fire by kicking the flare into the fireplace. Suddenly there was a tremendous explosion, wreaking bloody havoc. Mrs. Samuel's right arm was torn off at the elbow, and her eight-year-old son was killed. The others present also received serious injuries.[33]

Pinkerton steadfastly insisted that a flare and not a bomb had caused the explosion. He also claimed that he had given orders not to harm Dr. and Mrs. Samuel; however, a month earlier, he had written to Samuel Hardwicke, a local attorney under his employ, instructing him to "destroy the house ... burn the house down."[34]

The bungled attack gave the James boys more favorable publicity than they could imagine. The *St. Louis Dispatch* felt that the past acts of the outlaws should be forgiven: "All former guerrilla fighters who have turned to crime in desperation after the war must be allowed amnesty for their crimes committed during the war and full protection of the law for crimes committed after it."[35] Some members of the Missouri legislature introduced a bill providing for the pardoning of all ex-guerrillas for wartime deeds. But before the legislature could act on the bill, the gang was believed to be involved in a double murder of persons suspected of aiding and abetting the Pinkertons. This act of revenge undermined much of the good will previously built up for the Jameses.[36]

After the tragedy at the Samuel house, the outlaws laid low for most of the year. Jesse had good reason to stay at home; his first son, Jesse Edward James, was born on August 31, 1875. On September 1, 1875, the gang returned to action, robbing the Huntington National Bank in West Virginia. Before leaving, the bandits asked the cashier whether he had any of his own money in the bank. When he replied that he had a balance of seven dollars, the amount was returned to him. The outlaws explained that they did not believe that an employee should suffer a loss when a bank was robbed.[37]

During the spring and summer of 1876, the gang continued to pull off daring robberies with impunity. Now cocky, seemingly invincible after having robbed a stagecoach in Texas in May and a train in Missouri in July, they decided to complete a "triple play" by robbing a bank in Minnesota in September — all in the same year. One of the members of the gang, Bill Chadwell, convinced Jesse and the others that his home state of Minnesota would be a good hunting ground with easily accessible banks.[38] The rich bank in Northfield was picked for the target.

Near noon on September 7, 1876, three men rode into Northfield. On the road behind, two more horsemen appeared, part of the same party. Their plan called for Jesse, Frank, and Bob Younger to lead the way to town and then enter to rob the bank. In the meantime, Cole and Clell Miller would stand guard outside the bank to prevent any interruptions. Charles Pitts, Jim Younger, and Bill Chadwell would wait outside of town until they heard a shot, signaling to them to come into town to support the getaway.[39]

When Cole and Miller arrived, Jesse, Frank, and Bob Younger entered the bank. One of the bandits stuck his gun in the face of cashier Joseph Heywood and demanded that he open the safe. "It's on a timelock and cannot be opened now," he replied. Insisting that Heywood open the safe, one of the bandits slashed the blade of a knife across his throat. Heywood wriggled free and screamed, "Murderer!" When Jesse hit Heywood in the head with his gun, Alonzo Bunker, the other teller, made a dash for the back door. Bob Younger shot him in the shoulder, but he was still able to make his escape and give the alarm.[40]

Outside, Clell Miller had difficulty with a customer who was trying to enter the bank. Sizing up the situation, he ran up the street, shouting, "Get your guns boys; they're robbing the bank!" Quickly the citizens of Northfield armed themselves. Outside the bank, Cole attempted to keep people away by returning the fire.[41] Charles Pitts, Jim Younger, and Chadwell galloped into town, firing their revolvers and yelling. One of the bandits yelled for Jesse to hurry: "They're killing our boys!" In anger and frustration, Jesse shot and killed Heywood. Jesse and the others ran outside, empty-handed, only to be met with heavy gunfire. Chadwell and Miller were already dead in the street. Frank had been hit in the leg, and blood was pouring from Jim Younger's mouth.

Now the six remaining bandits were fighting for their lives. Bob Younger's horse was down, and Chadwell's and Miller's horses had run off when they were shot. Those who were able mounted their horses and charged down the street, guns blazing, hoping to avoid being hit. Bob Younger, who was still in the street, cried for help. "My God, boys, you're not deserting me. I'm shot!" Cole Younger, although wounded himself, turned his horse around and came back for his brother. With bullets flying all about him, he pulled his wounded brother up behind him and followed the others out of town.

As the outlaws fled, information about the robbery was telegraphed to all the small towns along the railroad.[42]

The robbery at Northfield had netted the bandits only $26.70, the money Jesse had taken from the counter. The ironic thing about the robbery was that the safe had been unlocked all the time — a turn of the handle would have opened it.

Although all of the survivors were wounded to some extent, they managed to make it to the swamps and heavy wilderness called the Big Woods. A posse was organized in Northfield, and other posses were organized all along the outlaws' line of retreat. Jesse and his gang were a long way from the friendly Missouri confines and, worse, a long way from friends to shelter and care for them. Word spread quickly that a large reward had been offered for the capture of the outlaws. Lawmen and ordinary citizens joined in the chase. It was the largest manhunt in the history of the United States up to that time. Over a thousand men attempted to apprehend the Northfield robbers.[43]

The six outlaws struggled through the swamp with little to eat and near exhaustion. Traveling by night and trying to sleep by day, they covered less than fifty miles in five days. Bob Younger was badly hurt and was slowing them down. He suggested they leave him behind so the others could escape. Cole and Jim wouldn't consider it; however, Jesse and Frank thought they should split up. It was decided that Jesse and Frank move on, hoping the posse would follow them, thus allowing those left behind to move on without the pressure of a chase. Jesse and Frank took off, leaving the three Youngers and Charles Pitts.[44]

The Youngers and Charles Pitts struggled off in the opposite direction, stopping at a farmhouse where they tried to buy food, claiming they were hunters injured in an accident. Seventeen-year-old Oscar Soble realized who they were and rode for help. When he finally convinced the authorities to believe him, pursuit was swift.[45]

When the posse caught up with the Youngers and called for their surrender, the fugitives opened fire. The posse returned their fire, killing Pitts and wounding the Youngers again. When captured, Cole Younger had eleven wounds. Bob Younger was the only outlaw who could stand up; bleeding from another wound in the chest, his arm in a bloody sling, he raised his good arm in surrender.[46]

The prisoners were taken by wagon to Madelia. The outlaws expected to be hung, but they were surprised by the kind treatment they received. Minnesota law provided that anyone confessing to a capital crime would receive life in prison rather than being hung. Without delay, the Youngers confessed. They stood trial for their part in the bank robbery and the murders of Joseph Heywood and Nicholas Gustavson, also killed at Northfield. Pleading guilty, they were sentenced to life imprisonment.

Ten days after leaving Northfield, Jesse and Frank crossed the Minnesota line into the Dakota Territory and finally home. It was another three years before the James boys were heard from again. The James brothers moved to Nashville, Tennessee, where they were not well known. In order to avoid suspicion, Jesse took the name of J. D. Howard and he settled down, farming, raising cattle, and racing horses. The family was well accepted by the community. Jesse even joined the local church and began singing in the choir. The only dark spot during this time was the early death of twins born to Zee.

After two years the family pulled up stakes and joined Frank and Ann on their farm. Frank, alias B. J. Woodson, had settled down and was enjoying life in Nashville. He disliked the life of a fugitive. The quiet years with his family on the farm were among the happiest of his life.[47]

Jesse, far too restless for a life of routine and order, was ready to form another gang, but Frank argued against it, telling him he would put his family's lives in danger again. Jesse ignored Frank's advice and returned to Kearney to form a new gang. Frank did not go with him. Jesse's new gang consisted of Ed Miller, Wood Hite, Bill Ryan, Dick Liddil, and Tucker Bassham. On the night of October 8, 1879, Jesse and his gang robbed a Chicago and Alton train as it stopped at Glendale, Missouri. They collected an estimated $6,000.

On July 15, 1881, the gang robbed a Chicago Rock Island and Pacific train at Winston, Missouri; this time Frank joined them. During the robbery, conductor William Westfall and a passenger, Frank McMillan, were killed. Public outcry was angry and loud over the two robberies and murders. Thomas Crittenden, the newly elected governor of Missouri, had pledged to rid the state of outlaw bands. A tempting reward of $15,000 was offered for the capture and conviction of Jesse, Frank, and the other gang members.[48]

William Wallace, the prosecuting attorney of Jackson County, vowed he would never rest until the James gang was destroyed. His first test came with the capture of Bill Ryan, one of its members. Ryan came to trial in September 1881 in the heart of James country. There was fear that the gang might try to rescue their old gang member, and threats were made against Wallace's life. With the help of the governor, who pardoned a key witness so he could testify, Wallace was able to get a conviction. For his part, Wallace paid dearly; his house was burned to the ground by gang supporters. But the tide had turned.

In a bold act of defiance during the Ryan trial, the James gang attacked the Chicago and Alton train at Blue Cut. After taking the passengers' valuables, the bandits took the engineer back to the cab and offered to clear the tracks so the train could continue on. One of the bandits gave the engineer two silver dollars and told him to use the money to drink to Jesse James.[49]

In the fall of 1881, Jesse, using the name Thomas Howard, and his family moved to St. Joseph, Missouri. The house he rented was on a hill with a good view of all the approaches. In his stable, he kept two saddled horses, ready for a quick getaway if needed.

Among the new members of his gang were two brothers, Charles and Robert Ford. Bob Ford and Dick Liddil had killed Wood Hite, Jesse's cousin, in a quarrel over a woman. The Ford brothers were fearful that Jesse would seek revenge for Hite's murder. They obtained assurances of leniency from Governor Crittenden if they helped in the capture of Jesse. They agreed to tell Clay County Sheriff Jim Timberlake of the time and place of the gang's next planned robbery. In return, Crittenden promised them immunity from punishment and a share of the reward money.[50]

The Fords were afraid to wait for Jesse to be captured. They made plans to kill him, hoping to catch him off guard and unarmed if possible. Jesse's ability with his revolver was well known, and the Fords knew they would never survive a face-to-face shootout with him. Late in March 1882, they went to Jesse's house in St. Joseph to plan for a robbery. When Jesse turned his back to dust a picture on the wall, Bob Ford pulled out his revolver and fired. The bullet tore through the back of Jesse's skull, and in Ford's own words, "Jesse fell like a log, dead."[51] Hearing the shot, Zee rushed into the room. When she saw Bob Ford with his gun drawn, she screamed, calling him a murderer. The Fords fled the scene. Zee attempted to comfort her husband. Jesse tried to speak to her but was unable to. He collapsed, dead, in her arms.

As the word spread that Jesse James was dead, a crowd formed outside his house. They followed the undertaker back to the funeral home in hopes of seeing or touching his body. A photographer was called in to take pictures of the body, and the crowd followed him back to the studio so they could get prints. The pictures were sold as quickly as they could be developed.[52] The next day the newspapers were full of the story. News of Jesse's death rocked the nation. The *St. Joseph Gazette* carried the banner headline: JESSE, BY JEHOVAH!

John Edwards gave his opinion of the death of Jesse James in the *Sedalia Daily Democrat*: "Why the whole state reeks today with a double orgy, that of lust and that of murder. . . . Tear the bears from the flag of Missouri. Put thereon in place of them as more appropriate, a thief blowing the brains out of an unarmed victim, and a brazen harlot, . . . and splashed to the brows in blood."[53]

The manner in which Jesse died and the cowardly treachery of it added to the Jesse James legend. Even William Wallace, the tireless prosecutor and enemy of the James brothers, said it was one of the most cowardly and diabolical deeds in history. "Jesse James was a lawless, bloodthirsty man, but that gave the Ford boys no right to assassinate him," he said.[54] Governor Crittenden, however, issued the Ford brothers a pardon and awarded them part of the reward. Bob Ford expected to be treated as a hero for killing Jesse. Instead, he is remem-

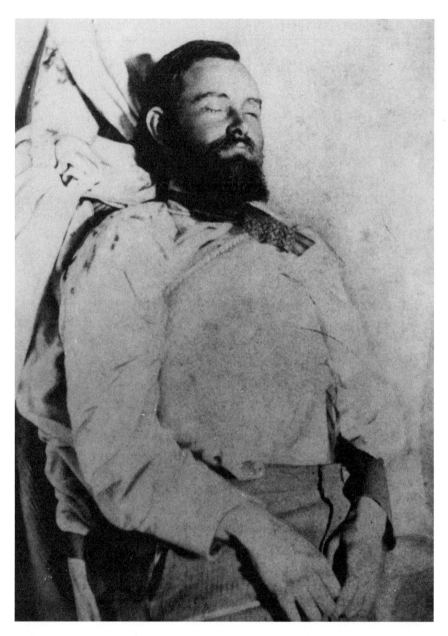

A lucky photographer made a fortune at Jesse James's expense, selling copies of this photograph to eager onlookers. (Used by permission, The State Historical Society of Missouri, Columbia, all rights reserved)

bered in history as "that dirty little coward that shot Mr. Howard and laid Jesse James in his grave." The public's emotional reaction to the treacherous act of the Fords made it impossible for them to enjoy their reward money. Newspapers called for their hanging. There were threats of lynching, and the governor was forced to get police protection for them.

Jesse James was buried in his mother's yard. On the stone that marked his grave was this inscription:

Jesse W. James
Died April 3, 1882
Aged 34 years, 6 months, 28 days.
MURDERED BY A TRAITOR AND A COWARD WHOSE
NAME IS NOT WORTHY TO APPEAR HERE.[55]

After Jesse's death, Frank decided to surrender and to try to clear the charges against him. Governor Crittenden promised Frank a fair trial if he "came in." On October 4, 1882, Frank surrendered to the governor, saying, "I want to hand over to you that which no living man except myself has been permitted to touch since 1861 and to say that I am your prisoner."[56] When asked why he surrendered, he said he was tired of an outlaw life.

On August 21, 1883, Frank was brought to trial for the murders of Detective James Whicher and John Sheets. The trial was held in the Gallatin Opera House to accommodate the large number of people who wanted to attend. The "show" ran for eight days to capacity crowds. Former gang member Dick Liddil testified for the prosecution. Frank's mother, his stepsister Susan James Parmer, Confederate war hero General Joseph Shelby, and even Governor Crittenden testified as character witnesses for Frank. It took the young, all Democratic jury three and one-half hours to acquit him. Several other charges were dropped because of legal technicalities.[57]

In April 1884, Frank was tried for robbery in Huntsville, Alabama. His lawyer produced witnesses who said that Frank was in Nashville, Tennessee, at the time of the holdup. Once again, the jury found Frank not guilty. Frank still had charges against him for an Otterville holdup. Just before the trial date, the charges were dropped because the prosecutor's main witness had died. Frank was free at last.

Except for a few weeks Frank James spent in custody waiting for trial, he did not serve a single day in prison for his many crimes. No other charges were made against him. Of all the gang members, he alone escaped punishment. John Younger, Clell Miller, Bill Chadwell, and Charlie Pitts were killed by law officers or by citizens in arms. Jesse James, Wood Hite, and Ed Miller were killed by members of their own gang. Jim Younger and Charley Ford committed suicide. Robert Ford fled the state and was killed in a quarrel over a woman. Bob Younger died in prison, and Clarence Hite was released from prison to go home and die. Jim Cummins died in the Missouri Confederate Home..

For the rest of his life, Frank was a model citizen. He worked at many different jobs: he sold shoes, worked as a doorman, herded horses, served as a starter at race tracks, farmed, acted in traveling shows.[59] He did not rob banks or trains. On February 18, 1915, Frank died quietly in the home where he lived as a child; his wife was at his side.

It is true that war breeds crime and criminals, and the American Civil War was no different than others in that respect. The claim that Jesse and his gang were driven to a life of crime by the war has a ring of self-justification. Not all ex-guerrillas or those who had suffered great losses during the war became outlaws. Not everyone who saw the railroads and banks as the enemy took their revenge with bullets. The truth of the matter is that they were violent, ruthless criminals who stole what they refused to earn honestly and killed all those who stood in their way. Jesse and his gang robbed twelve banks, seven trains, and five stagecoaches. In the process, they killed fifteen innocent people. This is not a record to be envied. Although the American Civil War ended in 1865, in many ways the aftermath continues even today.

Endnotes

Part 1. A Web of Deception: Blue and Gray Spies

1. Time-Life Books, *Spies, Scouts, and Raiders*, Alexandria: Time-Life Books, 1985, 8.
2. F. Linden, *Lincoln: The Road to War*, Golden, Colo.: Fulcrum, 1998, 198–199.
3. Ibid., 196.
4. P. Kunhardt, et al. *Lincoln*, New York: Alfred A. Knopf, 1992, 16.
5. Ibid., 16.
6. Time-Life Books, 8.
7. R. Luthin, *The Real Abraham Lincoln*, Englewood Cliffs: Prentice Hall, 1960, 225.
8. Time-Life Books, 8.
9. Ibid., 21.
10. Ibid., 21.
11. Kunhardt, et al., 19.
12. Luthin, 256.
13. Time-Life Books, 9–10.
14. E. Fishel, *The Secret War for the Union*, Boston: Houghton Mifflin, 1996, 1.
15. W. Davis, et al., *Civil War Journal: The Legacies*, Nashville: Rutledge Hill, 1999, 293.
16. Time-Life Books, 10.
17. Davis, et al., 293–294.

18. W. Tidwell, *April '65*, Kent, Ohio: Kent State University Press, 1995, 116.
19. Davis, et al., 294.
20. J. Brakeless, *Spies of the Confederacy*, Mineola, N.Y.: Dover, 1970, 2.
21. Ibid., 2.
22. Davis, et al., 294.
23. Ibid., 294.
24. D. Markle, *Spies and Spymasters of the Civil War*, New York: Hippocrene, 1994, 2.
25. Ibid., 2–3.
26. Ibid., 3.
27. Ibid., 4–5.
28. Brakeless, 3.
29. Markle, 5.
30. Ibid., 7–11.
31. Time-Life Books, 75.
32. Ibid., 76.
33. Ibid., 78.
34. Ibid., 78.
35. Ibid., 79.
36. Davis, et al., 319–320.
37. Time-Life Books, 80.
38. Davis, et al., 320.
39. Markle, 11–13.
40. Ibid., 14–15.
41. Time-Life Books, 46–47.
42. A. Axelrod, *The War Between the Spies*, New York: Atlantic Monthly Press, 1992, 49.
43. M. Antonucci, "Code-Crackers," *Civil War Times Illustrated*, (Aug. 1995): 47.
44. Ibid., 47.
45. Ibid., 47.
46. Ibid., 48.
47. Markle, 39–40.
48. Antonucci, 48–49.
49. Ibid., 72–73.
50. Ibid., 74–75.
51. Markle, 40.
52. Ibid., 37.

53. Ibid., 18.
54. Tidwell, 107.
55. Markle, 50–51.
56: Time-Life Books, 60–61.
57. Markle, 54.
58. Ibid., 54.
59. Ibid., 56.
60. Ibid., 58.
61. Davis, et al., 317.
62. Markle, 61–62.
63. Markle, 58–59.
64. Ibid., 85–86.
65. Ibid., 86.
66. Ibid., 87–91.
67. D. Gaddy, "Gray Cloaks and Daggers," *Civil War Times Illustrated* (July 1975): 27.
68. Davis, et al., 321.

Chapter 1. Union Private Eye: Allan Pinkerton

1. E. Fishel, *The Secret War for the Union*, Boston: Houghton Mifflin, 1996, 53.
2. P. Robbins, "Allan Pinkerton's Southern Assignment," *Civil War Times Illustrated* (Jan. 1977): 7.
3. Time-Life Books, *Spies, Scouts, and Raiders*, Alexandria: Time-Life Books, 1985, 11.
4. J. E. Raymond, review of *The Pinkertons: The Detective Dynasty That Made History*, *American History Illustrated* (May, 1969): 49.
5. R. Patterson, *The Train Robbery Era*, Boulder: Pruett, 1991, 185.
6. W. Davis, et al., *Civil War Journal: The Legacies*, Rutledge Hill, 1999, 295–296.
7. J. Mackay, *Allan Pinkerton, The First Private Eye*, New York: John Wiley & Sons, 1994, 71.
8. Ibid., 75.
9. D. Sabine, "Pinkerton's 'Operative': Timothy Webster," *Civil War Times Illustrated* (Aug. 1993): 33.
10. Ibid., 33.

11. Robbins, 7.
12. Sabine, 33.
13. Robbins, 7–8.
14. Time-Life Books, 22–23.
15. Fishel, 54.
16. Markle, 6–7.
17. Ibid., 7.
18. S. Sears, *George B. McClellan, The Young Napoleon*, New York: Ticknor & Field, 1988, 76–77.
19. Robbins, 8.
20. Ibid., 8–9.
21. Ibid., 10.
22. Ibid., 10.
23. Ibid., 11.
24. Ibid., 44.
25. Ibid., 44–47.
26. Robertson, 101.
27. Fishel, 113.
28. Ibid., 113–114.
29. Ibid., 115.
30. Davis, et al., 298–299.
31. Sears, 179.
32. E. Furgurson, *Ashes of Glory*, New York: Vintage, 1996.
33. Davis, et al., 315.
34. Ibid., 315–316.
35. Time-Life Books, 32.
36. Davis, et al., 303.
37. D. Markle, *Spies and Spymasters of the Civil War*, New York: Hippocrene Books, 194.
38. Patterson, 186–188.
39. Mackay, 235–237.
40. Ibid., 238–239.
41. Robbins, 7.
42. Sears, 107–108.
43. Ibid., 108.
44. Time-Life Books, 33.

Chapter 2. Union Double Agent:
Timothy Webster

1. D. Markle, *Spies and Spymasters of the Civil War*, New York: Hippocrene Books, 1994, 146.
2. Ibid., 144.
3. W. Davis, et al., *Civil War Journal: The Legacies*, Nashville: Rutledge Hill, 1999, 306.
4. Markle, 144.
5. D. Sabine, "Pinkerton's 'Operative': Timothy Webster," *Civil War Times Illustrated* (Aug. 1973): 33.
6. Ibid., 33.
7. Ibid., 33–34.
8. Ibid., 34.
9. R. Nash, *Spies*, New York: M. Evans, 1995, 506.
10. Sabine, 34.
11. Ibid., 34–35.
12. Ibid., 34.
13. Nash, 507.
14. Sabine, 35.
15. A. Axelrod, *The War Between the Spies*, New York: Atlantic Monthly Press, 1992, 135.
16. Time-Life Books, *Spies, Scouts and Raiders*, Alexandria: Time-Life Books, 1985, 38–39.
17. Ibid., 39.
18. Sabine, 35–36.
19. Ibid., 36.
20. Ibid., 36.
21. Nash, 507.
22. J. Mackay, *Allan Pinkerton, The First Private Eye*, New York: John Wiley & Sons, Inc., 1996, 139.
23. Sabine, 37.
24. Ibid., 37.
25. Time-Life Books, 40–41.
26. Sabine, 37.
27. Mackay, 141.
28. Markle, 146.
29. Mackay, 142–143.

30. Ibid., 143.
31. Nash, 508.
32. Ibid., 508.
33. Mackay, 144–145.
34. Ibid., 145.
35. Ibid., 146.
36. Nash, 508.
37. Markle, 147.
38. Mackay, 146.
39. Nash, 508.
40. Sabine, 42.
41. Nash, 509.

Chapter 3. "Crazy Bet": Elizabeth Van Lew

1. A. Axelrod, *The War Between the Spies*, New York: Atlantic Monthly Press, 1992, 104.
2. E. Anderson, "'Crazy Bet' Van Lew Was General Grant's Eyes and Ears in Richmond," *America's Civil War*, July, 1991, 8.
3. J. Nash, *Spies*, New York: M. Evans, 1997, 489.
4. D. Ryan, ed., *A Yankee Spy in Richmond*, Mechanicsburg, Pa: Stackpole, 1996, 4–5.
5. W. Davis, et al., *Civil War Journal: The Legacies*, Nashville: Rutledge Hill, 1999, 311.
6. Anderson, 8.
7. Ibid., 8.
8. Ibid., 8.
9. Nash, 490.
10. Time-Life Books, *Spies, Scouts, and Raiders*, Alexandria: Time-Life Books, 1985, 87.
11. Ryan, 7.
12. Anderson, 56.
13. Ryan, 7.
14. Time-Life Books, 87.
15. E. Leonard, *All the Daring of the Soldiers*, New York: W. W. Norton, 1999, 52.
16. Davis, et al., 311–312.

17. Anderson, 8.
18. Ibid., 8.
19. Ibid., 54.
20. Time-Life Books, 88.
21. Davis, et al., 312–313.
22. Ibid., 313.
23. Ryan, 13.
24. Nash, 490.
25. Ibid., 490.
26. Ibid., 491.
27. Anderson, 56.
28. Leonard, 55.
29. Time-Life Books, 89.
30. Nash, 491.
31. Time-Life Books, 89.
32. Anderson, 57.
33. Davis, et al., 314.
34. Ibid., 314–315.
35. Ibid., 315.

Chapter 4. Siren of the Shenandoah:
Belle Boyd

1. R. Scarborough, *Belle Boyd, Siren of the South*, Macon: Mercer University Press, 1997, Cover.
2. Ibid., 3.
3. Ibid., 4–6.
4. Ibid., 9–10.
5. W. Davis, et al., *Civil War Journal: The Legacies*, Nashville: Rutledge Hill, 1999, 308.
6. D. Markle, *Spies and Spymasters of the Civil War*, New York: Hippocrene, 1994, 155.
7. Davis, et al., 308.
8. R. Nash, *Spies*, New York: M. Evans, 1997, 115.
9. Davis, et al., 308–309.
10. Ibid., 309.

11. J. Brakeless, *Spies of the Confederacy*, Mineola, New York: Dover Publication, 1970, 149.
12. Scarborough, 49.
13. B. Boyd, *Belle Boyd in Camp and Prison*, Baton Rouge: Louisiana State University Press, 1998, 6–7.
14. E. Leonard, *All the Daring of the Soldier*, New York: W. W. Norton & Co., 1999, 28.
15. Markle, 156.
16. Scarborough, 59.
17. Ibid., 71.
18. Ibid., 72.
19. Ibid., 73–74.
20. Markle, 80.
21. Scarborough, 93.
22. Leonard, 32–34.
23. Ibid., 33–34.
24. Davis, et al., 310.
25. Boyd, 41.
26. Nash, 116.
27. Leonard, 35.

Chapter 5. Rebel Rose:
Rose O'Neal Greenhow

1. A. Axelrod, *The War Between the Spies*, New York: Atlantic Monthly Press, 1992, 45.
2. R. Nash, *Spies*, New York: M. Evans, 1997, 248.
3. E. Leonard, *All the Daring of the Soldiers*, New York: W. W. Norton, 1999, 36.
4. Ibid., 36.
5. Ibid., 36–37.
6. Axelrod, 45.
7. Leonard, 37.
8. D. Markle, *Spies and Spymasters of the Civil War*, New York: Hippocrene, 1994, 159–160.
9. Leonard, 37.
10. J. Brakeless, *Spies of the Confederacy*, Mineola, New York: Dover Publication, 1970, 10.

11. Axelrod, 46.
12. Time-Life Books, *Spies, Scouts, and Raiders*, Alexandria: Time-Life Books, 1985, 25.
13. Markle, 160–161.
14. Axelrod, 50.
15. Ibid., 51.
16. Leonard, 38.
17. Nash, 250.
18. Ibid., 250.
19. Leonard, 39.
20. Nash, 251.
21. W. Davis, et al., *Civil War Journal: The Legacies*, Nashville: Rutledge Hill, 1999, 302–303.
22. Time-Life Books, 28–29.
23. Markle, 161.
24. Time-Life Books, 29.
25. Ibid., 29, 31.
26. Axelrod, 64–65.
27. Nash, 252.
28. Time-Life Books, 31.
29. Nash, 252.
30. Ibid., 252.
31. Ibid., 253.
32. Axelrod, 68.
33. Nash, 253.
34. Ibid., 253–254.
35. Ibid., 254.

Chapter 6. The Death of a President: John Wilkes Booth

1. R. Fowler, "Album of the Lincoln Murder: Illustrating How It Was Planned, Committed, and Avenged," *Civil War Times Illustrated* (July 1965): 16.
2. C. Clark, *The Assassination, Death of the President*, Alexandria: Time-Life Books, 1987, 82.
3. Ibid., 16.
4. Ibid., 16, 21.

5. Ibid., 21–22.
6. D. Donald, *Lincoln*, New York: Simon & Schuster, 1995, 598.
7. P. Kunhardt, et al., *Lincoln*, New York: Alfred A. Knopf, 1992, 359.
8. T. Roscoe, *The Web of Conspiracy*, Englewood Cliffs: Prentice-Hall, 1959, 5–6, 13–15.
9. Clark, 16.
10. Ibid., 17–18.
11. Ibid., 18–19.
12. M. Kauffman, "John Wilkes Booth and the Murder of Abraham Lincoln," *Blue & Gray* (April 1990): 14.
13. Clark, 19–20.
14. Kauffman, 16–17.
15. Clark, 21.
16. Roscoe, 58–61.
17. Clark, 21.
18. Ibid., 21.
19. Roscoe, 50–51.
20. Ibid., 61–63.
21. Clark, 39–40.
22. Roscoe, 44–48, 50.
23. Fowler, 10.
24. Clark, 38.
25. Fowler, 10.
26. Kauffman, 24.
27. R. Luthin, *The Real Abraham Lincoln*, Englewood Cliffs: Prentice-Hall, Inc., 1960, 620.
28. Fowler, 10.
29. Donald, 593.
30. Fowler, 10.
31. E. Steers, *The Escape and Capture of John Wilkes Booth*, Gettysburg: Thomas Publications, 1992, 6.
32. Donald, 594.
33. Ibid., 595.
34. Luthin, 622.
35. Clark, 82–83.
36. Donald, 595.
37. Ibid., 596–597.
38. Fowler, 33.

39. Luthin, 665.
40. Clark, 111.
41. Fowler, 29.
42. Steers, 27–29.
43. Ibid., 30.
44. Fowler, 29.
45. Steers, 31–32.
46. Ibid., 32–34.
47. Fowler, 32.
48. Ibid., 33, 35.
49. Ibid., 36.
50. Clark, 114–116.
51. Fowler, 38–39.
52. Kunhardt, 367.
53. Fowler, 46–48.
54. Roscoe, 399, 543.
55. M. Kauffman, "Booth's Escape Route: Lincoln's Assassin on the Run," *Blue & Gray* (June 1990): 49.
56. Clark, 139.
57. Ibid., 140–141.
58. Fowler, 52.
59. Clark, 148.
60. Fowler, 58.
61. Ibid., 59.
62. Ibid., 60.
63. W. Hanchett, "Lincoln's Murder: The Simple Conspiracy Theory," *Civil War Times Illustrated* (Nov./Dec. 1991): 28–29.
64. W. Tidwell, *Come Retribution*, Jackson: University Press of Mississippi, 1988, 3.
65. Hanchett, 29.
66. Tidwell, 4.
67. Hanchett, 30.
68. Tidwell, 13.

Part 2. Warriors Behind the Lines: The Raiders

1. E. Longacre, *Mounted Raids of the Civil War*, Lincoln: University of Nebraska Press, 1975, 16–17.
2. T. Rodenbough, ed., *The Photographic History of the Civil War: The Cavalry*, New York: Random House, 1983, 122.
3. Ibid., 122, 124.
4. W. Davis, et al., *Civil War Journal: The Leaders*, Nashville: Rutledge Hill, 1997, 328.
5. Ibid., 223.
6. Longacre, 17.
7. Rodenbough, 120.
8. Davis, et al., 340.
9. Ibid., 323–325.
10. H. Hattaway, *Shades of Blue and Gray*, Columbia: University of Missouri Press, 1997, 164.
11. Time-Life Books, *Spies, Scouts, and Raiders*, Alexandria: Time-Life Books, 1985, 107–108.
12. Ibid., 108.
13. Longacre, 11–12.
14. Ibid., 12.
15. Ibid., 12.
16. Ibid., 14–15.
17. Ibid., 15–16.
18. D. Phillips, *Daring Raiders*, New York: Metro Books, 1998, 124.
19. Hattaway, 164.
20. Time-Life Books, 90, 93–94.
21. Ibid., 104.
22. Ibid., 111.
23. Phillips, 28–29.
24. Ibid., 30–31.
25. Time-Life Books, 112.
26. Phillips, 34–35.
27. Ibid., 36–38.
28. Ibid., 39–40.
29. Ibid., 43.

Chapter 7. Gray Ghost of the Confederacy: John Singleton Mosby

1. J. Ramage, *Gray Ghost,* Lexington: University Press of Kentucky, 1999, 65–66.
2. Ibid., 66.
3. B. Brager, "Combative to War's Very End," *Military History* (October 1986): 55.
4. Time-Life Books, *Spies, Scouts, and Raiders,* Alexandria: Time-Life Books, 1985, 119.
5. J. Wert, *Mosby's Rangers,* New York: Simon and Schuster, 1990, 25–26.
6. Ibid., 26–27.
7. Time-Life Books, 115.
8. W. Davis, et al., *Civil War Journal: The Legacies,* Nashville: Rutledge Hill, 1999, 397–398.
9. Time-Life Books, 116.
10. Davis, et al., 399.
11. J. Cooke, *Wearing of the Gray,* Bloomington: Indiana University Press, 1959, 110–111.
12. Davis, et al., 399.
13. M. Grimsley, *The Hard Hand of War,* New York: Cambridge University Press, 1995, 112.
14. Civil War Times Illustrated, "John Mosby, An Appraisal," *Civil War Times Illustrated* (Nov. 1965): 4–5.
15. Davis, et al., 399, 403.
16. Wert, 35.
17. Ibid., 105.
18. Ibid., 115.
19. Ibid., 117, 121.
20. Ibid., 124.
21. Ibid., 87.
22. J. Wert, "Inside Mosby's Confederacy," *Civil War Times Illustrated,* (Sept./Oct. 1990): 41.
23. Ibid., 42.
24. Davis, et al., 407–409.
25. Ibid., 409–410.
26. Ibid., 411.
27. M. Martin, "A Match for Mosby," *America's Civil War* (July 1994): 26.

28. Ibid., 28–29.
29. Ibid., 30.
30. Brager, 57.
31. Wert, *Mosby's Rangers*, 245–246.
32. Ibid., 249–250.
33. Civil War Times Illustrated, 53–54.
34. Davis, et al., 416–417.
35. K. Siepel, *Rebel: The Life and Times of John Singleton Mosby*, New York: Da Capo Press, 1977, 175.
36. V. Jones, *Ranger Mosby*, McLean: EPM Publications, Inc., 1944, 286–288.
37. Ibid., 288–289.
38. Ibid., 289–290.
39. Ibid., 299–301.
40. Ibid., 301.
41. Ibid., 302–303.
42. Davis, et al., 417.
43. Jones, 303.
44. Ibid., 304.
45. Siepel, 252.
46. Ibid., 252–253.
47. Jones, 305–306.
48. Ibid., 307–308.
49. Wert, *Mosby's Rangers*, 291.

Chapter 8. Bold Cavalier:
J.E.B. Stuart

1. P. Bolte, "Command Shift Dictated," *Military History* (June 1992): 50.
2. E. Thomas, *Bold Dragoon: The Life of J.E.B. Stuart*, New York: Harper & Row, 1986, 210.
3. Bolte, 52.
4. Ibid., 52.
5. B. Davis, *Jeb Stuart, The Last Cavalier*, New York: Holt, Rinehart and Winston, 1957, 18.
6. E. Thomas, "The Real J.E.B. Stuart," *Civil War Times Illustrated* (December 1989): 35.
7. Thomas, "Real," 35.

8. Thomas, *Bold Dragoon*, 9.
9. J. Thomason, *Jeb Stuart*, Lincoln: University of Nebraska Press, 1929, 18.
10. Thomas, *Bold Dragoon*, 13.
11. Thomas, "Real," 35.
12. Thomas, *Bold Dragoon*, 18–19.
13. Thomas, "Real," 35.
14. A. Mapp, *Frock Coats and Epaulets*, Lanham, Md: Hamilton Press, 1982, 440.
15. Davis, 27.
16. Ibid., 37.
17. D. Russell, "Jeb Stuart's Other Indian Fight," *Civil War Times Illustrated* (January 1974): 11.
18. Thomas, *Bold Dragoon*, 63–64.
19. Mapp, 441.
20. C. Anders, *Fighting Confederates*, New York: Dorset Press, 1968, 154.
21. Thomas, *Bold Dragoon*, 55–56.
22. Ibid., 56–58.
23. Thomas, "Real," 36–37.
24. Ibid., 40.
25. Anders, 156.
26. W. Davis, et al., *Civil War Journal: The Leaders*, Nashville: Rutledge Hill, 1997, 279–280.
27. L. Naisawald, "Stuart as a Cavalryman's Cavalryman," *Civil War Times Illustrated* (February 1963): 46.
28. Thomas, "Real," 37.
29. Davis, et al., 281.
30. R. Morris, "Richmond's Fate in Balance," *America's Civil War* (May 1988): 38–39.
31. Anders, 160.
32. E. Feldner, "Jeb Stuart's Daring Reconnaissance," *America's Civil War* (July 1995): 41.
33. Morris, 41.
34. Davis, et al., 282.
35. Anders, 164.
36. J. Hennessy, "Stuart's Revenge," *Civil War Times Illustrated* (June 1995): 42.
37. Ibid., 45–46.
38. Thomas, "Real," 41.
39. Anders, 166.
40. Mapp, 464–465.

41. C. Price, "Stuart's Chambersburg Raid," *Civil War Times Illustrated* (January 1966): 42.
42. Thomas, *Bold Dragoon*, 175.
43. Thomas, "Real," 75.
44. W. Brooksher and D. Snider, "Around McClellan Again," *Civil War Times Illustrated* (August 1974): 47.
45. Davis, et al., 284–285.
46. Thomas, *Bold Dragoon*, 188–189.
47. Ibid., 191–194.
48. E. Longacre, "Stuart's Dumfries Raid," *Civil War Times Illustrated* (July 1976): 18–25.
49. Ibid., 25.
50. Thomas, "Real," 75.
51. Thomas, *Bold Dragoon*, 212.
52. Anders, 173.
53. Thomas, *Bold Dragoon*, 217–218.
54. Anders, 174.
55. S. Fleek, "Swirling Cavalry Fight," *America's Civil War* (September 1989): 49.
56. C. Hall, "The Battle of Brandy Station," *Civil War Times Illustrated* (June 1990): 45.
57. Fleek, 47.
58. Thomas, "Real," 76.
59. Anders, 175–176.
60. Ibid., 176.
61. Thomas, "Real," 76–77.
62. D. Zimmerman, "J.E.B. Stuart: Gettysburg Scapegoat?" *America's Civil War* (May 1998): 50.
63. Zimmerman, 56–57.
64. Thomas, *Bold Dragoon*, 256.
65. Thomas, "Real," 77.
66. Davis, et al., 298.
67. J. Guttman, "Jeb Stuart's Last Ride," *America's Civil War* (May 1994): 35.
68. Ibid., 35.
69. Thomas, "Real," 77.
70. Davis, et al., 298.
71. Thomas, "Real," 77.
72. Thomas, *Bold Dragoon*, 294–295.
73. L. De Grummond and Lynn De Grummond Delaune, *Jeb Stuart*, Philadelphia: J. B. Lippincott Co., 1962, 155.

74. Davis, et al., 298.
75. Thomas, *Bold Dragoon*, 300.

Chapter 9. Brief Glory:
         Turner Ashby

1. D. Cochran, "First of the Cavaliers," *Civil War Times Illustrated* (February 1987): 22.
2. C. Dufour, *Nine Men in Gray*, Lincoln: University of Nebraska Press, 1993, 41.
3. H. Douglas, *I Rode With Stonewall*, Greenwich: Fawcett Publications, 1961, 87.
4. Dufour, 42.
5. Ibid., 42.
6. Ibid., 42–43.
7. J. Kerwood, "His Daring Was Proverbial," *Civil War Times Illustrated* (August 1968): 19.
8. Dufour, 43.
9. Ibid., 43–44.
10. T. Ashby, *Life of Turner Ashby*, Dayton: Morningside House, 1988, 39.
11. Cochran, 22.
12. Ibid., 22.
13. Dufour, 45–46.
14. Ibid., 46.
15. Kerwood, 19.
16. Ibid., 19.
17. Ibid., 20.
18. Cochran, 24.
19. D. Freeman, *Lee's Lieutenants, Vol. 1*, New York: Charles Scribner's Sons, 1942, 308–309.
20. Kerwood, 20.
21. L. Gainer, "Personality — Turner Ashby," *America's Civil War* (January 1992): 8.
22. Kerwood, 20–21.
23. Ibid., 21.
24. Dufour, 59.
25. Kerwood, 22.

26. Ibid., 23.
27. C. Clark, *Decoying the Yankees: Jackson's Valley Campaign*, Alexandria: Time-Life Books, 1984, 90.
28. Cochran, 25.
29. Dufour, 62–63.
30. Douglas, 89.
31. Clark, 92.
32. Ibid., 92.
33. J. Roberton, *Stonewall Jackson*, New York: Macmillan, 1997, 362.
34. Ibid., 362.
35. Dufour, 65–66.
36. Freeman, 433–434.
37. Cochran, 26.
38. Kerwood, 28.
39. Cochran, 27.
40. Kerwood, 28–29.
41. Ibid., 29–30.
42. Cochran, 28.
43. Ibid., 28.
44. Dufour, 73.
45. Cochran, 28.
46. Gainer, 74.
47. Cochran, 28.
48. Ibid., 28.

Chapter 10. Maryland's Gallant Harry: Harry Gilmor

1. Time-Life Books, *Spies, Scouts, and Raiders*, Alexandria: Time-Life Books, 1985, 108.
2. Ibid., 108.
3. T. Ackinclose, *Sabres & Pistols*, Gettysburg: Stan Clark Military Books, 1997, 4–5.
4. Ibid., 5–6.
5. Ibid., 9.
6. Ibid., 11.
7. Ibid., 13–14.

8. Ibid., 16–25.
9. W. Davis, et al., *The Civil War Journal: The Leaders*, Nashville: Rutledge Hill, 1997, 95.
10. Ackinclose, 38–41.
11. Ibid., 48.
12. Ibid., 48–51.
13. Ibid., 52.
14. Ibid., 52–53.
15. J. Brakeless, "Catching Harry Gilmor," *Civil War Times Illustrated* (April 1971): 36.
16. Ibid., 36.
17. Ackinclose, 59–60.
18. Ibid., 63–64.
19. Ibid., 72–74.
20. Time-Life Books, 124.
21. Ibid., 124.
22. Ibid., 126.
23. Ackinclose, 87.
24. Time-Life Books, 126.
25. Ackinclose, 90.
26. Ibid., 92.
27. Ibid., 97–98.
28. T. Alexander, "McCausland's Raid and Burning of Chambersburg," *Blue & Gray* (August 1994): 11.
29. Ackinclose, 99.
30. Ibid., 100–102.
31. Ibid., 104–108.
32. Ibid., 109–111.
33. Ibid., 115.
34. Alexander, 13.
35. Ackinclose, 129.
36. Ibid., 131–132.
37. Time-Life Books, 125.
38. Ackinclose, 153.
39. D. Phillips, *Daring Raiders*, New York: Metro Books, 1998, 104.
40. Ibid., 104–105.
41. Ackinclose, 175.
42. Ibid., 176–177.

43. Ibid., 181.
44. Ibid., 188–189.

Chapter 11. Kill-Cavalry:
Hugh Judson Kilpatrick

1. E. Longacre, "Judson Kilpatrick," *Civil War Times Illustrated* (April 1971): 25.
2. S. Martin, *Kill-Cavalry: The Life of Union General Hugh Judson Kilpatrick*, Mechanicsburg, Pa.: Stackpole Books, 2000, cover.
3. Ibid., cover.
4. Longacre, 25.
5. Martin, *Kill-Cavalry*, 15–16.
6. Longacre, 25.
7. Ibid., 25.
8. Ibid., 25–26.
9. Martin, *Kill-Cavalry*, 27–29.
10. S. Martin, "Kill-Cavalry," *Civil War Times Illustrated* (February 2000): 25.
11. Ibid., 25.
12. Longacre, 26.
13. Martin, "Kill-Cavalry," 26.
14. Martin, *Kill-Cavalry*, 58.
15. Longacre, 26.
16. Martin, *Kill-Cavalry*, 57.
17. Ibid., 57.
18. Martin, "Kill-Cavalry," 27.
19. Longacre, 26.
20. Martin, "Kill-Cavalry," 28.
21. Ibid., 28.
22. Ibid., 28–29.
23. Longacre, 29.
24. Ibid., 29.
25. Martin, *Kill-Cavalry*, 125.
26. Ibid., 126.
27. Martin, "Kill-Cavalry," 30.
28. R. Suhr, "The Kilpatrick Dahlgren Raid on Richmond," *Military Heritage* (June 2000): 50.
29. Martin, "Kill-Cavalry," 30.

30. Ibid., 30.
31. Suhr, 57.
32. Martin, 169–170.
33. Ibid., 171.
34. Martin, "Kill-Cavalry," 30.
35. Longacre, 30–31.
36. A. Lee, "Tangling With Kilcavalry," *Civil War Times Illustrated* (June 1998): 67–68.
37. Martin, 197.
38. Longacre, 32.
39. Ibid., 33.
40. Martin, "Kill-Cavalry," 59.
41. Martin, 262–263.

Chapter 12. Thunderbolt of the Confederacy: John Hunt Morgan

1. J. Ramage, *Rebel Raiders: The Life of John Hunt Morgan*, Lexington: University Press of Kentucky, 1986, 1–3.
2. Ibid., 5–7.
3. Ibid., 7.
4. E. Thomas, *John Hunt Morgan and His Raiders*, Lexington: University Press of Kentucky, 1975, xi.
5. Ramage, 11–17.
6. Thomas, 5.
7. Ramage, 19–20.
8. Thomas, 6–7.
9. Ibid., 7, 18.
10. Ramage, 39.
11. Thomas, 9–12.
12. Ibid., 15–16.
13. Ibid., 19.
14. Ibid., 27.
15. Ibid., 29.
16. Ramage, 57–58.
17. Ibid., 58–60.
18. Ibid., 61–62.

19. Thomas, 29.
20. Ibid., 30–32.
21. Ibid., 34–36.
22. Ibid., 36–37.
23. Ramage, 87–88.
24. Ibid., 89–91.
25. Thomas, 39–40.
26. W. Brooksher and R. Vickery, "Morgan Rides Again: Kentucky, 1862," *Civil War Times Illustrated* (June 1978): 8.
27. M. Ballard, "Deceit by Telegraph," *Civil War Times Illustrated* (October 1983): 22–23.
28. Brooksher and Vickery, 10, 43.
29. Ibid., 43.
30. Thomas, 44.
31. Ibid., 44–45.
32. Ramage, 108.
33. Thomas, 46–47.
34. Ibid., 48, 50.
35. Ibid., 51–52.
36. Ibid., 53–54.
37. J. Jones, *A Rebel War Clerk's Diary*, New York: Sagamore Press, 1958, 88–89.
38. Thomas, 59–61.
39. Ibid., 61–64.
40. D. Brown, "Morgan's Christmas Raid," *Civil War Times Illustrated* (January 1975): 12.
41. Thomas, 65–69.
42. Ibid., 69–71.
43. Brown, 19.
44. Thomas, 72–75.
45. W. Kingseed, "The Great Escape," *American History* (February 2000): 25.
46. Thomas, 76.
47. Ibid., 77.
48. D. Phillips, *Daring Raiders*, New York: Metro Books, 1998, 72–74.
49. Thomas, 78–82.
50. Kingseed, 26.
51. A. Keller, "Morgan's Raid Across the Ohio," *Civil War Times Illustrated* (June 1963): 36.

52. R. Creeks, "John Hunt Morgan's Ill-Fated Ohio Raid," *America's Civil War* (May 1998): 48–49.
53. D. Roth, "John Hunt Morgan's Escape from the Ohio Penitentiary," *Blue & Gray* (October 1994): 16–17.
54. Kingseed, 27.
55. Thomas, 87–90.
56. Ibid., 91.
57. Ibid., 92–93.
58. Ibid., 96–98.
59. Ibid., 100–101.
60. Ibid., 102–103.
61. Ramage, 219.
62. Ibid., 218.
63. W. Stier, "Morgan's Last Battle," *Civil War Times Illustrated* (December 1996): 84.
64. S. Foote, *The Civil War, A Narrative: Red River to Appomattox,* New York: Random House, 1974, 596.
65. Ibid., 596.

Part 3. Fighting Under the Black Flag:
Guerrilla Warfare

1. D. Sutherland, ed., *Guerrillas, Unionists, and Violence on the Confederate Homefront,* Fayetteville: University of Arkansas Press, 1999, 3.
2. D. Sutherland, "Without Mercy and Without the Blessing of God," *North & South* (September 1998): 14.
3. W. Davis, et al., *The West,* New York: Smithmark Publishers, 1992, 73.
4. R. Brownlee, *Gray Ghosts of the Confederacy,* Baton Rouge: Louisiana State University Press, 1958, 3–4.
5. R. Bruns, *The Bandit Kings,* New York: Crown Publishing, 1995, 6.
6. E. Leslie, *The Devil Knows How to Ride,* New York: Da Capo Press, 1998, 8–9.
7. Ibid., 9.
8. Time-Life Books, *Spies, Scouts, and Raiders,* Alexandria: Time-Life Books, 1985, 141.
9. Ibid., 141.
10. Brownlee, 10.
11. M. Brant, *The Outlaw Youngers,* Lanham, Md.: Madison Books, 1992, 18–19.

12. A. Castel, "The Guerrilla War, 1861–1865," *Civil War Times Illustrated*, (October 1974): 7.
13. Time-Life Books, 142–143.
14. Ibid., 143–144.
15. Ibid., 145–146.
16. Ibid., 146–147.
17. Ibid., 149.
18. Castel, 31–32.
19. Ibid., 49–50.
20. T. Goodrich, *Black Flag: Guerrilla Warfare on the Western Borders, 1861–1865*, Boomington: Indiana University Press, 1999, 160.
21. Ibid., 161–162.
22. Ibid., 164.

Chapter 13. Fanatical Abolitionist: John Brown

1. R. Webb, *The Raid on Harpers Ferry, October 16, 1859*, New York: Franklin Watts, 1971, 25.
2. S. Oates, *To Purge This Land With Blood*, New York: Harper & Row, 1970, 274–275.
3. Webb, 26–27.
4. Oates, 8.
5. Ibid., 10.
6. J. Scott and R. Scott, *John Brown of Harper's Ferry*, New York: Facts on File, 1988, 32–33.
7. W. Davis, et al., *Civil War Journal: The Leaders*, Nashville: Rutledge Hill, 1997, 5.
8. Scott and Scott, 36–37.
9. Oates, 15.
10. Ibid., 16–17.
11. Ibid., 17.
12. Ibid., 19–20.
13. Ibid., 21.
14. Ibid., 24–25.
15. Davis, et al., 6.
16. Oates, 33.

17. Davis, et al., 6.
18. Ibid., 7–8.
19. Ibid., 10.
20. Ibid., 10.
21. Webb, 7–10.
22. Ibid., 10, 14.
23. Ibid., 15.
24. Davis, et al., 13.
25. G. Ward, *The Civil War, An Illustrated History*, New York: Alfred A. Knopf, 1990, 4.
26. Davis, et al., 15–16.
27. Ibid., 17.
28. Ibid., 18–19.
29. Ibid., 18–19.
30. Webb, 51.
31. W. Davis, et al., *Brother Against Brother*, Alexandria: Time-Life Books, 1983, 88.
32. Davis, et al., *Journal*, 20.
33. Webb, 56-57.
34. Davis, et al., *Brothers*, 89.
35. A. Hemingway, "Meteor of the War," *America's Civil War* (July 1991): 48.
36. Davis, et al., *Journal*, 22.
37. Ibid., 23.
38. Scott and Scott, 156.
39. Ibid., 159.
40. Davis, et al., *Journal*, 23.

Chapter 14. Guerrilla with a Vendetta: Champ Ferguson

1. T. Sensing, *Champ Ferguson, Confederate Guerrilla*, Nashville: Vanderbilt University Press, 1942, 252–253.
2. Ibid., 253.
3. Ibid., 2–3.
4. Ibid., 3.
5. Ibid., 3.
6. Ibid., 36.

7. A. Castel, "The Guerrilla War, 1861–1865," *Civil War Times Illustrated,* (October 1974): 32.
8. Sensing, 39.
9. Ibid., 78–79.
10. Ibid., 80–81.
11. Ibid., 83–86.
12. Ibid., 94–95.
13. Ibid., 103.
14. J. Ramage, *Rebel Raider: The Life of John Hunt Morgan,* Lexington: University Press of Kentucky, 1986, 114–115.
15. Ibid., 101.
16. Sensing, 118–120.
17. Ibid., 129.
18. Ramage, 143.
19. Sensing, 141.
20. Sensing, 148.
21. Ibid., 165–169.
22. W. Marvel, "What Makes a Massacre," *Blue & Gray* (August 1991): 52–53.
23. Sensing, 177.
24. Ibid., 187–188.
25. Ibid., 189.
26. W. Jones, *After the Thunder,* Dallas: Taylor Publishing, 2000, 26.
27. Sensing, 12–13.
28. Ibid., 67.
29. Ibid., 247.
30. Ibid., 255.

Chapter 15. Deadly Duo:
William Quantrill and "Bloody Bill" Anderson

1. D. Schultz, *Quantrill's War: The Life and Times of William Clarke Quantrill, 1837–1865,* New York: St. Martin's, 1966, 72.
2. P. Wellman, *A Dynasty of Western Outlaws,* Lincoln: University of Nebraska Press, 1986, 26–27.
3. Schultz, 3.
4. Ibid., 3–4.

5. A. Castel, *William Clarke Quantrill, His Life and Times,* Norman: University of Oklahoma Press, 1962, 25.
6. Ibid., 31–32.
7. Schultz, 56–57.
8. Ibid., 69–70.
9. Ibid., 71–72.
10. L. Wood, "They Rode With Quantrill," *America's Civil War* (November 1996): 60.
11. Ibid., 62.
12. R. Bruns, *The Bandit Kings,* New York: Crown, 1995, 10.
13. Schultz, 78–79.
14. Ibid., 80.
15. Time-Life Books, *Spies, Scouts, and Raiders,* Alexandria: Time-Life Books, 1985, 149.
16. Ibid., 149.
17. Wellman, 35.
18. A. Castel and T. Goodrich, *Bloody Bill Anderson,* Mechanicsburg, Pa.: Stackpole Books, 1998, 17.
19. R. Brownlee, *Gray Ghosts of the Confederacy: Guerrilla Warfare in the West, 1861–1865,* Baton Rouge: Louisiana State University Press, 1958, 138.
20. Castel and Goodrich, 19.
21. Time-Life Books, 149.
22. Castel, 101–102.
23. Wellman, 38.
24. Schultz, 131–132.
25. Ibid., 132–133.
26. Schultz, 137–138.
27. Ibid., 139.
28. Ibid., 81.
29. Ibid., 139–140.
30. Ibid., 130.
31. Ibid., 142–143.
32. Castel and Goodrich, 27.
33. D. Brugioni, "The Meanest Bushwhacker, Bloody Bill Anderson," *Blue & Gray* (June 1991): 33.
34. Time-Life Books, 152.
35. Wellman, 39.
36. Time-Life Books, 153.

37. D. Stinson, "The Bloodiest Atrocity of the Civil War," *Civil Times Illustrated* (December 1963): 44.
38. Time-Life Books, 153.
39. Stinson, 44.
40. Time-Life Books, 153.
41. Stinson, 45.
42. Brownlee, 123.
43. Ibid., 124.
44. G. Ward, *The West, An Illustrated History*, Boston: Little, Brown, 1996, 194.
45. Brownlee, 124.
46. Castel and Goodrich, 29.
47. Brownlee, 124.
48. Ward, 194.
49. Wellman, 18.
50. Ibid., 44.
51. D. Moore, "Raiders' Savage Attack," Wild West (December 1988): 41.
52. Time-Life Books, 153–154.
53. Ward, 195.
54. Wellman, 47.
55. Bruns, 16–17.
56. Castel and Goodrich, 32.
57. Brugioni, 34.
58. Time-Life Books, 126.
59. A. Castel, "Quantrill in Texas," *Civil War Times Illustrated* (June 1972): 22.
60. Ibid., 23.
61. Ibid., 24.
62. Ibid., 27.
63. B. Kerrihard, "Bitter Bushwhackers and Jayhawkers," *America's Civil War* (January 1993): 31.
64. Brugioni, 34.
65. R. Morris, "Gunfighters and Lawmen," *Wild West* (February 1989): 64.
66. Castel, 187–188.
67. Ibid., 188.
68. Schultz, 285.
69. Castel, 188–189.
70. Schultz, 286–287.
71. Brugioni, 35.
72. Castel and Goodrich, 90–91.

73. Brugioni, 35.
74. Ibid., 35.
75. Castel and Goodrich, 35.
76. Brugioni, 35.
77. Schultz, 291–292.
78. Brugioni, 35.
79. R. Morris, "Editorial: 'Bloody Bill' Anderson," *America's Civil War* (January 1993): 6.
80. Castel and Goodrich, 125.
81. Ibid., 130.
82. A. Castel, "The Guerrilla War, 1861–1865," *Civil War Times Illustrated* (October 1974): 48–49.
83. S. Sanders, "Quantrill's Last Ride," *America's Civil War* (March 1999): 47.
84. Ibid., 47-48.
85. Ibid., 48.
86. P. Trachtman, *The Gun Fighters*, New York: Time-Life Books, 1974, 59.

Epilogue: The Aftermath of Violence

1. M. Brant, *The Outlaw Youngers*, Lanham, Md.: Madison Books, 1992, 73.
2. P. Wellman, *A Dynasty of Western Outlaws*, Lincoln: University of Nebraska Press, 1986, 71.
3. J. Wukovits, "Raiders Repulsed by Fire," *Wild West* (October 1988): 20.
4. R. Love, *The Rise and Fall of Jesse James*, Lincoln: University of Nebraska Press, 1990, 33–34.
5. Ibid., 34.
6. M. Brant, *Jesse James, The Man and the Myth*, New York: Berkley Books, 1998, 16.
7. W. Settle, *Jesse James Was His Name*, Lincoln: University of Nebraska Press, 1977, 44.
8. J. Horan, *Desperate Men*, New York: Bonanza Books, 1949, 10–11.
9. Brant, *Outlaw*, 14.
10. M. Baldwin and P. O'Brien, *Wanted Frank and Jesse James*, New York: Julian Messner, 1981, 30.
11. Brant, *Outlaw*, 24.
12. Baldwin and O'Brien, 40.
13. Brant, *Outlaw*, 58.
14. Wellman, 66.

15. Ibid., 66.
16. Brant, *Outlaw*, 64.
17. R. Bruns, *The Bandit Kings*, New York: Crown, 1995, 32.
18. Ibid., 32–33.
19. Wellman, 65.
20. Ibid., 65.
21. Ibid., 72.
22. Wellman, 68–69.
23. M. Brant, *Outlaws: The Illustrated History of the James-Younger Gang*, Montgomery: Elliott and Clark, 1997, 62–63.
24. Ibid., 69.
25. Ibid., 70–71.
26. Ibid., 71.
27. Settle, 45.
28. R. Patterson, *The Train Robbery Era*, Boulder: Pruett, 1991, 2–3.
29. J. Ernst, *Jesse James*, Englewood Cliffs: Prentice-Hall, 1976, 27.
30. P. Trachtman, *The Gun Fighters*, New York: Time-Life Books, 1974, 67.
31. Brant, *Outlaws*, 97–99.
32. Wellman, 91.
33. Ibid., 97.
34. H. Soltysiak, "The Pinkerton Bomb," *American History Illustrated* (May/June 1992): 55.
35. Bruns, 39.
36. Brant, *Outlaws*, 111–112.
37. Ibid., 113.
38. Wellman, 99.
39. Brant, *Outlaw*, 126.
40. Ibid., 128–129.
41. Ernst, 47.
42. D. Gilmore, "Showdown at Northfield," *Wild West* (August 1996): 86.
43. Brant, *Outlaw*, 187.
44. Ibid., 193.
45. Brant, *Jesse James*, 190.
46. Baldwin and O'Brien, 102.
47. Ernst, 59.
48. Brant, *Outlaw*, 159–160.
49. Ernst, 63.
50. Castel, 17.

51. Ibid., 17.
52. Baldwin and O'Brien, 139.
53. M. Brant, "Jesse James Defender, John Newman Edwards," *Wild West* (December 1998): 34.
54. Wellman, 123–124.
55. Ibid., 124.
56. Brant, *Outlaw*, 248.
57. Ibid., 249–250.
58. Wellman, 128–129.
59. Ernst, 69.

Bibliography

Ackinclose, Timothy. *Sabres & Pistols*. Gettysburg: Stan Clark Military Books, 1997.

Alexander, Ted. "McCauland's Raid and the Burning of Chambersburg." *Blue & Gray*. August 1994.

Anders, Curt. *Fighting Confederates*. New York: Dorset Press, 1968.

Anderson, Ella. "'Crazy Bet' Van Lew Was General Grant's Eyes and Ears in Richmond." *America's Civil War*. July 1991.

Antonucci, Michael. "Code-Crackers." *Civil War Times Illustrated*. August 1995.

Ashby, Thomas. *Life of Turner Ashby*. Dayton: Morningside House, 1988.

Axelrod, Alan. *The War Between the Spies*. New York: The Atlantic Monthly Press, 1992.

Baldwin, Margaret, and Pat O'Brien. *Wanted Frank and Jesse James*. New York: Julian Messner, 1981.

Ballard, Michael. "Deceit by Telegraph: 'Lightning' Ellsworth's Electronic Warfare." *Civil War Times Illustrated*. October 1983.

Bennett, Kevin. "Morgan's Luck Runs Out." *Blue & Gray*. April 1998.

Bolte, Philip. "Command Shift Dictated." *Military History*. June 1992.

Booksher, William, and David Snider. "Morgan Raids Again: Kentucky, 1862." *Civil War Times Illustrated*. June 1978.

Boyd, Belle. *Belle Boyd in Camp and Prison*. Baton Rouge: Louisiana State University Press, 1998.

Brager, Bruce. "Combative to War's Very End." *Military History*. October 1986.

Brakeless, John. "Catching Harry Gilmor." *Civil War Times Illustrated*. April 1971.

_____. *Spies of the Confederacy*. Mineola, N.Y.: Dover, 1970.

Brant, Marley. "Jesse James Defender, John Newman Edwards." *Wild West.* December 1998.

____. *Jesse James, The Man and the Myth.* New York: Berkley Books, 1998.

____. *The Outlaw Youngers.* Lanham, Md.: Madison Books, 1992.

____. *Outlaws: The Illustrated History of the James-Younger Gang.* Montgomery: Elliott and Clark, 1997.

Brennan, Patrick. "The Best Cavalry in the World." *North & South.* January 1999.

Brooksher, William, and David Snider. "Around McClellan Again." *Civil War Times Illustrated.* August 1974.

Brooksher, William, and Richard Vickery. "Morgan Rides Again: Kentucky, 1862." *Civil War Times Illustrated.* June 1978.

Brown, Dee. "Morgan's Christmas Raid." *Civil War Times Illustrated.* January 1975.

Brownlee, Richard. *Gray Ghosts of the Confederacy: Guerrilla Warfare in the West, 1861–1865.* Baton Rouge: Louisiana State University Press, 1958.

Brugioni, Dino. "The Meanest Bushwhacker, Bloody Bill Anderson." *Blue & Gray.* June 1991.

Bruns, Roger. *The Bandit Kings.* New York: Crown, 1995.

Castel, Albert. "Bleeding Kansas." *American History Illustrated.* July 1975.

____. "The Guerrilla War, 1861–1865." *Civil War Times Illustrated.* October 1974.

____. "The James Brothers." *American History Illustrated.* Summer 1982.

____. "Quantrill in Texas." *Civil War Times Illustrated.* January 1972.

____. *William Clarke Quantrill, His Life and Times.* Norman: University of Oklahoma Press, 1962.

Castel, Albert, and Thomas Goodrich. *Bloody Bill Anderson.* Mechanicsburg, Pa: Stackpole Books, 1998.

Civil War Times Illustrated. Staff. "John S. Mosby, An Appraisal." *Civil War Times Illustrated.* November 1965.

Clark, Champ. *The Assassination, Death of the President.* Alexandria: Time-Life Books, 1987.

____. *Decoying the Yankees: Jackson's Valley Campaign.* Alexandria: Time-Life Books, 1984.

Cochran, Darrell. "First of the Cavaliers." *Civil War Times Illustrated.* February 1987.

Cooke, John Esten. *Wearing of the Gray.* Bloomington: Indiana University Press, 1959.

Creeks, Robert. "John Hunt Morgan's Ill-Fated Ohio Raid." *America's Civil War.* May 1998.

Current, Richard. Ed. *The Confederacy.* New York: Simon & Schuster, 1998.

Davis, Burke. *Jeb Stuart: The Last Cavalier.* New York: Holt, Rinehart and Winston, 1957.

Davis, William, et al. *Brother Against Brother.* Alexandria: Time-Life Books, 1983.

_____. *Civil War Journal: The Leaders.* Nashville: Rutledge Hill, 1997.

_____. *Civil War Journal: The Legacies.* Nashville: Rutledge Hill, 1999.

_____. *The West.* New York: Smithmark Publishers, 1992.

De Grummond, Lena, and Lynn De Grummond Delaune. *Jeb Stuart.* Philadelphia, Pa.: J. B. Lippincott, 1962.

Donald, David. *Lincoln.* New York: Simon & Schuster, 1995.

Douglas, Henry. *I Rode With Stonewall.* Greenwich: Fawcett Publications, 1961.

Dufour, Charles. *Nine Men in Gray.* Lincoln: University of Nebraska Press, 1993.

Ernst, John. *Jesse James.* Englewood Cliffs: Prentice-Hall, 1976.

Feldner, Emmitt. "Jeb Stuart's Daring Reconnaissance." *America's Civil War.* July 1995.

Fellman, Michael. *Inside War.* New York: Oxford University Press, 1989.

Fleek, Sherman. "Swirling Cavalry Fight." *America's Civil War.* September 1989.

Fishel, Edwin. *The Secret War for the Union.* Boston: Houghton Mifflin, 1996.

Foote, Shelby. *The Civil War, A Narrative: Red River to Appomattox.* New York: Random House, 1974.

Fowler, Robert. "Album of the Lincoln Murder: Illustrating How It Was Planned, Committed, and Avenged." *Civil War Times Illustrated.* July 1965.

Freeman, Douglas Southall. *Lee's Lieutenants, Vol. 1.* New York: Charles Scribner's Sons, 1942.

Furgurson, Ernest. *Ashes of Glory.* New York: Vintage, 1996.

Gaddy, David. "Gray Cloaks and Daggers." *Civil War Times Illustrated.* July 1975.

Gainer, Lucia. "Personality — Turner Ashby." *America's Civil War.* January 1992.

Gilmore, Donald. "Showdown at Northfield." *Wild West.* August 1996.

Goodrich, Thomas. *Black Flag: Guerrilla Warfare on the Western Border, 1861–1865.* Bloomington: Indiana University Press, 1999.

Grimsley, Mark. *The Hard Hand of War.* New York: Cambridge University Press, 1995.

Guttman, Jon. "Jeb Stuart's Last Ride." *America's Civil War.* May 1994.

Hall, Clark. "The Battle of Brandy Station." *Civil War Times Illustrated.* June 1990.

Hanchett, William. "Lincoln's Murder: The Simple Conspiracy Theory." *Civil War Times Illustrated.* November/December 1991.

Hattaway, Herman. *Shades of Blue and Gray.* Columbia: University of Missouri Press, 1997.

Hemingway, Albert. "Meteor of the War." *America's Civil War.* July 1991.

Hennessy, John. "Stuart's Revenge." *Civil War Times Illustrated.* June 1995.

Horan, James. *Desperate Men.* New York: Bonanza Books, 1949.

Jones, John. *A Rebel War Clerk's Diary.* New York: Sagamore Press, 1958.

Jones, John. *A Rebel War Clerk's Diary.* New York: Sagamore Press, 1958.

Jones, Vergil. *Ranger Mosby.* McLean: EPM Publications, 1944.

Jones, Wilmer. *After the Thunder.* Dallas: Taylor Publishing, 2000.

Kauffman, Michael. "John Wilkes Booth and the Murder of Abraham Lincoln." *Blue & Gray.* April 1990.

___. "Booth's Escape Route: Lincoln's Assassin on the Run." *Blue & Gray.* June 1990.

Keller, Allan. "Morgan's Raid Across the Ohio." *Civil War Times Illustrated.* June 1963.

Kerrihard, Bo. "Bitter Bushwhackers and Jayhawkers." *America's Civil War.* January 1993.

Kerwood, John. "His Daring Was Proverbial." *Civil War Times Illustrated.* August 1968.

Kingseed, Wyatt. "The Great Escape." *American History.* February 2000.

Kunhardt, Philip, et al. *Lincoln.* New York: Alfred A. Knopf, 1992.

Lee, Angela. "Tangling With Kilcavalry." *America's Civil War.* June 1998.

Leonard, Elizabeth. *All the Daring of the Soldiers.* New York: W. W. Norton, 1999.

Leslie, Edward. *The Devil Knows How to Ride.* New York: Da Capo Press, 1998.

Linden, Frank. *Lincoln: The Road to War.* Golden, Colo.: Fulcrum, 1998.

Longacre, Edward. "Judson Kilpatrick." *Civil War Times Illustrated.* April 1971.

___. *Mounted Raids of the Civil War.* Lincoln: University of Nebraska Press, 1975.

___. "Stuart's Dumfries Raid." *Civil War Times Illustrated.* July 1976.

Love, Robertus. *The Rise and Fall of Jesse James.* Lincoln: University of Nebraska Press, 1990.

Luthin, Reinhard. *The Real Abraham Lincoln.* Englewood Cliffs: Prentice-Hall, 1960.

Mackay, James. *Allan Pinkerton, The First Private Eye.* New York: John Wiley & Sons, 1996.

Mangum, William, II. "Kill Cavalry's Nasty Surprise." *America's Civil War.* November 1996.

Mapp, Alf. *Frock Coats and Epaulets.* Lanham, Md.: Hamilton Press, 1982.

Markle, Donald. *Spies and Spymasters of the Civil War.* New York: Hippocrene, 1994.

Martin, Michael. "A Match for Mosby." *America's Civil War.* July 1994.

Martin, Samuel. "Kill-Cavalry." *Civil War Times Illustrated.* February 2000.

____. *Kill-Cavalry: The Life of Union General Hugh Judson Kilpatrick.* Mechanicsburg, Pa: Stackpole Books, 2000.

Marvel, William. "What Makes a Massacre." *Blue & Gray.* August 1991.

Mogelever, Jacob. *Death to Traitors.* New York: Doubleday, 1960.

Moore, David. "Raiders' Savage Attack." *Wild West.* December 1988.

Morris, Roy. "Editorial: 'Bloody Bill' Anderson." *America's Civil War.* January 1993.

____. "Gunfighters and Lawmen." *Wild West.* February 1989.

____. "Richmond's Fate in Balance." *America's Civil War.* May 1988.

Naisawald, L. Van Loan. "Stuart As a Cavalryman's Cavalryman." *Civil War Times Illustrated.* February 1963.

Nash, Robert Jay. *Bloodletters and Badmen.* New York: M. Evans, 1995.

____. *Spies.* New York: M. Evans, 1997.

Oats, Stephen. *To Purge This Land With Blood.* New York: Harper & Row, 1970.

Patterson, Richard. *The Train Robbery Era.* Boulder: Pruett, 1991.

Phillips, David. *Daring Raiders.* New York: Metro Books, 1998.

Price, Channing. "Stuart's Chambersburg Raid." *Civil War Times Illustrated.* January, 1966.

Ramage, James. *Gray Ghost.* Lexington: University Press of Kentucky, 1999.

____. *Rebel Raider: The Life of John Hunt Morgan.* Lexington: University Press of Kentucky, 1986.

Raymond, Colonel J. E. Review of *The Pinkertons: The Detective Dynasty That Made History. American History Illustrated.* May 1969.

Robbins, Peggy. "Allan Pinkerton's Southern Assignment." *Civil War Times Illustrated.* January 1977.

____. "Audacious Railroad Chase." *America's Civil War.* September 1991.

Robertson, James. *Stonewall Jackson.* New York: Macmillan, 1997.

Rodenbough, Theo. Ed. *The Photographic History of the Civil War: The Cavalry.* New York: Random House, 1983.

Roscoe, Theodore. *The Web of Conspiracy.* Englewood Cliffs: Prentice-Hall, 1959.

Roth, Dave. "John Hunt Morgan's Escape from the Ohio Penitentiary." *Blue & Gray.* October 1994.

Russell, Don. "Jeb Stuart's Other Indian Fight." *Civil War Times Illustrated.* January 1974.

Ryan, David. *Four Days in 1865: The Fall of Richmond.* Richmond: Cadmus Communication Corp., 1993.

____. Ed. *A Yankee Spy in Richmond.* Mechanicsburg, Pa.: Stackpole, 1996.

Sabine, David. "Pinkerton's 'Operative': Timothy Webster." *Civil War Times Illustrated.* August 1973.

Sanders, Stuart. "Quantrill's Last Ride." *America's Civil War*. March 1999.

Scarborough, Ruth. *Belle Boyd, Siren of the South*. Macon: Mercer University Press, 1997.

Schiller, Lawrence. "A Taste of Northern Steel." *North & South*. January 1999.

Schultz, Duane. *Quantrill's War: The Life and Times of William Clarke Quantrill, 1837–1865*. New York: St. Martin's, 1996.

Scott, John, and Robert Scott. *John Brown of Harper's Ferry*. New York: Facts on File, 1988.

Sears, Stephen. *George B. McClellan, The Young Napoleon*. New York: Ticknor & Fields, 1988.

Sensing, Thurman. *Champ Ferguson, Confederate Guerrilla*. Nashville: Vanderbilt University Press, 1942.

Settle, Wilham. *Jesse James Was His Name*. Lincoln: University of Nebraska Press, 1977.

Siepel, Kevin. *Rebel: The Life and Times of John Singleton Mosby*. New York: Da Capo Press, 1977.

Smith, Robert Barr. "The James Boys Go to War." *Civil War Times Illustrated*. January/February 1994.

Steers, Edward, Jr. *The Escape and Capture of John Wilkes Booth*. Gettysburg: Thomas Publications, 1992.

Stier, William. "Morgan's Last Battle." *Civil War Times Illustrated*. December 1996.

Stinson, Dwight. "The Bloodiest Atrocity of the Civil War." *Civil War Times Illustrated*. December 1963.

____. "Quantrill's Lawrence, Kansas Raid." *Civil War Times Illustrated*. December 1963.

Suhr, Robert. "The Kilpatrick Dahlgren Raid on Richmond." *Military Heritage*. June 2000.

Sutherland, Daniel. Ed. *Guerrillas, Unionists, and Violence on the Confederate Homefront*. Fayetteville: The University of Arkansas Press, 1999.

____. "Without Mercy and Without the Blessing of God." *North & South*. September 1998.

Thomas, Edison. *John Hunt Morgan and His Raiders*. Lexington: University Press of Kentucky, 1975.

Thomas, Emory. *Bold Dragoon: The Life of J.E.B. Stuart*. New York: Harper & Row, 1986.

____. "The Real J.E.B. Stuart." *Civil War Times Illustrated*. December 1989.

Thomason, John. *Jeb Stuart*. Lincoln: University of Nebraska Press, 1929.

Tidwell, William. *April '65: Confederate Covert Action in the American Civil War.* Kent, Ohio: Kent State University Press, 1995.

Tidwell, William, et al. *Come Retribution.* Jackson: University Press of Mississippi, 1988.

Time-Life Books. *Spies, Scouts, and Raiders.* Alexandria: Time-Life Books, 1985.

Trachtman, Paul. *The Gun Fighters.* New York: Time-Life Books, 1974.

Ward, Geoffrey. *The Civil War, An Illustrated History.* New York: Alfred A. Knopf, 1990.

____. *The West, An Illustrated History.* Boston: Little, Brown, 1996.

Webb, Robert. *The Raid on Harpers Ferry, October 16, 1859.* New York: Franklin Watts, 1971.

Wellman, Paul. *A Dynasty of Western Outlaws.* Lincoln: University of Nebraska Press, 1986.

Wert, Jeffry. "Inside Mosby's Confederacy." *Civil War Times Illustrated.* September/October 1990.

____. *Mosby's Rangers.* New York: Simon and Schuster, 1990.

Wood, Larry. "They Rode With Quantrill." *America's Civil War.* November 1996.

Wukovits, John. "Raiders Repulsed by Fire." *Wild West.* October 1988.

Zimmerman, Daniel. "J.E.B. Stuart: Gettysburg Scapegoat?" *America's Civil War.* May 1998.

Index